Spitfire Attack

Flight Lieutenant W T Rolls, DFC, DFM, AE

FORTUNES OF WAR

Spitfire Attack

FLIGHT LIEUTENANT W T ROLLS
DFC, DFM, AE

CERBERUS

First published by William Kimber & Co Limited, in 1987

PUBLISHED IN THE UNITED KINGDOM BY;
Cerberus Publishing Limited
22A Osprey Court
Hawkfield Business Park
Bristol
BS14 0BB
UK
e-mail: cerberusbooks@aol.com
www.cerberus-publishing.com

British Library Cataloguing in Publication Data.
A catalogue record for this book is available from the British Library.

ISBN 1 84145 041 3

PRINTED AND BOUND IN ENGLAND.

Contents

For
Mr J R Pepper, thoracic surgeon
and
Squadron Leader A M Worger-Slade
without either of them,
this book could never have been written

Introduction

I do not usually like to see the word Introduction in any book I am about to read. Usually it is used to explain something that is not in the book or sometimes is used to cover a lot of the preliminaries in the story; to me it is a cheap way of explaining the content of the book.

However, since completing the book I have let several people read it in order to get some idea of public reaction to a book of this kind. Most of them asked me the same question when they returned the book: 'Why have you left it so long to write it?' Good question that! and one that needs answering, hence the reason I have included this foreword.

On the evening of Saturday, 6th September 1980, I was watching the television programme from the Royal Albert Hall, featuring the promenade concert. The orchestra had just finished playing 'Land of Hope and Glory'; the reaction of the youth in the audience was spontaneous applause and waving of Union Jacks. It was a very touching moment for me to see the youth of this country of ours so patriotic, especially after all the bad press they had been getting over some of their exploits. It was a sight I would never forget; unfortunately this beautiful scene was marred for me by the Australian conductor who, in his speech of thanks to the audience, likened the young, free-standing audience who were waving and cheering to a football crowd.

I was suffering from angina at the time and I was so incensed by this attitude, that I got severe chest pains which continued until the Monday morning when I was rushed to Southend Hospital with a bad heart attack. It was while I was here that I met the young doctors and nurses, who, by information disclosed in conversation with my son, found out that I was an ex-RAF Spitfire pilot who flew in the Battle of Britain. This was because it happened to be Battle of Britain week. I was amazed at the interest these young people took in asking me questions about 1940 during the three weeks I was there.

The same thing happened when I was sent to the London Chest Hospital for a heart by-pass operation. The surgeon who was to do the operation had already seen me in Southend Hospital and he had evidently told his team that I was a Battle of Britain pilot because a couple of the young doctors came up to see me and discuss what they were going to do. One of them told me it was their turn to help pay me back for what I had done in 1940. It was suggested that when I had recovered from the operation I should write a book about those days but to write it in language they could understand. He said that most books on that period of history were too technical as far as the RAF were concerned and that I should write a book for the younger people to understand as they were interested to know what went on.

I did not take much notice at the time and was quite fit after a year had passed but had done nothing about writing, until one day when my younger brother and my son told me that I owed it to the younger generation to write down as much history as I could. There must be some lessons to be got from it.

I decided that I would have a go at it, but I was not very enthusiastic as I had no idea where to start and, as I had not thought much about the war years since I left the RAF, it was going to be difficult to remember what to write about. There was only one way to do it and that was by using my pilot's logbook as a reference and hope that it would jog memories. I had not looked at the logbook for over thirty years and was surprised how readily the events in the logbook came to mind. It was like looking at a video of each entry, I could almost see every detail of those actions and people I had met during those times.

In writing down my memoirs I had some very pleasant times remembering people I had known and old pals whom I had lost. It was suggested that I had a ghost writer to help me write the book, but I had many real ghosts helping me every time I sat down to the typewriter.

All the incidents in this book are as true an account as I can remember.

CHAPTER ONE

POSTING TO 72 SQUADRON, ACKLINGTON

It was on 14th June 1940 that I was standing at attention on the parade ground at RAF South Cerney, Number 3 Flying Training School, Advanced Training Squadron. It was one of those lovely June days with the sun shining but at the same time a nice cool breeze blowing; on this breeze could be heard the sound of the RAF band in the distance, gradually getting louder. I glanced round and saw the rest of the No 1 Course, standing in perfect formation – at attention. The wings over their left top pockets seemed to be lit up by the sun, or perhaps the wearers were pushing out their chests in pride – after all, we were now pilots in the RAF and our operational squadrons were now in sight.

The band was now coming onto the parade ground and orders were quickly given for the march past as the commanding officer was taking the salute. The music was stirring something up inside me and I felt so proud at being part of this moving ceremony. It made worthwhile all that hard work I had put in over these past few months and the course I had attended at Gatwick before the war started.

After the parade was over, we were stood at ease and the adjutant stood in front of us. He gave us a pep talk and told us that he was now going to read out our posting notices. You could have heard a pin drop; at long last this was the moment we had been waiting for, although we were all a bit fearful, lest the posting be one we did not want. We knew that the posting could be the most important thing in our lives with the chance of being sent to Bomber, Fighter, Coastal or Army Cooperation Commands.

The adjutant started to read out the names and postings but I was not interested as I was only listening for my name to be called out. After a time I heard him say that he would now read out the Fighter Command postings and I was listening hard this time for my name must be in this lot. I knew that I could be on some kind of fighter and as my three mates' names had not been read out, there was the chance that perhaps a couple of us might be posted to the same squadron.

After five minutes we knew. He had read out four more names who were going to Hurricane squadrons and at last he put us out of our agony.

In a loud and very clear voice he called out: 'Pilot Officer Males, Sergeants Glew, Gilders, Rolls and White are posted to 72 Squadron, RAF Acklington, where they will be flying Spitfires.' I looked at the others and we shouted 'Hooray' together, not a thing to do on a parade ground but as we were the only ones from a course of forty, it was well justified. The Spitfire was the finest aircraft in the world as far as I was concerned and I was going to fly it.

The next hours were spent collecting our documents and saying our goodbyes to the instructors and friends we had made. Little did we know what to expect in the future, but at least I knew that with my mates with me that it was going to be good.

I had been told earlier by my flight commander, Worger-Slade, to go and see him before I left the station. I made my way to his office for this purpose.

He greeted me as he had done, when he was my instructor at Gatwick in April 1939. 'Hello, laddie! So you are off to your new station. You have got what you set out for and I know you will be a credit to us.'

He came over to me to shake my hand and then I pointed to my wings and said, 'Sir, there is a little bit of you in these.' He pointed to underneath the wings and said, 'When you have the Distinguished Flying Medal here, you come and see me.'

As he was going back to his chair he said, 'You'll be back with one some day.'

The next few days were spent with my wife and baby who was now growing quickly. Life was very good to me and even though the war was not going very well I never once had any thoughts that I would not survive it.

I caught the night train to Acklington via Newcastle on 18th January 1940. The journey from Newcastle to Acklington would be on a local train and I was going to meet the others at Newcastle. On arriving at Newcastle early next morning I went into the buffet feeling very hungry. I asked the woman behind the counter if she had any bacon and eggs for breakfast. She was a big lady and fat and I was stunned by her reply, she almost shouted at me, 'Where have you been? Don't you know there is a bloody war on?' and this in a Geordie accent was enough to scare anyone. I was glad there were not many people in the buffet. The thing was that I had on my best tunic with nice shining sergeant's stripes on my arm and a lovely pair of Royal Air Force wings. Did I know there was a war on? A few minutes later Sergeant J White came in and I told him about the woman behind the counter, but he ignored it and with one of his smiles went up to the lady and said something I could not hear.

In a short time he was called up to the counter and to my amazement came back with a nice hot bacon sandwich. 'Trouble with you, Bill, is that you don't speak the same language as I do.'

'What has a Glasgwegian got in common with a Geordie?' I asked him.

'Well, you must admit that I am better looking than you.'

It was not a long journey to Acklington and Johnny remarked that we soon should be able to see the aerodrome from the train and we opened the window to look out for it. As we went by a grass mound we saw a Spitfire only a few yards away. It was fantastic to see one so close. I even noted the number, K 9949 and the squadron marking, RN. D. We looked for as long as we could and then standing back in the carriage, we hugged each other in sheer joy. We had arrived.

When we arrived at the station the adjutant asked us if we would like some breakfast and told his sergeant to take us to the mess. It was a very good one and we thanked the sergeant in charge and he remarked, 'This is an operational squadron and pilots are on what is called special rations because they never know where or when they are going to come down in the sea or mountains.'

INTRODUCTION TO SQUADRON PERSONNEL AND SPITFIRE

On 19th June 1940 I had become a member of a fighter squadron which had been formed on 8th July 1917, from the Central Flying School at Netheravon. It had seen many actions in various parts of the world during World War I. At the outbreak of war in 1939 the squadron was operating from Leconfield and had been equipped with Supermarine Spitfire 1. It had shot down two Heinkel He 115 floatplanes in October 1939, helped cover the evacuation of Dunkirk from Gravesend and had only just returned to Acklington, when we joined it. Of its former members who had been posted to other squadrons, one had won the Victoria Cross and another a Distinguished Flying Medal. The squadron badge was 'SWIFT'.

With a background such as this, we had something to live up to.

John White and I had just finished breakfast when in came Stickey and the other John, Gilders. They told us that they had been in a cafe outside the station where the owner had given them a slap up breakfast when he knew they were going to 72 Squadron at Acklington. He told them that as they would be helping to protect him and his family from enemy bombers it was the least he could do. After my own experience I was pleased that at least all northerners were not like that woman in the buffet.

At 10.30 sharp we went to the adjutant's office and saw that Pilot Officer Males had already arrived and was making himself known to the Adj. We introduced ourselves and sat down with Males. The Adj then had us sign the usual forms and explained the station lay-out and the Official Secrets Act etc. He told Pilot Officer Males that he would be billeted in the officers' mess. The rest of us would be billeted together in a long hut type of building. We would sleep and have our lockers here but we would have our meals in the sergeants' mess and use the same facilities as the ground sergeants. Evidently the idea of the community sleeping quarters was that in the event of a scramble we would not be obstructed in any way and it would save time in getting us all together. We had no objections, in fact we welcomed it; we could have a card school sometimes.

I think we all felt sorry for Pilot Officer Males as he was on his own as a new boy and he felt the fact that only a week before he was with us in the mess, and had been with us at Cambridge and South Cerney. We all thought that it was a bad idea putting us in the same squadron, for it could prove embarrassing if he started to give us orders.

When we had completed the forms, the adjutant took us to the squadron leader's office so that he could meet us. As he knocked on the door we saw the name Squadron Leader R.R. Lees.

The adjutant handed the CO the file he had made on us and after a few seconds he turned to Pilot Officer Males:

'Pilot Officer Males, will you introduce your colleagues?'

Males introduced us one at a time and the CO shook hands with us all and welcomed us to his squadron. I gathered from his voice that he was an Australian.

'For the purpose of getting familiar with the Spitfire you will come under Flying Officer Elsdon who will ensure that you will learn the operational facts of the machine. I will test each one of you in a Harvard when he is satisfied that you are capable of flying a Spitfire. You will be allocated your flights when you have been solo in it.'

He told us a bit about the squadron history and hoped we would become valued members of the squadron. He rang the bell and a sergeant came in and was told to take us down to Flights for Flying

Officer Elsdon, after we had put our luggage in our billet. This did not take long and we were soon on our way to the flights and we saw several Spitfires in their pens. It was marvellous; in a few days we would be flying one of those machines.

When we arrived at Flights, they were on readiness and were sitting around in their Mae Wests. Flying Officer Elsdon was not in flying kit and as we walked in the flight room he came over and introduced himself to us.

Flying Officer Jimmy Elsdon looked to me to be younger than I was and with his innocent round face I hardly imagined him to be an experienced fighter pilot, but one thing he did have in abundance was personality. Within minutes he made us feel as if we had been on the squadron for ages. He was quiet-spoken and had a good memory, as we soon found out. In no time at all he was calling us by our names and introducing us to the flight commander of 'B' Flight, Flight Lieutenant E. Graham, Ted to his brother officers. A few words from him and we went into the crew room where we were introduced to the rest of the flight.

We were then introduced to 'A' Flight and met the members of that flight. It seemed to me that there were a few characters in this flight as there seemed to be much argument going on amongst them. It was good-natured but it was obvious to me that a couple of the pilots stood out from the rest although they were probably smaller than the others. One was nicknamed 'The Deacon' and the other 'Pancho'. I was going to see a lot of them in future.

The next step from flights was to meet some of the ground crew. Flight Lieutenant Elsdon had impressed on us that next to the pilots, the ground crew were the most important people on the station. He had told us, 'Every time you take up one of these aircraft you readily accept that it will be working properly and as efficiently as possible. Maybe up until now you have accepted this as part of the service and have not really appreciated what the ground crew of a Spitfire have to do in order to keep your aircraft serviceable. I suggest that during the coming week or so while you are not operational that you make time to come down to flights and watch these chaps at work and see for yourself just how important their job is. Another thing there is no bullshit on this squadron and if you wish to call them by their nicknames or Christian name, no one is going to worry about it. Don't worry, they will still call you sergeant.'

It was obvious the way the ground crew greeted him that 'Jimmy', as he was known to us, was very popular with them, but to him it was always Sir. We were introduced by the flight sergeant in charge of the ground staff and having met the lads he told 'Jimmy' that he had arranged for a Spitfire near 'B' Flight so that we could get to know the cockpit and what the machine looked like at close quarters.

Our first taste of Pilot Officer Males' rank came as we stood around the cockpit:

'Pilot Officer Males, climb into the cockpit and we will go through the cockpit drill.'

Back at Cemey we had gone by the alphabet and usually it was Sergeant Glew who was the first of the five to go first. Males looked at us, shrugged his shoulders and got in the cockpit. 'Jimmy' went through every item in the cockpit explaining their function and at the same time did a dummy take-off by telling Males exactly what he had to do to get airborne. The rest of us were perched on the side and back of the fuselage looking as best we could at what was being done and listening intently to what was being said. One at a time we got the same treatment and it was a little easier as we had heard it once before. By the time we had all had a turn, there was not much about the aircraft we did not know.

Our first lesson over we went back to the billets to unpack. We met two of the sergeant pilots who had been off for the day, Sergeants Plant and Gray. We learned later that they were known as Laura and Mabel to the other pilots. We all got called the usual: Johnny White became 'Chalky', Glew became 'Stickey'. In time we got called a lot of other names as well.

We had unpacked and as it was a large quarter we had plenty of room and rather liked the feeling of togetherness. I had not been living in at South Cemey so I had very little experience of mess life. After having had a shower and changing, we made our way to the sergeants' mess. No bother this time about being new boys. Some of the sergeants were in the bar and because we were early for dinner we went in as well. We did not get a chance to order a drink as one was put in our hands within seconds. A flight sergeant said, 'Cheers, and welcome to Acklington, one of the outposts of the Empire.' In no time at all we had got to know the rest of them and half a dozen beers later we wandered into dinner and I do mean wandered.

The rest of the evening was spent in the bar and lounge talking to the sergeants who had been on readiness that day. In all, now that we had arrived there were eight sergeants and one flight sergeant attached to the squadron as pilots. The flight sergeant had been a pilot for about ten years and at first I wondered why he had not been commissioned but after a while when I got to know him better, I understood why he had not wanted one. Two of the other sergeants had been recommended for a commission and were waiting for the results.

During the conversation we learned that we would do a couple of trips in a Miles Magister first to get to know the area we would be flying over. It would give us an idea of what a monoplane was like again, for after flying the Hart during our time at South Cerney it would be difficult to go on a Spitfire without a single trip on a monoplane. After these trips the squadron leader would give us a flight on a Harvard Trainer which was much more advanced than the Magister. None of us had seen a Harvard close up and did not know any of the cockpit layout.

Sergeant Plant suggested that he should give us some instruction on the Harvard cockpit the next time he was off readiness. We accepted his offer with thanks. We knew that Flying Officer Elsdon was to be our instructor but if we could get a little bit on the side who cared. He also told us that the CO would expect us to take over directly we were in the cockpit; there would be no tuition from him.

I thought this was a bit drastic from Harts to Harvard in one go as it were, but Sergeant Plant soon explained: 'You can't get dual instruction on the Spitfire and so you only have the cockpit drill learned on the ground, to get you airborne, and back on the ground again. If you can't do it with the Harvard, you certainly won't do it with the Spitfire.' It made sense when put that way. Another point he told us to watch was that when taxying out to take off, 'Observe all the airfield rules; keep your eyes open, observe RT procedure. The CO will do it, so that you can remember what you have to do when you go solo on the Spitfire.'

The next couple of days we did our trips in the Magister and it was nice to be back in one again. While I was familiarising myself with the local terrain I was gradually gaining height and when I reached 5,000 feet I decided to do some aerobatics. I could see the airfield in the distance quite clearly so I knew I could not get lost. I went through every acrobatic I knew and found that I had not forgotten anything I had learned when at Gatwick. For a few moments I remembered my old instructor. Flight Lieutenant Worger-Slade. I was determined to make good as a Spitfire pilot, so that one day I might see him again and prove what a good job he had done on me. I did a few turns down to 1,000 feet and in no time at all I was back at dispersal very pleased with myself. I expected the other chaps who were waiting for the aircraft to say something pleasant, but instead from Johnny White I got:

'You're up the creek, man. Not only are you overdue but you have been doing aerobatics without authorisation from Flying Officer Elsdon.'

'He booked me out for familiarisation flight, so what's the trouble?'

'He meant with the area and landmarks, not the bloody aircraft. We all know how to fly that, you are only wasting time,' he barked.

I turned to the corporal standing near me, 'Oh, corporal, that nasty sergeant's shouting at me.' The ground crew started laughing and so did Johnny. I had been forgiven by the angry Scot.

On the morning of 25th June 1940, Squadron Leader R. Lees took me up for the test in the Harvard and thanks to the cockpit drill I had received both from Sergeant Plant and Flying Officer Elsdon, I had no trouble in flying the machine. At first it seemed very noisy but it felt nice and powerful. I felt at the time, if this is only a trainer what is the real thing like the Spitfire going to feel like with all that power behind it. I did two take-offs and landings and climbed to three thousand feet and did some minor and steep turns. I found the turns much more severe than the Hart but the handling qualities of the machine were great.

After 30 minutes and having requested permission to land, we landed and I taxied over to 'B' flight.

I climbed out of the cockpit after the CO and undid my parachute, the CO had left his in the cockpit for his next test.

I was waiting for him to tell me the result of the test but all he said was, 'Put your parachute on the wing of that aircraft,' pointing to one standing near our aircraft, 'and come into the flight office.' The short walk to the office seemed to take a hell of a long time. I was worried. He had not told me how I had done, but perhaps he was waiting until there were no other people about. In about one minute a thousand things passed through my mind – talk about when someone is drowning.

I finally reached the office and saw the CO talking to Flying Officer Elsdon. He turned to me and said: 'Are you ready for your Spitfire solo?'

I replied, 'Yes, sir.'

He smiled, 'I thought you would be,' then he went out to the Harvard to take Johnny White for his test.

Flying Officer Elsdon went to a locker and took out a Mac West lifejacket and handed it to me. We walked out to the Spitfire and I put on my parachute over the Mae West and climbed into the cockpit.

'The aircraft has already been run up so you do not have to test the magnetos. The petrol is already turned on. Push your RT connection in tight and call control to see if you have contact. For the purpose of this flight your coding will be Green Three, the station code is Bluebell.'

I switched on the RT to transmit and called, 'Hello, Bluebell, Green Three, are you receiving me? Over.'

I got the reply immediately, 'Hello, Green Three, Bluebell calling, receiving you loud and clear, out.'

I then had another run through the cockpit drill with Flying Officer Elsdon and he was now satisfied and told me to prepare for take-off. The airmen were waiting for me and so I got comfortable and the next thing I knew was that Flying Officer Elsdon had climbed on the wing and said to me:

'This time I want you to do the exercise only. No aerobatics until I give you permission.'

I did not need telling this. I had been warned off enough about the trip in the Magister, and you don't make the same mistake twice.

My exercise was to fly out to the coast and have a good look round, do some different rate turns to get the feel of the aircraft, come back for a landing and then take off again for a complete circuit of the airfield. The time allowed was thirty minutes. I was to keep in RT contact all the time and cany out landing and take-off procedure at all times.

I put my brakes on by the lever on the handle of the control column looked out to the crew to see that they were on position on each wing tip and on the starter trolley. I primed the engine and then called out to the trolley man, 'Switches on, contact.' He pressed his button on the trolley and with a bang the engine started. The airman then pulled the cable from out of the cowl on the engine and dosed the flap, and then pulled the trolley clear of the aircraft. I knew that I had to move as quickly as possible because the engine had a habit of heating up quickly when the wheels were down as one of them obstructed the vent of the radiator. The wing man held on while I turned the aircraft towards the runway and after I had got straight they both left and waved me on. I found that I had continually to use my rudder on the rough grass to keep straight and owing to the narrow undercarriage the aircraft dipped its wings from side to side, and what with swinging the nose from side to side to see where I was going, it was quite a handful. During the taxying out I had called control for permission to take off.

'Hello, Green Three, you are cleared for take-off came the reply and so I turned onto the runway ready for take-off. I closed my hood, did a quick check of the instruments, looked around to see that I was clear and then turned into wind on the runway. I set my radiator flap and elevator trim, locked my gyro compass, put the airscrew in fine pitch and closed my hood. I opened up my throttle fully and looking out the side of the aircraft, I pushed the control column forward to get the tail up so that I could look ahead over the nose of the engine; a little rudder to correct and I felt the aircraft leave the ground.

I pumped the undercart lever three times, selected wheels up, continued pumping for about fifteen times and then saw the undercarriage lights come on and that the undercarriage indicators on the wings were out of sight. While I had been pumping with my right hand and holding the control column with my left hand I had been performing a switch back motion at first, but had quickly put my left elbow onto my thigh and stopped the up and down motion. I then adjusted the radiator, put the airscrew into coarse pitch for cruising and unlocked my gyro compass. By the time I had done all this I found I was at two thousand feet and near the coast, I was cruising at 185 mph. I now had time to look round while I continued to fly straight and level having trimmed the aircraft once more. I tried out the controls and was amazed how light they seemed and how responsive, almost immediate, they were, to the slightest touch, either of rudder or elevator. Compared with the Hart, which up till then I had thought was the perfect machine, the Spitfire was like a greyhound, so sleek and fast. I climbed to five thousand feet in no time at all and did various turns. I played with the controls to get the feel of them and waggled my wings from side to side, used the rudder and trimmer to see their response. It was magic. I felt that I was an integral part of the aircraft and that the wings were fixed to my arms and I could fly just like a bird. The cockpit was so small that there was no room to move and this made it feel as though you had it strapped on you.

I now tried some mild turns and the smoothness of them and the grace of the aircraft in performing the moves was unbelievable. I had heard that in a steep turn, it was possible to black out and so I decided to try one and see how far I could go, before I felt myself blacking out. I had never blacked out in any of the aircraft I had flown in, so I thought, the sooner I learn what to expect the better. I decided that I would go into a shallow dive and then go into my turn on the pull out. As I went into the turn I pulled the control column over to my left and back at the same time, and then it happened, I felt a terrific pressure on my body and as the nose was dropping I had to give more rudder and a tighter hold on the control column. I did not black out but I did not like the feeling I had experienced, I was not quite prepared for such a quick reaction of my controls. I decided that I would come out of the turn in a half roll, and so I throttled back, pulled hard over on the control column, levelled the rudder and pulled back the control column and, hey presto, I was coming out of the turn in a well controlled bottom half of a loop.

I now returned to base because I had to do another take-off and landing. I was already at 1,000 feet and in the direction of my approach so I called up on the RT:

'Hello, Bluebell, Green Three requesting permission to land.'

'Hello, Green Three, permission to land granted, over and out.'

I thought, what a polite lot of chaps they are down there in control! I was going to like RT. It was so civilised even with a war on.

I selected wheels down and pumped the lever until I saw the green lights go on and the wing indicators were up, I then put down my flaps. This caused the aircraft to drop its nose sharply and I had to correct it quickly. I adjusted the radiator and finally put the airscrew into fine pitch and turned into wind over the runway approach. I motored in at 95 mph and gradually lost height. When a few feet from the ground I cut the throttle and pulled back on the control column, I felt a slight bump and I was on the ground. I used the hand-brake on the control column to pull up the aircraft and kept straight with the aid of the rudder. When I had stopped I raised the flaps. I had done my first trip in a Spitfire and I was going to do another one directly I could get to take-off point again.

The second trip was–a repeat of the first except this time I did not switch back the aircraft, as I had on the first trip. When I landed, and was taxying to dispersal I said my usual little prayer, 'Dear God, thank you'. Some pilots carried lucky charms, but the words had kept me safe all the other times I had flown, I did not intend to change now. In fact it was meant in two ways, one for the flight, and one for having let me achieve my ambition to fly a Spitfire.

I taxied back to dispersal where the lads were waiting for me and as I approached two airmen came running over to me and took hold of each wing tip to guide me in over the grass. They both put their thumbs up to me. I had been accepted by the boys who look after your aircraft. This was very important as your life depended on these chaps every time you were airborne. I was to find out in the future just how brave and how important were the ground crews of the RAF. Up till now I had not taken too much notice of them as at Gatwick and Hatfield they had been civilians and at South Cerney I had been too worried about learning to fly to consider what other people had been doing to keep you in the air.

I switched off the engine and climbed out of the cockpit. Johnny White was waiting to take over the aircraft and I wished him luck and told him it was a piece of cake, flying it. I then went up to Flying Officer Elsdon, 'Well, what do you think of the Spit?' he asked.

'Marvellous. I can't describe the feeling but I feel as though I have been flying it for ages, it is so easy to fly, and what a graceful lady she is to look at!'

In the office I handed him the Mae West I had by now taken off. He did not take it but said instead, 'That is now your personal equipment which you will sign for and you will put your name in a convenient place for identification, and take care of it because some day if you ever come down in the sea, your life will depend on it.'

He told me of my faults in taxying out too fast and not swinging the nose sufficiently to see what was ahead of me, but stated that I taxied back better. He also explained that we would be having full explanation of the RT procedure at a later date,

'By the way, enter up those two trips in your logbook,' he called as I was going out to see Johnny off.

'I will put them in gold block,' I said, laughingly, and went to the aircraft which was now ready for Johnny.

It was lovely to see the way Johnny handled the taxying out to the runway. He swung from side to side as though he were waltzing the aircraft. His take-off was quick and perfect; in fact his wheels were up almost before he had left the edge of the airfield. 'Cunning bugger, our John!' I thought. 'He has been getting some private advice!'

After fifteen minutes he came on the approach, did a perfect turn straight in line with the runway, wheels and flaps down and a lovely final glide with a perfect touch-down. He quickly taxied back to take off again, repeating his same performance: a perfect take-off and later a perfect landing.

The grin on his face as he went to get out of the aircraft was as good as him saying to me, 'Beat that, mate!' We were good pals but were also competitive whenever we could be.

We did not see the other three do their solo because we were told to go into the flight dispersal and talk to the pilots who were there on readiness. Jimmy Elsdon was putting Pilot Officer Males and myself under Flight Lieutenant E Graham in 'B' Flight. White, Glew and Gilders were going into 'A' Flight.

The flight commander appeared to be a very quiet and good-tempered man, very soft-spoken and not a bit what I thought an experienced fighter pilot would be like. Some of the officers however looked proper tearaways and were game for anything. In fact they were often playing pranks on each other and it made it a happy place to be in when they were around. We were made welcome by all of them and we already knew the sergeants so we did not feel a bit strange.

That same evening after dinner we went to the bar for a minor celebration but only had a couple of half pints each. I think we had been well and truly mentally sapped because of the excitement of the day. We agreed that an early night would be the best for us as we all wanted to write letters home to let the families know we had arrived and what is more important, that we were now Spitfire pilots.

We hardly spoke to each other in the billet, and so we started our letters home. I wrote to Rene telling her about my first solo on the Spitfire and told her that looking at her photo was no substitute for the real thing. I also told her how much I was missing the baby, although it had only been days away it seemed a long time to me since I had last seen them. I also told her that I had to share a billet with the other four sergeants. This was due to operational requirements and I explained what that meant. However as we had the full run of the sergeants' mess for meals and leisure we had nothing to worry about. I told her Johnny White and I were in the same billet and as she knew Johnny and I were good friends I knew she would be pleased.

I put Rene's photograph back in my jacket pocket and got ready for bed.

To my amazement I had a very good night's sleep that night and by breakfast time next morning I was ready for another flight. I actually did two trips that day, one of 40 and the other of 30 minutes' duration. The first trip was booked out as General Handling and Landings, and I assumed that this meant some aerobatics if I wished.

I climbed up after take-off and flew out to sea at about 8,000 feet by the time I levelled out and decided I would have a go at doing a loop first. My first attempt was a wash out, I almost blacked out as I went over the top of the loop. I had taken the loop much too tight and too fast and as I pulled back the control column at the top of the loop as I saw the horizon coming up I also saw it go grey and wondered what had happened. I throttled back and finished the bottom half of the loop and by that time I was seeing properly once more. I did not like the feeling at all and climbed again and tried a few slow rolls; these were easy and I then did a stall turn. This meant diving and then pulling the control column back until you were vertical in the climb. As your speed decreased you had to put full rudder and stick over to fly over the stall. If you were not quick enough you could spin in and I did not intend to do that. This gave you a quick height advantage and a chance to change direction, without doing a tight turn. I decided that I would have to have another go at the loop – no point in waiting until the next trip – and as I had the height I was in position for it. This time I took my time in the climb and did not pull back so hard going over the top of the loop, I saw the horizon quite clearly this time and throttled back and made for base. This time no bother with the landing and cockpit drill was automatic.

That afternoon Johnny and I were told to do some formation flying and take it in turns to lead. We had done this on the Hart many times so we decided to do a bit of tail-chasing like we had done at South Cerney. This was good fun and it was up to the one leading to lose the one chasing him and to finish up on the chaser's tail if possible.

Johnny took the lead at first and I sat on his tail all the time and then I took the lead, for a while it was just chasing and a few minor climbs and turns. Then I remembered what had happened to me when I tried a full rate turn and almost blacked out. I went into a tight turn and Johnny followed me and I gradually increased my turn to make it steeper, Johnny was still there behind me. Quickly I opened to full throttle, pulled the control column right back, applied full rudder and was in about the tightest turn you could get in a Spitfire. I did not grey out this time, although there was a terrific pressure on my body. I looked round for Johnny and he had gone from behind me. I came out of the turn, levelled out and saw Johnny below me and in front, so diving down I formated on him, and this way we flew back to base.

After we had landed and got back to dispersal, having parked our aircraft we walked back to the flight office and as I met Johnny he almost shouted at me:

'You bastard, you pulled a fast one on me, doing that turn'. Only if you have seen a Glasgow Scot in a temper could you know what the look on his face was like. I had never seen him so angry. I was annoyed because I could see Flying Officer Elsdon inside and I knew he must have heard what was said. I pulled at John's arm to hold him back from going inside,

'John!' I said quietly, 'do you expect that when you eventually meet a German fighter pilot he is going to let you know what kind of turns he is going to do? Besides remember what Jimmy told us, "When you are up there, you are not practising, you are up there for real. You never know when your trip will turn into an operational sortie, so be prepared at all times." '

At this he smiled, put his arm round my shoulder and said, 'You are still a bastard doing that to a mate. I almost spun in and only just caught it in time.'

Flying Officer Elsdon came up to us, 'I see you've had a good trip, chaps.'

The next few days we were kept busy doing various exercises and Flying Officer Elsdon took John and me up for some formation flying. I was on his right side and John was number three on the left. We did some reasonably tight formations in vie pattern and line astern and then we were told we were going to do a battle climb to 25,000 feet. As we had never been higher than 10,000 feet in the Hart, 25,000 feet seemed bloody high.

We climbed up in vie formation and were reminded of the oxygen by Jimmy and we then turned it on. I had only tried it out once in my previous trips and felt it quite easy to breathe with it and a mask over your face. The climb was not steep but by the way the altitude meter was going we were gaining height very rapidly and we were at almost full throttle. After about 15 minutes we were at 20,000 feet and when I looked down it felt as though the earth had stood still. At first I thought I was going to stall but one look at the leading aircraft showed that we were still climbing. At 25,000 feet the aeroplane felt very light and as though we were wallowing somewhat; it felt uncomfortable but then we levelled out and it was not so bad. I took a good look round because we were in open formation now and had plenty of room to see the Northumberland coast for miles and even the mountains in the distance.

We got the order to close formation and when in position Jimmy started his descent. It was only a shallow dive but soon we had reached just over 300 mph on the dock. The sense of speed was exhilarating and we held formation all the time. Soon we were down to three thousand feet and Jimmy told us to tighten up a bit. We were now tucked in between his tail plane and wings. Then I noticed that we were going over the aerodrome. We did two rounds of the circuit to get acclimatised to the height, because at altitude you tend to get disorientated and that was the reason for the two circuits.

On the landing approach we put our wheels down at the same time as Jimmy and he gave us the order 'line astern'. I dropped behind him and Johnny dropped behind me. We were now all in a landing configuration.

We put our flaps down and Jimmy turned onto the runway and started to make his descent. As I saw him touch down I was making my approach; Johnny was still on the last leg, waiting for me to touch down. Eventually we were all down and taxying to dispersal. I thought it the best trip I had ever had. What with the sensation of height and speed in the dive and the feeling that I could fly in formation, it could not have been better.

When we got into the flight dispersal office the flight commander congratulated us on keeping the formation and one or two of the others said, 'Good show'. One of the wags of the flight said, 'Oh, is that was it was supposed to be? I thought it was some wild geese.' Jimmy said one word only.

From then on we did as much flying as we could: more battle climbs in formation to 25,000 feet; more RT communication with control; more take-offs, this time operational take-offs which involved your sitting in dispersal; when the bell went you raced off to your aircraft and got in as fast as possible whether on the grass or runway as long as you were airborne at speed.

During these days every time Johnny and I went into flights some of the officers would say 'Here come the Sprogs'. It was well meant and we even thought we would expand it a bit. That night in the bar the four of us decided that we would paint on the back of our Mae West in bright lettering. Sprog 1, which we decided should be for Pilot Officer Males; the others we picked out of a hat. Johnny White was Sprog 2. I was Sprog 3, Johnny Gilders was Sprog 4 and Stickey Glew was Sprog 5.

The next morning we went down to the parachute section and got the Mae West painted with the respective nicknames. We would show those officers that we were proud of being Sprogs. We were not on duty till the afternoon and when we eventually arrived at flights wearing our Mae West, the officers had a good laugh and thought it was a good idea. When the ground crew saw what we had done they thought it funny and very sporting of us and I am sure they had a bit more respect for us after that day.

We had now been on the squadron ten days and we were told to make up our log books for Squadron Leader Lees to sign. My total flying time in those ten days was 11 hours 10 minutes. I began to think about what was happening down south and the enemy raids on our shipping and the South Coast. Surely we must soon go down to replace one of the other squadrons who were fighting every day and we were losing quite a few pilots as well.

I started to get a guilt complex again. I thought, my wife and baby are closer to the Germans than I am. I would have a word with Flying Officer Elsdon tomorrow.

The next day was unfit for flying and the squadron was at 30 minutes' readiness, so the four of us decided to go over to flights to see what the ground crew were doing and to get to know a bit about the aircraft we were now flying. We saw the sergeant in charge and told him what we would like to see and he called an LAC and detailed him to take us into the hangar where a Spitfire had its cowls off and all the engine was visible. The LAC was obviously used to doing this with pilots because he went through the workings of everything in the cockpit and engine explaining the pitch of the airscrew and how it worked. It was a most interesting couple of hours.

After lunch we were told to be over at flights as Flying Officer Elsdon wanted to have a talk with us about the squadron. He arrived with Pilot Officer Males who had settled down in the officers' mess by the look of him. We sat down in the armchairs. Johnny and I had intended to ask him how long we would be before we went down south, but I did not have the nerve to do so. Jimmy commenced by telling us that the next few days we would spend on air firing and almost the same things we had done on the Hart and after that we would be put on readiness like the other sergeants in the squadron. We would do practice flying mostly in pairs or flights, such as battle climbs to 25,000 cloud flying and later, night flying.

He then continued, 'I may as well tell you that you are likely to be up here at Acklington for a month or two, subject to operational requirements. The reason for this is because the squadron has been down south for the Dunkirk evacuation and is now on rest. This does not mean that we have nothing to do but sit on our asses in these armchairs all day long. The squadron will be at readiness for any attack which might come by German bombers. They can just as well reach here as London and Command have no crystal ball to let them know where it is going to come. Hence we are just as operational as any 11 Group station, except that their chances of meeting enemy aircraft are higher than ours at the moment.'

He paused a while, then carried on, 'I know that you have been a long while training for operational duty but you are lucky. When you do meet the German pilots – and let me tell you this, they are bloody good pilots and have had lots of experience in Spain and Poland – you will be glad you have had so much training. Some of your RAFVR colleagues who were at

Dunkirk have finished their flying days, so don't let the CO, the flight commander or especially me hear you moaning about getting on operations. The war is going to last a bloody long time. When the men at the top think the time is right, we will be tossed into the middle of the fray, hook, line and sinker.'

When he had finished, we felt embarrassed. We should have known this, you don't put all your eggs in one basket and obviously the C-in-C Fighter Command knew exactly the way he was going to fight the air war.

I was surprised by his next words: 'Have you been out on the town yet? You can get a bus into Ashington or Newcastle and as long as you are not on readiness next morning there's nothing to stop you enjoying yourselves. If you only want a walk out there is a local pub called *The Trap* in Broomhill. I hear there are two lovely daughters serving in the bar.'

This pleased us as we had not been outside the station as yet and sometimes the local pub is a better place to have a drink than the mess.

I MEET THE HAMILTONS AND *THE TRAP*

That evening after dinner one of the ground sergeants told us that he was going to *The Trap* that evening and would be pleased to give us a lift and introduce us to the owners, a Mr and Mrs Hamilton, and to Cissie the elder daughter and Nellie the younger daughter. The way he spoke about them I thought he must have been one of the family. Stickey was awaiting the arrival of one of his pals from the other squadron so there were only the three of us going.

It did not take long to get to the pub which was in a small village. In the distance you could see the slag heap of the local colliery, so we thought we would probably see some of the local miners in the pub. To my surprise when we got inside they were nearly all sergeants including a couple of sergeant pilots who I understood, were from another squadron. We had never seen them before. One of them was talking to the young lady, so he was no stranger to the pub.

We went up to the bar and the ground sergeant insisted on getting the first round. The man who took the order and pulled the four beers and put them on the bar in front of us. He wiped his hands on a cloth and to my surprise held out his hand to me, and said, 'Well, Ted, introduce me to the lads.' Ted looked at me and said 'Sergeant—' he paused. 'Rolls,' I replied. 'Ah yes, I knew it was some sort of car.' He turned to the man. 'Mr Hamilton, meet Sergeant Bill Rolls who is a newcomer to my squadron; this is Sergeant Gilders and finally this is Sergeant White.'

The lady who had been serving at the other end of the bar walked up to her husband. He took hold other arm. 'My dear, meet Sergeant Bill Rolls.' I shook hands with her. He then introduced the two Johns, White and Gilders, and said, 'This is my wife, and pointing to a young lady who had been taking some drinks to a table, he said, 'and there is our daughter Nellie.'

We had a few minutes, between them serving other customers, to tell them a little about ourselves. Johnny White was doing most of the talking. Meanwhile the lovely young lady was at a table taking an order from some sergeants who evidently knew her very well from the way they were teasing her.

It was starting to get busy and so we decided to sit at a table. There were already two people at one end, a man and a lady and when I asked them if they minded moving up a little or us sitting there with them, there was a waving of arms. I could not understand a word that they were saying to John but they looked very happy whatever it was about. I had yet to learn what true Geordie sounded like. I saw that Nellie was not serving anyone so I called out, 'Nellie dear, can you come over here?'

She was soon at our table and the first thing she said was, 'Who told you my name was Nellie dear?'

I laughed as did Johnny Gilders who was a Londoner like myself.

I replied, 'In London we call all ladies dear whether they are old or young good-lookers like you.'

She laughed and said, 'You married ones are the worst.'

'How do you know that I am married?' I asked.

'You wear the advertisement on your hand.' She took my left hand and pointed to my ring, which of course was my wedding ring.

After time was called Mrs Hamilton asked us if we would like to stay for a bite of supper. By this time Cissie the elder daughter had come home. She was married but her husband was away and so she lived with her parents. It was the first of many a pleasant evening we spent at *The Trap* and time was flying when we decided that we had better get back. No one took any notice and Ted told us not to worry.

After a while Johnny White whispered to me, 'How the devil are we going to get back? We can't walk back?' We had forgotten that we had no means of transport back to the aerodrome and that it was a long walk. No one seemed to care and as we were not on readiness until after lunch, we had no need to rush. I think it must have been turned midnight when we eventually decided to make our way back and so we said our cheerios and got a little kiss from the two girls as a friendly token. We thanked our hosts for their excellent hospitality and told them that we looked forward to our next visit.

When we reached the front door we saw a small RAF van and Ted went up to it and told us to get in the back. In minutes we were back at our base. As we were walking to our billet I asked Ted how the van got there. 'I phoned the MT Section', he replied, and added, 'We sergeants have got to stick together.' That was a beginning of a friendship that lasted all the time I was in the squadron. In fact we were friendly with all the ground crews; they were a great lot of chaps, most of them being regulars of many years' standing. They did not worry about our having come into the RAF as direct entry sergeants; they had seen the aircraft come back from operations, riddled with bullet holes and knew the risks both officers and sergeant pilots took.

When we got to our billet, poor old Stickey was in bed but not asleep. He had been let down by his friend who had not turned up. He had missed a good night out and we did not spare his sorrows because we told him about what he had missed. Perhaps next time he would come with us.

For the next week, we were doing practice flying and in between periods at readiness. This meant that you would only fly if you had to take off on a scramble for enemy aircraft. Most of us played cards or read one of the many sexy books which always seem to abound in crew rooms.

During these periods we had the chance of getting to know our officers a bit better. The CO had been posted to Group and my flight commander had been made our new squadron leader. One of the flying officers had taken over 'B' Flight and again we were lucky; we could have had a stranger posted in as CO and flight commander. As it was we could not have wished for a better arrangement. What I liked about the officers was that they never talked down to the sergeants, like some I had met. If you did something silly they did not bawl you out but quietly hinted that next time you should do it their way; you might find it easier. Most of them called the sergeants by their Christian names.

We had by now become regular visitors to *The Trap*. I don't think it was the beer so much as Cissie and Nellie. We had been into Ashington to a dance with them and it had made a lovely change from all the weeks of only male company. They made every one of the RAF welcome when they visited the pub, but I would like to think we, that is Johnny White and myself, had made two good friends, always eager to listen to you talk about your own family, which because of the baby had been of interest to them.

MY FIRST SCRAMBLE

One day when I was at readiness as Green Three, I looked out of the window and wondered how long it would be before I actually had a chance to see the enemy. I had been waiting for that vital telephone call telling us to scramble but although it rang several times, causing an awful feeling in the pit of my stomach, it was never for us to scramble. I looked at the Spitfires which were at readiness with the ground crew sitting near their respective aircraft. The aircraft could be airborne within a couple of minutes if an alert was called. As I looked at this scene, I thought to myself here I am, a member of a famous Spitfire squadron, waiting to take off to do battle with enemy aircraft, if need be. It was far beyond my wildest dreams when an uncle of mine who had been in the Royal Flying Corps in the First World War, made models of those aircraft for me when I was a youngster. I had never thought that one day I would be in the Royal Air Force. I had come a long way since those happy childhood days.

Suddenly I came to my senses as I heard the telephone ring and immediately after the call: 'Green Section Scramble'.

This was it, this was for real and the three of us in Green Section raced to our aircraft. By the time we had reached them, the ground crews had started the engines and the straps of our parachutes were open ready for us to jump in the cockpit. The airman put the straps round you and you hooked the leads up and the harness was put over you and the pin inserted in a matter of seconds. The leader had started to taxi out and number two and myself were soon in position ready for a formation take-off. The weather was very cloudy and, at about 2,000 feet, we were going up through cloud in tight formation. A bandit had been reported off the coast at 6,000 feet. We broke cloud which was very ragged cumulus; there was no clear all round view. We received various directions as to which course to steer, when suddenly it appeared ahead of us. We could see even from this distance that it was an Anson twin-engine trainer aircraft, but as yet we did not know who was flying it. It could have been a captured one from the fall of France.

Green Leader tried to contact its pilot but like control there was no reply from it. They did not even fire a Very pistol giving the colour of the day; as far as Green Leader was concerned it could have been an enemy plane on reconnaissance. He ordered us to echelon port and number two came up under me on my left side. The Leader then flew close to the Anson and you could see the pilot but he could not understand what he was supposed to do. At the time I thought how dim the pilot must be, but it was not for me to reason why.

Green One then flew ahead of the Anson and number two went underneath me and formated on the port side of the Anson and I closed in on the starboard. It was now hemmed in and short of committing suicide the pilot had to follow. Base were informed that the Anson was being escorted back to base. Green One changed course and we went down through thin cloud and flew on to the aerodrome.

Green One put his wheels and flaps down on the approach run and the Anson did the same. Green One then went into land and Green Two and myself motored in formation still, until the Anson touched down. We then climbed away and landed in the normal manner. By now a RAF police van was waiting at the Anson door. We taxied back to dispersal and the aircraft were soon re-fuelled and we were again back in readiness.

It was my first scramble and although we could not claim it as a victory it was a successful interception. I had learned a lot on this trip and it gave me a lot of confidence in the way control had handled the whole situation. If it had been a German aircraft it would have had three Spitfires shooting it down.

A few days after this I was in another scramble but we were recalled within twenty minutes.

On the night of 6th August which was my birthday we all went to *The Trap* and the less said of that night the better. Johnny and I finished up behind the bar serving pints to all and sundry. We made the most of it because we knew that for the next week or so, weather permitting, we would be doing night flying and even patrols out to sea. Not a pleasant prospect to look forward to even sober.

Night-flying a Spitfire was about the most dangerous thing you could do in an aircraft. Owing to the long nose and the proximity of the two exhausts to your eyes it was almost blind flying until you .were airborne and then if you had no horizon to look at it was head in cockpit for most of the time.

Normally you lined your aircraft up on the runway, pointed it dead ahead, opened the throttle fully and, as you went forward, looked quickly out of the side of the aircraft to see if you were still straight. Then you lifted the tail and tried to see over the nose. If you could see the horizon you were all right; the take-off was bloody but bearable. If you saw a black cloud merging into the horizon, then the only thing to do was head in the cockpit and hope your artificial horizon was reading right. On most of my night flights, the horizon was obscured by black clouds.

On my second night's flying I was flying over Newcastle having been vectored by control. Enemy aircraft were in the region and I was at 23,000 feet and it was bloody dark. I was on instruments quite a lot of the time and if there were any enemy aircraft about I had no chance of seeing them unless I was behind them and could see the exhaust. It would have to have been pretty close even for that. I was ordered to descend to Angels twelve and given a course to vector which I was sure would take me right over Newcastle. I saw ahead and below a dark shape which according to control was a Heinkel 111. I dived down and the shape suddenly grew much larger and then I realised it was not an aircraft but a balloon I could see in the distance. At the same time I saw ack-ack flashes way ahead of me. Then two searchlights came on and at that moment I was well away from the whole scene. I had instinctively climbed steeply to get above the balloon barrage. I thought for a moment that the ack-ack had been firing at me, but it was too far away. I was now getting low on fuel as I had been airborne for almost an hour and had received no instructions to return to base.

On the RT I heard that one of the other Spits had crashed on landing and that did not make me feel very good. I did not know if it was Johnny White or one of the officers and did not know how bad the crash was. After about ten minutes I got the order to return to base and as I turned on to my course for home I heard the all clear for landing given to one of the other aircraft. It was not long before I had another instruction to orbit base as the runway was obstructed by another crash. I was now getting very worried. If I did not land soon I would be out of petrol and I would be number three on the runway. I had now been airborne for 1 hour 15 mins out of 1 hour 30 duration. Taking into consideration that I had done a speed climb to 23,000 feet I doubted if I could last 1 hour 30 minutes.

I could see that the crash aircraft was now clear of the runway and so I called up control and told them I was getting low on fuel and the only reply I got was that they had everything under control, which was more than I had as I watched the seconds ticking away on the clock.

'Hello, Green Two, are you receiving me?' What a bloody silly question at a time like this.

Quick as a flash I replied, 'May I now pancake?'

'Hello, Green Two, permission to land, watch out for obstacles at far south side of runway.'

By the time he had finished talking I had my wheels and flaps down and short-circuited the approach leg and straight on to the runway. I taxied to the far end and saw the two damaged aircraft at the side of the runway. At least I had made it, I had landed safely. Because of my shortage of petrol I opened my throttle and raced back to dispersal whistling because I was so happy when there was a sudden jolt and a noise of twisted metal and I came to a full stop. The engine had cut and there was this terrible silence for a moment or two. I jumped out of the cockpit and saw to my utter confusion that I had gone head on into another Spitfire which was taxying out for a take-off.

I had damaged two Spitfires through sheer bloody negligence, unforgivable in ordinary circumstances. By now the flight commander had reached the scene of the accident. The other pilot, an officer, was out of his aircraft and he said quietly, 'Wait for it, here it comes'.

I knew what he implied and was waiting for a rocket from the flight commander. To my surprise he looked very concerned and asked us if we had been hurt at all. He then took us back to dispersal in the car and immediately I was given a cup of hot coffee by one of the officers. I was trembling, not from fear but because I was wondering what was going to happen to me after such a silly accident. The telephone rang and he answered it and spoke to the CO of the squadron, or a superior officer that I did know.

After the flight commander had put the phone down, he came into the room, came over to me and sat down near me, 'You have had a nasty experience tonight what with the searchlights and waiting to land with very little petrol. I think we can safely say that your accident on the ground was caused by drcumstances beyond one's normal control. I suggest that you stand down for the rest of the night.'

I was only able to mutter, 'Thank you, sir'. My mouth had dried up.

When he had returned to his office I asked one of the other officers what would happen to me because of my carelessness.

'Nothing,' he replied. 'You see it was as much the fault of the officer in the other aircraft. He is far more experienced than you and should have seen you coming.' He looked at the office door and then quietly said to me, 'The CO has settled it with the flight commander so you will not hear any more about the matter.'

It took some time before I realised that even after I had done all that damage, I was still going to be allowed to fly.

The next day I was back on duty and we had a scramble. There were only the two of us. Green One and myself. Green Two. We were ordered to 25,000 feet, as bandits were coming from the east at that height. It was bad weather and ten-tenths cloud when we took off. I tucked myself in at the number three position on the left of the leader and we started to go into cloud. It was very dense cloud and I had to keep my eyes on the other wing tip every second as the slightest shift in my position and I would not be able to see the other aircraft. I was not unduly worried because I thought that after about ten minutes we would break cloud and see nice blue sky above. The ten minutes passed and we were still climbing in cloud. It was getting very trying, having to be so precise with my flying. I had never been so long in cloud and I was getting worried. There was no RT talk so I just had to follow the leader whatever he did, I doubted whether I could get down through so much cloud on my instruments especially if I was told to change course. The only way I knew we were in cloud was by the instruments because looking at the other aircraft without any background was like flying straight and level. At last we broke cloud and continued to climb to 25,000 feet. This did not take long but it was a relief to be able to see a background once more. We vectored out to sea for some fifteen minutes and were then told by control that the bandits had gone back so we could return to base.

That sounded such a simple order but we were at 25,000 feet and had about 18,000 feet of cloud to go through with a cloud base at about 4,000 feet. All kinds of thoughts were going through my head. I was thinking,

'Suppose you lose Green One in the let-down and suppose you dive down much too fast and can't control your descent. (This had happened to me on the Hart.) Will you have enough room to pull out at about 340 miles an hour?'

Green One brought me back to the present situation by asking me if I felt confident for a formation let-down. Eagerly I replied, 'Yes.'

'OK then, if you lose me turn to starboard and continue in a straight line.'

I then tucked myself in as close as I dared and we went into cloud at a shallow angle, the airspeed reading 200 mph. This continued for a while and I noticed that the airspeed was gradually increasing. When I looked at the artifical horizon I knew why. We were now in a steep dive. I watched the other aircraft more than ever now. I did not like the speed going up so quickly but I had to put up with it for what seemed to me to be ages. At one point we touched 340 mph and then gradually dropped down to about 250 mph. This was more like it, a few more minutes and we should break cloud, which we did. Oh, what a glorious feeling that was, and what a first class flight commander I had as my number one.

We landed and taxied back to dispersal. We had been airborne one hour exactly – I could have sworn it was at least two hours.

I was just behind the officer as we went to dispersal and when I got in he said in front of all the other pilots, 'Bloody good show, Rolls.' If he had given me a medal I could not have been more pleased, especially as it was said in front of the other sprogs.

I told the others about the height of the clouds and that I had kept formation all the time. I also told them that it was fear more than skill what made me do it, I am sure I would have been a worried man if I had tried it on my own.

Two nights later I was again on night readiness and had been told to patrol Blue Line which was an imaginary line about 100 miles off the Northumberland coast. Again the weather was not very good. I had started to climb through some cloud towards the coast; it seemed to get darker and darker and I did not like it at all. I had been flying for about twenty minutes when I had a call on the RT to return to base as quickly as possible as the weather was getting worse. I turned back on a reciprocal course and as the aircraft started to buffet it got hard to control. I opened up the throttle to offset the bumps and called up control for a QDF; this gives you the barometric pressure for the height of the aerodrome. Normally you get it when you take off but because of the bad weather coming up I knew that it must have changed since I took off. I set the millibars on my altimeter and I was at about 2,000 feet. I thought that the glim lamps were bright for that height – normally you could hardly see them. I decided to come in on a long approach on engine because of the bumpiness. I was about to lower my flaps when it happened.

I felt a terrific bang on my head and back and heard the rending sound of metal; the aircraft pitched up into the air and I saw a blinding light go past me. I saw the front of the aircraft fall away and felt the bang as my right wing hit the ground and tore itself away from the fuselage. I was bouncing up the runway and then over to my left wing which was torn off. I vaguely remember a howling wind as the fuselage went up the runway and a lot of noise but by then I was too dazed to care.

The first thing I remember when I came to was a voice saying, 'Don't touch him, don't move anything, wait.' I then saw the fire engines and ambulance and saw a lot of airmen running around, then an officer – I think it was the medical officer – was undoing my harness very slowly and asking me if I had any bad pains. I told him I only had a bad knee as it was bleeding and a headache, but I could get out of the cockpit with a bit of help. I got out of the side with his aid and they put me into the ambulance and off we went to the Hospital Wing. By the time we reached there I was fully aware of what was happening and I knew that there was very little wrong with me.

After a full examination the only damage I had sustained was a piece of skin taken off my right knee cap, this was soon plastered and I was able to get dressed again. Both our CO and my flight commander came to see how I was and I convinced them that there was nothing wrong with me. I was going to talk about the accident but the CO told me not to worry about it as long as I was all right; they could replace the machine, but not me. At the back of my mind I was thinking of the artificial horizon, there was something I had to do about it, but I could not think what it was. I remember thinking at the time I crashed that someone had made a cock-up and it wasn't me.

I was taken back to my billet and told that I could have the next day off. The sergeants in the billet were all awake and discussing the crash and I quickly learned that the machine was a complete write-off. Even the back of the fuselage had broken in half; nothing was salvageable. 'That's right, you bastards, rub it in,' I was thinking. My biggest worry was that the aircraft K9959 was the one I had done my first solo in and now I had killed it stone dead. Johnny White said that he would go with me and see the crash before breakfast as they had not cleared it yet.

The next morning about five o'clock we got up and walked over the other end of the aerodrome to the runway. The fuselage had already been shifted onto the grass verge. I could hardly believe my eyes, to think that I had escaped from that crash with a minor cut. We went along the runway and I saw the wings away on the grass flanking the runway, the biggest shock was to come because the engine was on the grass approach to the runway. I must have hit well before the flood light, that must have been the blinding light I saw as I bounced past. Johnny took some pictures of the wreck for me, I did not accept the prints, as I did not want a reminder of how I lost my first Spitfire.

During the morning I went to see the commanding officer and my flight commander and filled in the report, stating the change of barometric pressure I had been given and also the one I had been given prior to take-off. I also told the CO that I did not have my landing light on as my altimeter was reading 1,100 feet and I did not use a landing light at above 500 feet. I asked the CO if I could go on readiness at the afternoon session as I was quite able to fly and would like to do so. One reason I asked for this is because I was anxious to see whether I was to be banned from flying pending an investigation into the cause of the accident. He agreed and said to the flight commander, 'You have a visit to Wolsington this afternoon; he can go with you.' I felt relieved for I knew that if he had thought my crash was due to my own carelessness, he would not have let me fly until after the enquiry.

Another reason I wanted to be at flights that afternoon was because all the squadron would be there and the Five Sprogs had a special duty to perform that afternoon. After Flying Officer Elsdon had finished training us we decided that we would like to buy him something that would remind him of us whenever he had a beer. We had chosen a silver tankard and Johnny White was going into Newcastle that morning to pick it up from the engraver. Johnny arrived back before lunch and showed us the tankard. On the front was engraved:

To Flying Officer T A F Elsdon
For Patience and Devotion to Duly
From The Five Sprogs

It was something to be proud of and it was with this admiration for such a fine officer and friend, that we had chosen it.

After Johnny had packed it into its case, I asked him where the Iron Cross was. After all, the Five Sprogs had damaged at least five aircraft between them.

We had not told anyone else about the surprise we had for Flying Officer Elsdon and when we had settled down at the flight dispersal, we got together and handed the case to Pilot Officer Males who was Sprog One. We thought it would be more friendly as he could call him by his Christian name, whereas none of us sergeants could. He asked for a bit of hush as he had an important task to carry out. He then walked over to Flying Officer Elsdon and handing him the box said:

'Jimmy, on behalf of the Five Sprogs, I would like you to accept this gift as a token of appreciation from us, for all the patience and devotion to duty you have shown in teaching us amateurs to become professionals.'

The other officers and sergeants looked surprised and then Jimmy opened the case and took out the tankard; he did not speak for a few moments as he read the inscription that was engraved on it. He then read it out aloud to all of us and there was the usual clapping on such an occasion. Jimmy could not say a lot, but his look said it all. 'Thanks, chaps,' he said very quietly, but it was enough. It had been worth the effort to get the tankard engraved.

Later that afternoon I went with Green One to Wolsington, another fighter base. It was a quick trip; but I was back in the saddle again, and that was all that mattered as far as I was concerned.

Four nights after my crash I was on night readiness and I was scrambled to do the Blue Patrol. This consisted of flying out to sea about 100 miles and patrolling up and down an imaginary line between Newbiggin-on-Sea and Newcastle at a height of 25,000 feet; the idea was to intercept and shoot down any German bombers attempting to bomb Newcastle.

I had never been to that height on my own at night, and even in the daytime I did not like the feel of the aircraft at that height. It felt too light on the controls and having to fly on instruments exaggerated that feeling.

It was made worse because I had to turn 180 degrees after each leg.

I had been on patrol for almost an hour when I got the message to return to base and pancake. I immediately went into a dive and turned on to my course for base, pleased that I was now at a better height with more visibility. I landed without difficulty, having been airborne for almost the limitation of the aircraft. I had been up one hour and thirty minutes.

I was not afraid ot flying at night so near to my crash because I knew that the fault was not caused by my flying but my misdirection. I had heard no more about the episode, except what I had heard from one of the flight sergeant engineers. He told me that both the propellers from my head-on collision had been repaired as they were only bent; no damage had been done to either aircraft. I felt a lot better at that news and then he told me I would hear no more about my crash and writing off the Spitfire. You could say that I was feeling quite happy when I took off on Blue Patrol.

On these patrols you were in touch with base control all the time, but you could not transmit, except in an emergency. This was to stop the German aircraft beaming on your frequency and knowing where you were in relation to them.

I had climbed to 25,000 feet and was on patrol flying almost on instruments for the first leg so that I could get the airspeed and timing for my turns correct as I could not see the ground, I had to rely on dead reckoning using my clock and compass mainly. I was also on maximum oxygen. For the first two turns I was getting settled and used to the aircraft and the little red lights in the cockpit, then I saw what I thought was a ball of white fire coming straight at me -then it broke up into hundreds of pieces. I had never seen anything like it at night before – at least, not in the air. I could not call up on the RT to ask them what it was and I was very glad that I had not been able to or I would have looked an idiot. A few minutes later from another direction the same thing happened and then I realised that I had seen two shooting stars and the darkness gave a false impression of distance. They were miles from me. During the back and forth trips I had plenty of time to think, but unfortunately it was a very unpleasant think I was having. Suppose something goes wrong with the engine and I am in the drink, would they find me? Would my parachute open? Suppose there are enemy aircraft near me and I can't see them. They have gunners with free mounted guns and can fire from any angle, I can only fire forward and have to fly the plane as well.

'Calm yourself, laddie, don't panic, nobody asked you to join.'

Who was that? Must have been me, only another ten minutes and I would be free to return to base. The ten minutes passed and still no call from base to pancake; for over an hour I had heard nothing over the RT. I would wait another five minutes as I would be getting low on petrol if I did not start my let-down soon. I still remembered my other trip over Newcastle only a few days ago.

At last I heard those marvellous words: 'Hello, Green One, are you receiving me?'

'Hello Bluebell, Green One, loud and clear.'

'Green One, pancake, vector 260 degrees.' 'Hello, Bluebell, message received, out.'

While I was talking I was already in a pretty steep dive, I intended to get down as fast as possible this time. There is not much sense of speed at night so I hardly realised how quickly I had come down except that I thought I could see the aerodrome beacon very quickly after my descent. I was soon doing my circuit of the aerodrome and this time made a perfect landing and this time taxied more carefully and arrived in one piece at dispersal. As I was taxying, I thought of a hymn I used to sing as a child, 'Nearer my God to Thee'. After a flight like that at night that was as near as I ever wanted to get to Him, especially if that's the way you have to, up, up, up, up. I had been airborne for one hour and thirty minutes. A Spitfire should have a spare can of petrol with a long funnel in case of an emergency.

That was my last flight for the time being as I had done my quota of night flying and I was quite satisfied about that. There is an old saying:

Only birds and fools fly at day
Only fools and bloody idiots fly at night.

Things were beginning to hot up down south and we knew it was not going to be long before we were posted from Acklington. The signs were there but we did not know when or where. Our personal gear had already been packed.

On 31st August 1940 at early morning we knew where we were going and we were on our way to Biggin Hill. We were flying all the aircraft we could muster and would re-fuel on the way. We arrived at Biggin Hill after lunch and the ground crew who had travelled ahead of us the day before were there to re-fuel our aircraft. We were now in the thick of the Battle of Britain.

CHAPTER TWO

BIGGIN HILL AND CROYDON

We had shown the flag on the way down as we had sixteen aircraft in perfect formation and on arriving at Biggin, owing to the state of the airfield and the fact that there could be no formation landings, I had plenty of time to get a good look at the bombed-out aerodrome below. I was shocked to see the number of bomb craters which had been hastily filled in and which littered the grass field. I could see clearly the hangars which had been blown up the day before. Very little except the walls was left standing and several buildings were just a pile of rubble. My immediate thoughts went out to those poor buggers who had been in the thick of it for the past month whilst my pals and I had been enjoying ourselves at Acklington. It's true there had been some scrambles but we knew that it was only for the odd German aircraft, whereas we knew that when there was a scramble from Biggin Hill, it was to meet dozens or even hundreds of enemy planes.

The landings took a bit longer than usual, having to pick a path through the bomb craters but eventually we were all conducted to the far corner of the airfield to our dispersal area. Here our aircraft were taken over by our ground crew who had started off the day before by road as did the rest of the pilots who did not have an aircraft to fly down. We had hardly got out of our cockpits when the aircraft was taken over by another member of the squadron who had been there waiting for us to land.

When we went into the dispersal office we saw that the squadron had been put at 30 minutes' readiness and the flight plan was already on the wall. Only the CO's and flight commander's names were on the list so the rest of us were sent off to the mess to get a meal.

There was something about Biggin that you felt the minute you had landed on the airfield. Whether it was the smell of burning, cordite, the sight of the bombed-out hangars and buildings, or just plain anticipation of the danger to come, I did not know, but I did know one thing – we were now in the war with a capital W. Now would be the time to prove the value of the excellent training we had received all those months before. Our immediate worry for the moment was to get something to eat; we had had a busy morning and the flight down of two hours twenty minutes, plus the stop to refuel on the way down, had made us hungry and so after a little pep talk from our CO we were stood down from further duties for the day so that we could see our billets and have a meal.

A small van was ready to take us all to our respective messes and we all piled in for the trip to the mess. It was hard to leave the other chaps because we knew that it would not be long before they were in the air, possibly fighting for their lives while we were eating. This was enough to put all thoughts of food out of my mind, I would have preferred a tot of whisky or something hot but unfortunately the RAF rations did not run to this luxury.

The journey to the mess took us all through the bombed-out buildings and hangars. There was a burnt-out ambulance perched on the only bit of roof left on one of the hangars. By the time we had seen the other bomb damage, we knew that we would have to contend with it in the weeks to come. It was obvious the German High Command were out to destroy our airfields especially the fighter ones, as a prelude to the Invasion of Great Britain. It was up to us to stop the bastards from doing it.

None of us felt much like eating, because as we entered the mess, we heard on the tannoy 72 Squadron called to readiness. We went to our billets after having had some tea and toast which was about all we could manage. I decided that I was going to unpack only the essential personal things as I had a hunch that we would not be there very long. It did not look as though the airfield could take much more bombing. I went in to Johnny White's room and Stickey was already there. They were talking about the van that took us to dispersals and thought we ought to have a car of our own as some of the others had their own. One of the 79 Squadron sergeants, who were also at Biggin, had told them that unless you had a car to go out of a night with you would virtually be a prisoner on the aerodrome. He also told them of the local pubs and said, 'If you don't drink now, you will in a few days' time after you have been airborne a few times.'

I told Johnny and Stickey that we would discuss it with Johnny Gilders when he was off readiness. He had come down by road the previous day and was one of those who took over from us.

We were interrupted by the tannoy, telling 72 Squadron to scramble.

We took a quick look at each other and without a word we all raced out of the billets to the sergeants' mess where the transport van was parked. The driver was about to go and pick up the officers from their mess, but we piled in the back of the van first and then went to pick them up. As we were on the way, we saw our squadron get airborne in record time and after picking up the officers, we went to our dispersal to wait for the squadron's return.

We had just reached the huts when the siren went and unlike the first siren I had heard the day war on Germany was declared, this one was for real. We could hear on the dispersal RT of the number of bombers and fighters which were approaching Biggin Hill. A few minutes later we saw them in the distance and seconds after we saw the bombs leave the enemy aircraft. I was standing in the doorway with an officer looking at the bombs falling while John and Stickey were listening to the RT. The next thing I knew was a blast of hot air and some terrific explosions where the bombs had hit; some were on the grass and some were on the buildings. The next thing that happened was that all of us were lying on the floor. There was no air raid shelter anywhere near us and it was the safest place to be at that moment.

When the noise had died down we rushed out of the hut and watched the Spitfires who were attacking the bombers as they turned for home. It was so frustrating watching because they were so low I felt that if there had been some more aircraft on the ground we would have been able to take off and catch them before they reached the coast.

We could see the ground crew who were filling in the craters as fast as they could so that the aircraft would be able to land when they had run out of ammunition. Some of our aircraft were coming in the circuit. Our flight commander told us to get ready in case we had to take off again as we did not know if there would be any casualties.

We watched anxiously as the aircraft returned in one's and two's until we knew there were only eight of the twelve to return to base. One officer had been killed and one injured and baled out; two had landed at another base either to refuel or because something was wrong with their aircraft. The squadron's first sortie was costly as they had only claimed four Dornier 215's damaged.

We were stood down from readiness in time for dinner and we were a sorry crowd that climbed into the vans that evening. Our first day had been our baptism, and we all knew that this was only the start. Things could only get worse if Hitler's threat to invade our shores was to be carried out. It was a long way from *The Trap* at Acklington; tonight there would be no lovely ladies to welcome us at the bar. By what we had heard, we would be lucky to see a pub for a long time.

At dinner that evening we got the news that 31st August had been one of the hardest days so far, with forty of our own aircraft shot down with a loss of 11 pilots killed. The Germans had lost seventy-three aircraft. Our own aerodrome was almost out of action and a lot of work would be required to fill the craters in time for the next day's take-offs.

In that short time I had learned that it was probably safer up in the air fighting the enemy bombers than it was dodging bombs on the ground. We had heard stories in the press about pilots who raced to their aircraft and took off whichever way they could, to get into the air quickly. Some people must have thought they were mad. I now had my suspicions that they were not so silly as it looked.

John White, Stickey and myself were on dawn readiness so we did not go beyond the mess although one of the 79 Squadron sergeant pilots had offered to take us to the local pub, The Jail, in his car. Instead we had the chance to talk to some of the ground crew sergeants who had been at Biggin for most of the battle.

They told us about the previous day's bombing, twice in one day and that on 30th August, thirty-nine persons had been killed, some of them WAAF. It was estimated that during the days 30th and 31st August the

Germans had put up over 1,500 aircraft each day to bomb our airfields.

I excused myself because I wanted to go up to my room for some cigarettes. I walked down the corridor towards the staircase and saw some luggage which had been piled up by the door. As I approached my room, I thought I saw an airman come out of it, carrying some suitcases and I asked him if we were moving already.

'No, serge,' he replied, 'These belong to the sergeants who were killed recently.'

I could not reply, I had seen him coming from near my room though it was actually the one next to it.

In those few seconds I saw the ugly truth; these few precious belongings of the pilots killed would be all that their families would see of their loved ones. I thought of my wife at home with the baby. I said a silent prayer 'Dear God, please don't let my wife have to go through that.'

I went downstairs to the others and was greeted by Stickey with, 'Christ, mate, you look as though you have seen a ghost.'

I replied, 'I have, Stickey. Two of them in fact.' I did not elaborate on that statement, it was no good letting them know what I had just seen.

Johnny Gilders came in and sat down with us. He looked tired but we did not want to ask him what had happened on the first sortie. He said he had been talking to one of the officers of the other squadron whom he knew in Civvy Street; he told us that there was a garage in Bromley where you could buy old cars for next to nothing, owing to the cost of insurance and petrol rationing. He had also been told that it was essential to have a means of transport at night otherwise you would go round the bend. We told him that we had been considering it before he came in and so we decided that we would go into Bromley on our first afternoon off and buy a car. We decided that we could only afford about twenty pounds and were not interested in what it looked like so long as it went along the road.

I slept well that night and although there had been some raids, I did not hear anything. Consequently I was looking forward to getting over to flights on readiness; perhaps today we would get our chance to meet the enemy fighters.

It was 1st September and at 7.45 am when I had my first scramble from Biggin Hill. I was flying Green Two with Flying Officer Elsdon as Green One. I had complete confidence in whatever might lie ahead in the next twenty minutes or so. I was watching him all the time to keep good formation; I was also watching my instruments, oxygen, magnetos and everything that could be looked at, I intended that when the time came for me to make combat, I was going to be ready. I listened to the controller telling us to climb and giving our CO a vector and I assumed it would not be long before we saw the enemy. I had never been in such a high pitch of readiness either physically or mentally. I checked my gun sight and firing button, switched the camera button on and waited. I was now ready along with eleven other pilots to show the Germans that they were now up against 72 Squadron. I was waiting for the sighting of the enemy formations when after about twenty minutes I heard the instruction for our squadron to pancake. I was puzzled, we had not even sighted any enemy and we were about to land, I looked out of the cockpit and saw we were approaching Croydon Airport and that was where we were going to land. It would be hard to explain how I felt at that moment, in one sense I was annoyed that I had not seen action; in another sense I knew that I was still alive and that we were away from Biggin Hill and the bombing.

The real disappointment came when. we had landed. Our dispersal consisted of large bell tents on the west side of the airfield in sight of the airport offices and lounges and bars but not available to the sergeants, only officers. Our quarters were two semi-detached houses bordering on the airfield, no furniture and only the old iron bedsteads with straw palliasses. Our breakfast would be brought to us in the tents while our officers had the use of the restaurant; we had the use of the canteen for lunch and dinner. It was not a very good first impression of Croydon and all of us sergeants readily agreed that we would prefer the bombs to this Spartan way of living under operational conditions. We also knew that it was essential that we got our car quickly, otherwise our nights would be unbearable.

We had hardly got refuelled when we were brought to readiness and within an hour we were airborne once more. This time was for real, we had heard the CO get the information on the telephone. There was no tannoy available there. We scrambled to 15,000 feet and were told where the attack was coming from.

Once again I was all keyed up and ready for action when we sighted the enemy formations about two thousand yards away, we were being vectored towards the starboard side of the formations and I wondered why because we would have the sun behind us, I am sure our CO felt the same way. Suddenly it happened. There was call to break, and there right above and behind us were yellow-nosed Me 109s. It was a question of every man for himself. Before I realised what was happening I was in a steep turn to get this yellow nose from out of my rear mirror; at the same time I could see other Spitfires and Hurricanes milling around firing at everything. I had no time to get my sight on an aircraft although I saw enough crosses. I had lost the Me 109 which was on my tail and by now I was well underneath the formation which had turned back. I saw Green One, formated on him and heard the order for us to pancake. Flying Officer Elsdon looked across to me and put two fingers up and at first I thought he was being rude but I realised that he had shot down two Me 109s as they were the aircraft we had attacked. He confirmed this on landing.

When all our squadron had landed we saw that we were one short and that an ambulance was rushing towards one of them. One of our officers had been killed and another badly wounded. Our only claim was two Me 109s destroyed. Most of us had not even fired our guns; it was all over so quickly; one minute you were in the thick of it, the next minute you had lost height and it was impossible to climb up quick enough to engage again. A lesson I learned on that sortie was that some Me 109s would act as dummy in front of and below the bombers so that the Spitfires would dive down on a likely target and keep away from the bombers. It was something I would remember from then on.

When we were in the tent, very little was said about the sortie, either by our officers or the sergeants. We were more concerned about the wounded officer and the one killed. Two days running we had our losses; it did not bode well for the future.

Later that day we were again scrambled but it was only for a short time, we did not meet the enemy this time. The day had been a terrible anti-dimax for us sprogs and our billet did not help us forget. Our corporal promised to get us some better beds and furniture the next day and our CO was going to do something about us eating in the airport restaurant with the officers. He told us that as we were on early morning readiness the next day, we would have our breakfast in the tent but from then on it would be with the officers.

Sergeant Gray had a car and offered to take us into Croydon in the evening and we gladly accepted his offer. We went to a local pub not so much for a drink but to get away from those depressing billets. It also gave us a chance to meet some of the local residents with whom we had a few drinks and to have a chat with the owner of the pub.

The next morning we were to be at thirty minutes' availability and we arrived at the dispersal about six o'clock. Breakfast would be at seven-thirty in the tent – that is, if it was sent in time to eat it. The officers were having theirs in the restaurant in comfort. There was no rush for them to be at dispersal because at thirty minutes' availability they could easily be ready when required.

There were eight sergeants in the tent. Some had been marked down for squadron readiness, the others were there because it was better to know what was going on than to sit somewhere waiting for news.

At 7.30 am the telephone rang and the flight sergeant answered it. He put the phone down and told us all to get airborne immediately. No one asked why. We simply ran to the nearest aircraft, yelling to the crews to start up the engines and in no time we were taxying out to take off. The flight sergeant took the first four aircraft and I took the second four as Green One. There were no officers with us as the squadron had not even been called to readiness from the thirty minutes' availability state. It was only because we were in the tents waiting for breakfast that we were able to take off. The combat report for this action is J/2/15 dated 2-9-40.

SECRET   FORM F

COMBAT REPORT

Sector Serial No.	(A)
Serial No. of Order detailing Flight or Squadron to Patrol	(B)
Date	(C) 12-9-40
Flight, Squadron	(D) Flight: 'B' Sqdn: '72'
Number of Enemy Aircraft	(E) 30 Bombers + fighters
Type of Enemy Aircraft	(F) Do 17, Me 110, Me 109
Time Attack was delivered	(G) 08.00
Place Attack was delivered	(H) approx. MAIDSTONE
Height of Enemy	(J) 13,000-30,000
Enemy Casualties	(K) Me 110, Do 17 destroyed
Our Casualties Aircraft	(L) Nil
Personnel	(M) Nil

GENERAL REPORT   (R)

I took off from Croydon as Green One and followed Blue Section in wide formation and was instructed to climb to 15,000 ft. We saw the enemy approaching from ESE and Blue Section led the attack on the bombers while I followed above them. I saw Blue Section break away and the enemy was then turning to South as I approached. I saw one Me 110 leave the formation and dive on to the tail of a Spitfire and as no other Spitfire was near enough, I dived after it and came in at the Me 110 from 15° above and astern from port. I aimed at the Me 110 port engine and put about 640 rounds into it. It caught fire and appeared to fall away with part of the wing and the machine went over on its back and then went down with flames from the port wing. I had opened fire at 200 yds but did not see any return fire. I dived down to the starboard side of it and saw 17 Do 17 below me at about 12,000 feet. I had one in my sights and I fired all my other rounds at it. The fuselage blew to pieces and then the engine (port) caught fire. I closed my fire at about 175 yds to 50 yds and then dived again to starboard and went into a spin to avoid the Me 109 behind. I found myself flying at 4,000 feet when I pulled out of the spin. Above me rather separated I saw three parachutes drifting down and to my starboard I saw the Do 17 coming down in flames and it crashed into the wood NE of MAIDSTONE. I went up to investigate the parachute being as I could not see the enemy again. I saw that one was empty, another appeared to be a Sgt Pilot with Mae West, and the other had no Mae West and I circled round him and he landed near a factory at Chatham. I climbed up again to 3,000 feet and made for base as we were ordered to return.

Sgt Rolls
'B' Flight, Green Sect
72 Squadron

When we later landed back at Croydon we were faced with some very irate officers. The audacity of sergeant pilots taking off without their officers was something unheard of and they seemed at a loss to know what to do about it, until our flight commanders took over. They had been on the phone in one of the tents while we were landing and when we were all together they came into our tent to ask us how many enemy aircraft we had destroyed. Control had kept them informed as to what had happened. My own flight commander came over to me and said, 'Bloody good show, Rolls.' The other sergeants were likewise congratulated.

This time we had had no order to break and we were at the right height and distance when we made our attack, with maximum fire power. The enemy did not know what had hit them as they went down fast and furious. I had got two confirmed destroyed, Johnny White had a Dornier 17 destroyed and one damaged and also one Me 110 probable. Stickey had one probable and Johnny Gilders one Do 17 destroyed. The flight sergeant had been successful also. I think each one of us had made contact, if only to damage the enemy aircraft.

When we were making out our combat reports I asked Johnny White what position he was flying in and he told me was Blue Three. He also told me that he had been hit by a Me 110 on his tail but someone took it off him. I had the pleasure of telling him that it was me and that it had crashed at the edge of Birling woods near Maidstone. We were very happy at the results we had achieved without any officer to lead us and this fact only went to prove the value of the training Flying Officer Elsdon had put us through. Some of the credit for these victories should go to him.

That afternoon six of our squadron were scrambled to go to forward base at Kenley. When I was airborne I noticed that after a few minutes when we started to climb I was losing power and the engine was not sounding so good. As the flight was not likely to be long I decided that I would continue and get it seen to at Kenley. It was forty minutes before we landed and by then the aircraft was losing pressure in the oil system and I was glad when I arrived at dispersal. I told the flight sergeant to see if he could see what was wrong with the engine and went into the flight room to wait as we were supposed to still be at readiness.

Within the next ten minutes we had been ordered to scramble and I ran to my aircraft and the flight sergeant told me it was u/s as the magneto was not working on either mag. I had to watch the others take off after having tested the mags to satisfy myself that they were too bad for an operational sortie.

I went back to dispersal and listened to the controller on the RT set in the hut. Our flight of five aircraft was being vectored onto the target and I felt sick. Johnny White was up there and here I was on the ground without an aircraft. I could not listen any more so I went out onto the grass to lie and wait for their return.

About forty minutes later I saw two aircraft returning and watched them land. One had been hit and had made a bad landing, I thought immediately that the pilot must be injured. I then saw two others return and land and saw with relief that Johnny had landed and seemed to be all right. There was no sign of the fifth aircraft as I walked over to Johnny. I knew what had happened by the bullet holes in the aircraft which had landed.

As we were walking to dispersal I told Johnny what had happened to my aircraft.

'It's a good job it was u/s, Bill because we were jumped by Me 109s and did not have a chance. Blue Leader was hit and he did not bail out. I got hit on the tail unit and only just managed to break away in time.' He paused for breath and then continued, 'You know, Bill, I was scared out of my life when I saw all those Me 109's coming down on us. We had no time for avoiding action before they hit us.'

'Perhaps if I had been there as well, it might have made a difference,' I said.

'Don't be a bloody fool. It would have given them a better chance to knock another one down. At least you are here to fight another day. Poor old Snowy has had it'.

The flight commander agreed that it would have made no difference to what had happened even if there had been a dozen aircraft there at that particular moment. He asked about my own aircraft and I told him that they were changing the magneto, but that although it would be ready later in the day to fly back to Croydon, it would not be operational until a full inspection of the aircraft was done by our own ground staff. An inspection of the other aircraft showed that they could be flown back to Croydon to be serviced there. When this was reported to the controller he stood the flight down so that they could return to Croydon, having brought the flight that was still there to readiness again.

My aircraft was not ready until about an hour after the others had gone and although I still did not like the sound of the engine I took off and landed at Croydon in time to be stood down with the rest of the squadron.

That evening we went out to celebrate our day's victories and Johnny White was the first up to the bar and had whispered something to the barmaid and then turned to ask us what we wanted as there were six of us altogether and two were tee-total. Johnny gave the girl the order and then took from her a glass of whisky which he came up to me with; he put his arm round my shoulder and kissed me lightly on my cheek. I was flabbergasted and so were the others.

Stickey was the first to retort: 'Christ, I knew you two were bosom pals but I had no idea it had reached this stage.' The others were laughing but Johnny still had his hand on my shoulder, he said, 'Bill took a 110 off my tail this morning, otherwise I might not have been here tonight.'

'Cheers, Johnny, perhaps you'll do the same for me one day,' was my reply.

A gentleman who was standing near to us walked the couple of paces up to the middle of our group. 'Congratulations, lads, on today's effort. May I have the pleasure of asking you to join me in a drink?'

'It will be our pleasure, sir,' Stickey replied, and the gentleman told the barmaid to repeat the order for us. We duly toasted the gentleman's health and thanked him for his kind thoughts.

As more people came into the bar, we seemed to be the centre of interest. I don't think they had seen RAF sergeant pilots before, only officer pilots by the interest we seemed to be causing. After a short while the barmaid came up to us and pointed to the drinks on the bar; when asked where they had come from, she pointed to a man and presumably his wife. We all looked over to them and the man waved his hand to us and called, 'Cheers, lads.'

This was amazing, two free drinks in four minutes, it was just like being back at *The Trap*.

We had started on this second free drink when Johnny Gilders, pint in hand, walked over to the table where the man and wife who had bought us the drink were sitting. He spoke to them but not loud enough for us to hear what he was saying, but as the people on the other tables were all looking at him, we were beginning to wonder. He came back to us and we asked him what he had been telling them.

'I think their gesture was worthy of our personal thanks and so I thanked them for their round of drinks and told them that we would try and shoot down another half dozen bloody Jerries tomorrow.'

Needless to say, we did not have to buy any more drinks that night, and after a while had drunk as much as we could and still appear respectable. Good old Sergeant Gray was still sober and so our ride back to the billets was uneventful. That night even our metal bedsteads seemed comfortable.

SECRET FORM F   COMBAT REPORT

Sector Serial No.	(A)
Serial No. of Order detailing Flight or Squadron to Patrol	(B)
Date	(C) 4-9-40
Flight, Squadron	(D) Flight: 'B' Sqdn.: '72'
Number of Enemy Aircraft	(E) 30
Type of Enemy Aircraft	(F) Me 110+Junk 86
Time Attack was delivered	(G) 13.30
Place Attack was delivered	(H) Ashford and Tunbridge Wells
Height of Enemy	(J) 15,000
Enemy Casualties	(K) Two Ju 86's
Our Casualties Aircraft	(L) Nil
Personnel	(M) Nil

GENERAL REPORT   (R)

I took off from Croydon as Blue 3 in leading section at 12.50. We intercepted the enemy who were approaching us from the NE at right angles to our course. The leader gave the order line astern and turned to port to attack. His first burst hit the leading machine and the rest started to form a circle. I turned steeply to port and did a quarter attack on one of the end Ju 86. The port engine started to fire and two of the crew baled out as I went beneath. I turned steeply again to port and came up from the quarter on another Ju 86 which was in a steep bank. I gave a ring and a half deflection shot and my bullets hit the fuselage at about 200 yds range, and I saw the port engine smoke and the machine fall in. I followed it down and it was burning before it hit a wood SE of Tunbridge Wells. As I was about to climb up I saw another one crash not far away and it was followed down by Sgt Gray who joined up on me. We then went to investigate 3 parachutes and saw that 2 were German and one was an officer from our own squadron. I then flew back to base as I had run out of ammunition.

Rounds in First machine: about 800 to 1000

Rounds in Second machine: the remainder

Speed of Ju 86 about 160 to 180 mph

Firing cannon from back and what appeared to be cannon from the side window. Also tracer and incendiary bullets.

W Rolls, Sgt, Blue sect 3, 'B' Flight

The next day was rather a quiet one for me and I only did one sortie, but had no action. The 4th September saw us taking off at 12.50. I was Blue Three in the leading section and we were told the enemy were a mixed bunch of aircraft, making for Ashford in Kent. We intercepted them near Tunbridge Wells and made our attack. (See combat report page 53.)

That evening we had another interception over the London Docks, but I did not destroy any enemy aircraft. The same evening we again went into Croydon. It had not taken us long to understand what the 79 Squadron sergeant had said about getting away from the camp at night and also that if you don't drink now, you will after a few days here. I am not trying to excuse our desire to go out on the binge. We had seen some of our officers killed and wounded and some who had bailed out, all of this in a few days. It was no wonder that we thought our turn would soon come for the high jump, so why not enjoy ourselves while we could? That was the kind of mentality most of the fighter pilots had adopted for the first few days in action, but directly you realised you had survived some aerial battles and had got the better of the enemy, you tended to sober up and take it easier of a night. I even found time to write some letters home and this made my fight for survival necessary, even more than my mates who were all single, though they were of the same opinion as I was. We would have a drink at night when we were not on dawn readiness.

The next morning I was in a flight which was ordered to forward base at Hawkinge in Kent on the coast. We met some Me 109's and attacked them but it was impossible to get your sights on one of them long enough to get the right deflection. Unfortunately we lost one of our officers.

We returned to Croydon after lunch and the rest of the squadron were again scrambled later in the day but I did not go on that trip. One of our officers had to bale out and we lost one aircraft in sight of the aerodrome. He was right behind a Heinkel 111 and from the ground it seemed that the Heinkel was afire. At that moment a 109 dived down on the Spitfire and the Heinkel and the Spitfire fell to earth not very far from Croydon.

Those of us who were in the dispersal tent, waited anxiously for news as to who baled out and who was shot down. We knew that two of our aircraft had not yet returned but as other squadrons were involved we hoped the one we saw crash was not one of ours. The period of waiting was one of the worst I had encountered to date and it was a relief when the Ops phone rang to give us the news. The flight commander told us that our Australian officer, one of the nicest officers in the squadron, had baled out and was wounded. He looked at the sergeants who were by the tent opening:

'Sorry, chaps, have some bad news for you. Sergeant Gray has been killed.'

Until now we had lost some of our officers and had some injured and others who had baled out, but this was the first sergeant we had that had been killed and the fact that it was our dear old mate, Mabel, to those that were his friends, made it very hard to take. We had got used to it when we heard that one of the officers had been killed, you kind of expected that as they were the leaders, for they were more vulnerable, but when it came to our mate, who had taken us out each night, it was now personal and a great shock to all, as he was such a likeable chap. He would drink only a shandy so that he would be able to drive us home safely.

When we had finished for the day, we decided that we would get off the airfield as quickly as possible. We would go into Croydon and have something to eat and then have a drink in our local pub. We had a duty to perform. Later that evening after having had a meal we went back to the pub we had been using since we arrived at Croydon.

It was quite full and as we got near the bar Stickey called out for the usual four beers and a shandy. People soon made way at the bar for us and the manager asked where the other chap, the quiet one was. I pointed my finger towards the ceiling and the people round us all stopped talking. It went right through the lounge and yet no word had been spoken. We picked up our four beers and just said quietly, 'Cheers, Mabel' and took a few mouthfuls. Stickey then picked up the glass of shandy and poured it into each of our glasses. People were still looking at each other and did not say a word. They all seemed to know what it was all about and as most of them had seen Mabel on the other occasions, I think they were as shocked as we were.

Within a couple of minutes we were talking to the manager and things started to get back to normal. In the conversation I managed to tell him that we had agreed a long time ago that if one of us were killed, the others would drink his health and share his drink among us. We had even suggested that it might even come to one of us having to get drunk in order to carry out this request. We did not stay until closing time, I think we had depressed the other customers for long enough and so we caught a cab back to our billets for a more miserable night's rest.

I did not fly at all on the next day as our flight was at 30 minutes' availability and was not called to readiness.

That night we did not go out at all and wrote letters home instead.

On 7th September at late afternoon, we were scrambled and met 50 plus Dornier 17's with fighter escort going for the London Docks. Johnny White and I were in the section led by Flying Officer Elsdon and it was just like the training flights we had been doing with Jimmy back at Acklington. As we approached the enemy aircraft, he ordered echelon to port and I went underneath to come up on John's port side. This way we went into the bombers. As we were almost head on there was little chance to get a single target in your sight so it left you to open fire at everything in front of you as you flew through the formation of enemy bombers. At the same time the gunners in the front and rear turrets of the bombers were firing at us.

I saw a hell of a lot of crosses, but did not see any going down and by the time I had got through the formation, I was on my own without ammunition and was diving as fast as I could away from a Me 109 that I saw in my mirror. There were dozens of Spitfires from other squadrons attacking the bombers and I could see the fires down by the docks.

I was now over the reservoir at Chingford and not far from my parents' home at Edmonton. I flew low over the house and waggled my wings, I knew that if my parents did not see me, one of the neighbours would and they would tell my mother. They had seen me do the same thing when I was at Hatfield.

I then flew back to Croydon and landed. Flying Officer Elsdon and Johnny White had not yet returned and I was getting worried as I had not seen either of them after the attack had started. On landing I learned that Flying Officer Elsdon had baled out and that Johnny White had crash-landed somewhere near the docks. They had been seen by one of the other officers. It was now getting dark and we were stood down from readiness and would soon be going for our dinner, I decided that I would wait a while to find out where Johnny had landed as I knew he would phone in as soon as he was able. It was not very long before the phone rang and we got the message that he was in a pub in Rotherhithe and the MT driver who knew the pub would soon be going to pick him and his gear up. I asked our CO if I could go with the car to pick Johnny up and he readily agreed.

He rang the MT Section and ordered the car to come and pick me up; he asked me if I would like to go now or after dinner and I said 'He may be hurt and I don't want to wait if the driver is ready.' In minutes the driver had arrived to pick me up. I had not even had the time to have a wash, but that could wait.

As we were approaching the East End we could see the glow of the fires round the dock area; it looked as though London was going to be the target for the German bombers from now on. It was not long before we reached the pub, where the driver had been before. I expected that it would be busy, being a Saturday night, but as I pulled the blackout curtain aside, I was met with a solid wall of people and the noise was deafening. The people near the door saw us go in and immediately made way for us to get to John who was seated at the end of the room. He was surrounded by a bevy of ladies and had obviously had a couple of scotches by the looks of him. On the floor by his side was his Mae West and parachute. His arms were round two ladies' waists.

As I got nearer to him, he saw me and jumped up and put his arms round me and lifted me off the floor.

'I knew you would come for me,' he told me, and with that he put me down and sat me in his chair and one of the ladies stood up to let him sit down next to me. I had hardly sat down when a large whisky was put in my hand and I was told to drink up. I stood up and called, 'Cheers, everyone, and thanks for looking after my pal.' Then I saw myself in the mirror behind the bar.

My hair was a mess and looked dirty, my face was spotted with oil blobs some of which had been rubbed and my white scarf about my neck was likewise spotted with oil. I put my drink down and took my scarf off and tried to wipe my face and as I was doing so, an elderly lady whom I presumed was the owner of the pub came over to me and wiped my face with a nice warm flannel and got the spots off. She then took a comb and combed my hair back. The noise had by now died down considerably and we were the centre of interest. When the lady had finished she took my face in her two hands and kissed me saying afterwards, 'Thanks, son, for what you have been doing for us.' The next few minutes I did not know where I was because the other ladies young and old were kissing John and me and at the same time their men folk were slapping our backs and saying,

'Good show, mate.' Eventually sanity returned and another drink was put in our hand. One of the men asked me how the one who had baled out was, and I told them he was safe and unhurt. Someone asked me if I had been with John when he crash-landed and I told them I was the other one of the three they saw go head-on to attack.

I noticed that my scarf was missing and was looking for it when one of the ladies told me not to worry because the lady of the house was washing it to get the oil out before it dried in. I learned that her name was Edna and a few drinks later she came up to me and handed me the scarf which was still damp but clean. One of the ladies gave her a seat next to us and she asked why it was that all fighter pilots wore silk scarves round their neck, and nice black leather boots lined with lambs' wool. Johnny told her that the boots were for keeping one's tootsies warm and this caused some laughter. I told them that the scarf had two uses; one was for wiping any oil off your goggles or even your windscreen and in case you were wounded you might be able to use it as a tourniquet or bandage. I stopped here and one of the ladies asked, 'What is the other use then?'

I answered, 'Pure vanity. It looks good.'

This made them laugh even more and another drink was on its way down. I noticed at this point that our driver was not drinking at all but was enjoying himself talking to the women. It was now getting late and the driver asked if we were ready for the trip back and we said we were. There was a little bit of pushing from the back of the crowd and a large fat lady came and looked at us as though we were monkeys in a cage or something. She was obviously well known as it had gone quieter.

'Why, they are only a couple of ordinary blokes!' she exclaimed and with that she took a beautiful silk white scarf from around her neck and tied it round mine, then folded it into my tunic neck and patted my shoulder,

'Can't have you catching cold on the way back,' Emma said.

I did not know what to say to this very generous gesture so I bent down and lightly kissed her and said, 'Thanks, ma.' I was almost in tears and Johnny was the same. It was worth all the flying and danger to meet people like these, who really appreciated what we were doing.

After much kissing and back-slapping we crawled into the car and went back to our billet.

When we arrived back, Stickey and Johnny Gilders were waiting for us, they had not gone out on their own. We had hardly got in the room when

Stickey came over and pulled something from John's side pocket, and then came over to me and did the same.

'Where have you two been to? We expected you back two hours ago. And what's this stuffed in your pockets?'

We both put our hands in our side pockets and pulled out what seemed to be a lot of old papers but instead turned out to be pound and ten shilling notes; they were in the side pockets, the top pockets and even in the trouser pocket although I can't remember any unfamiliar moves by any of the ladies we had been with earlier.

We then related as best we could what had gone on in that pub.

'Next time any of us comes down in London, I will come and get him,' said Stickey.

When I was on my own I had another look at the white silk scarf. It was about a yard square but very fine and warm. I knew that it was going to see a lot of service in the future and I would not forget her remark when she saw us,

'They are only a couple of ordinary blokes.' How right she was. We were all ordinary blokes fighting for ordinary people, like that lovely lady and all those lovely ordinary people in an ordinary pub and all of us in an extraordinary land of Great Britain and most of all the Eastenders of London.

The next morning I was on readiness again and we were scrambled to patrol near Maidstone at 25,000 feet. It was a very cold and cloudy day and involved a lot of cloud flying to get above them. It was while climbing that I got something in my eye as at the time I had my goggles above my eyes, which gave you a much better all round view. You would pull them down over your eyes when going into the attack. I tried wiping my eyes with my scarfbut to no avail; it only made it worse. I decided that I would have to take my gloves off to be able to get a finger into the eye socket and pull the lid down over the other one. I removed my three pairs of gloves and felt the cold immediately and tried to clear my eye. My eyes were now watering so much I had a job keeping in formation as we were still climbing. I was attempting to pull the lid down when we went into a steep turn and I changed hands and just managed to keep the aircraft in formation, but in doing so my gloves fell from my knee into the bottom of the cockpit and I was unable to recover them.

My hands were getting colder and we were now at 25,000 feet and being vectored onto the enemy bombers and in desperation I again wiped my eyes with my scarf and this time I was successful although my eyes were still watering and I was not able to see very clearly. I knew we were now getting very near to the enemy. I went to put my firing button on to Fire but could not turn the switch, my fingers were numb. I could hardly hold the control column and I was getting out of formation. I only had seconds left to decide what I should do. I dare not use the RT to tell the CO what had happened. Then it suddenly came to me. The silk scarf round my neck! I pulled it off and tied it round my hand onto the control column and decided that I would have to follow the rest of the squadron even if I did not fire my guns, it would help break them up. I went into the attack with the rest of the squadron and kept as close to my number one as I could. They made a few kills but I did not fire my guns and my hand was still freezing but the silk scarf was beginning to have its effect in warming the hand. At least it was keeping my hand tied to the control column. Without it I would have had difficulty in controlling the aircraft.

I returned to base a very unhappy man but grateful that the feeling was now back in my hands. I untied the scarf and put it back round my neck. I remembered thinking that if I had the cotton scarf on I could not have tied it round in the same way as I could this lovely silk scarf and it wouldn't have had the warmth of the silk one. I would liked to have thought that perhaps the lady who gave it to me had given with it a little bit of her own warmth. God bless you, Emma.

I had learned a very valuable lesson though, and that was, never take your gloves off at altitude on an operational patrol.

On 9th September we had one short trip only, as the weather was not very good. On 10th September we had a day off and I decided to go to London and see my parents and in-laws. John Gilders was also going to see his parents. Stickey and Johnny White had decided to go down to the coast tor the day. The money we had been given was as good as a week's pay for each of the four of us and so we could afford a bit of luxury.

I decided that I would leave after having had some tea and catch a train to London and stay the night with my parents. As I was approaching Holborn Viaduct I could see the fires still burning and I thought at first that it was the station which was burning but on arrival I saw that it was on the other side of the road and quite a lot of buildings were burning round the whole area of St Paul's. It was frightening and I wanted to walk to

Holborn Viaduct to catch a tube train. I had hardly got out of the station when I saw these firemen pulling away some wreckage of a building which had been on fire. I went nearer to them and started to help them when I soon felt someone taking my arm and pulling me away; I turned to see who it was and saw that it was a fireman,

'What's that for?' I asked him.

'You have done enough work for one day. You are more important up there than down here. I can't take the risk of your getting hurt by falling masonry. Besides it's an experienced job which my men can handle.' He then let go of my arm.

'Now, son, I suggest you go down the shelter until it's all over.'

I thanked him, but told him that I was going to Edmonton to see my parents to put them at ease a bit. I then shook hands with him and started to walk the short distance to Holborn tube station. I had only gone a few paces when a young lad about twelve years of age came up beside me and took hold of my right hand and held it tight. I looked down at him and asked him what he was doing out of an air raid shelter and where were his parents?

'Don't worry about me, Guv. I'm used to the raids. You told the firemen you are going to Holborn tube station. Can I walk with you to keep you company?'

I did not want to upset the lad so I said it was all right by me.

'Are you a fighter or bomber pilot?' he enquired after a few moments of looking me over.

'A fighter pilot,' I replied.

'Well, why haven't you got your bleeding top button undone?'

'Because I am not on duty at the moment and I would be improperly dressed if I did not have my buttons done up.'

'Do you mean to tell me that someone is going to put you on a charge for one bleeding button, in the middle of a bleeding war?'

I admit that this conversation was taking my mind off what was going on around me, but there were too many bleedings in the conversation and from such a young lad I did not like it so I asked him why he had to swear. I also mentioned casually 'anyway it's not a bleeding button, it's a brass button, young man.'

At this remark he roared out laughing, 'You must be a stranger to London, if you don't know that that word ain't a swear word. Everybody says it where I live.'

By now we had reached the entrance to the tube and there were a lot of people about and some of them were looking at us as the boy was still holding my hand. I was anxious to get to my parents and as much as I liked this youngster I did not want to delay any longer but so many people were looking at us I was figuring how to say goodbye to him without people wondering what he was doing with me and holding my hand.

I saw a space on a seat near the ticket office and I walked over to it and put my arms under the lad's and lifted him on the seat, in a standing position. I quickly put my arms round him and kissed him on the cheek and said loudly so that the people would hear me.

'Cheerio, little brother. Don't forget to look after your mum while I'm away.'

I put a ten shilling note in his top pocket and walked quickly to the top of the escalator and as I reached it I felt a tug on my arm. It was him again. He handed me the folded ten shilling note and said, 'Thanks, brother, I did not help you for the sake of money'. He was crying as he ran away.

I was standing waiting for the train and a man and woman came up to me. The woman said, 'Your little brother was upset at you leaving him, it's a shame you have to go back to your squadron.'

I only nodded in reply. I could not talk, I was too choked up myself and all the way to Edmonton I thought of this young lad. I had become a brother to a complete stranger, if only for a little while. I also thought of the moaning we had been doing over our billets etc and when I saw in the past two days what the people of London had to contend with, sleeping in shelters and tube stations, I vowed I would never again complain of what was happening to me.

When I reached my parents' home I found my mother and sisters in the Anderson shelter at the bottom of the garden. My father was with the air raid warden just along the road. No need to enlarge on the greetings from my family. They had seen me fly over two days earlier and were surprised to see me because I had not let them know that I was going to visit them because of the short notice I had received of my day off.

The air raid was still on and as my mother was not very well she had a bed in the shelter. I was appalled at her having to live under these conditions but as she pointed out to me there were a lot worse than she was. It was at that moment that I realised the full horror of what this war was like to the civilian population who could do nothing but wait and take it. I was more than grateful that my own wife and baby and younger sister were away in Gloucestershire, so far out of the way of the bombings.

I wanted to get outside the shelter to see my father but my mother said that he would be back soon and did not want me to leave her. That night was a night I would not forget in a hurry. I realised how ill my mother was and the claustrophobic effect the shelter was having on me made it unbearable, but for my mother's sake I had to put up with it. I spent the next day visiting some aunts and my in-laws, but I was thankful when it was time to go back to my squadron and once again help to stop the bombers from reaching London.

The next morning I was at readiness and we talked about our respective days off and in the afternoon we were scrambled at 1500 hours to intercept 100 plus Dornier 17's escorted by Mc 110's and Me 109's. We met them east of Maidstone (see combat report page 64.)

Johnny White destroyed a Do 17 and a probable Do 17. Johnny Gilders got a Me 109. There were other claims for destroyed and damaged and we all returned safely to base. We had helped pay back the Germans for what they had done to the people of London the night before, but better still was that there would be a few aircraft less for them to use another night.

That evening one of my old pals from the other squadron which had arrived at Biggin Hill came to visit us in his car and took us to a pub way out in the country. We had a wonderful evening away from it all and even the regulars let us enjoy our evening together to talk of old times at Cambridge.

On the morning of 12th September we took off to intercept a 100 plus raid and once again it was a question of breaking up the formation for other squadrons to get at more easily and although I fired all my ammo I did not wait to see any results and hoped the camera gun would show something. I was about to pull up and turn after diving on the formation with the rest of our squadron when I felt my aircraft judder and felt something hit my throttle which stunned my hand. I felt a terrific draught coming into the cockpit and I knew that I had been hit somewhere although I could not see any aircraft near enough to me that could have fired at me.

When I landed back at Croydon, and having taxied over to our dispersal point I saw the holes in the cockpit; one of the insstruments had been smashed too. Then I saw holes on the other side of the cockpit and wondered how I had got hit both sides at the same time. I soon found out because before I could get out of the cockpit, I saw a metal rod coming through one of the holes and an airman on my wing put his hand on the rod and pushed it through the other side of the cockpit. The rod was now four inches from my Mae West at chest height.

COMBAT REPORT

Sector Serial No.		(A)	
Serial No. of Order detailing			
Flight or Squadron to Patrol		(B)	
Date		(C)	11.9.40.
Flight, Squadron		(D)	Flight: 'B' Sqdn.: 72
Number of Enemy Aircraft		(E)	100+
Type of Enemy Aircraft		(F)	Do 17 Me 110 and 109
Time Attack was delivered		(G)	15.50
Place Attack was delivered		(H)	East of Maidstone
Height of Enemy		(J)	20,000
Enemy Casualties		(K)	One Do 17 and 1 Do 17 probable
Our Casualties	Aircraft	(L)	Nil
	Personnel	(M)	Nil
		(R)	See Below
Searchlights: (Did they illuminate enemy if not, were they in front or behind		(N.I)	
A.A. Guns: (Did shell bursts assist pilot intercepting enemy?)		(N.2)	
Range at which fire was opened in each attack delivered, together with estimated length of bursts.		(P)	200 yds closed one No 1 at 25 to 30 yds 6 sec burst'on No 1
Total No. of Rounds fired			2,600
Name of Pilot (Block Letters)			ROLLS, W T Sgt

GENERAL REPORT   (R) See Below

I took off from Croydon as No 3 in Yellow section and we met the enemy at Ashford region where they were flying on a NW course. We attacked them from the beam and by the time our section had got into position we were attacking dead astern of the Do17. We dived down from 25,000 to 20,000 and made our attack. I saw return fire from the Do17 and immediately I opened fire it stopped and I saw pieces flying away from the machine and smoke start coming from the engine. I closed range at about 25 to 30 yds as it hauled over to starboard and went on its back as I did a steep turn to watch it go down. It continued to spin with smoke and flame coming from it and I saw it crash over a wood and lake at an estimated position Cranbook. I started to climb up again and I saw the other enemy machines above me. I continued to climb up below them from astern and saw the Mel 09s above me but they did not attack then. I was about 300 yds below them and I aimed full deflection on the leading machine and directly I fired I saw pieces flying off the underneath of it. I pulled the stick back gradually and finally saw the machine slip in but no smoke or fire came from it. By this time I had stalled and found myself in a spin. When I had pulled out I saw 3 Me 109s coming down towards me and I had to get them off my tail. They opened fire and I got hit on the tail plane and I kept doing steep turns and finally got rid of them at 3, to 5,000 feet and then I dived down to about 800 feet and came back home to Croydon. I had 13 rounds left in each gun approx. Before I fired my guns I saw Yellow 1 hit a Do 17, which went down between the hills near my own Do 17.

Sgt Rolls
'72' Squadron, 'B' Flight

The airman then said, 'Sergeant, do you realise that one ten-thousandth of a second later that bullet would have gone right through your heart.'

I looked at him and thought he had gone mad. I climbed out of the aircraft and told him not to do a stupid thing like that again. As an afterthought I asked him how he had worked that out so quickly. He showed me a chart he had made out showing various speeds of the aircraft and how far the aircraft would travel in one second, he had reduced this to inches and was thus able to calculate immediately how long it would take for the aircraft to travel the number of inches the bullet was away from you. This is why they used the cleaning rod of the Browning guns on the aircraft as it was the right size to penetrate the bullet holes on either side of your cockpit.

We had not been refuelled very long and I had only just put my parachute into another serviceable machine, when we were again ordered to scramble. This time the instructions from the controller were music to our ears. We were told to return to Biggin Hill for future operations.

Although we had some very good memories of some very nice people at Croydon, nothing could compensate for going back to a sergeants' mess where the other squadron pilots were. We had missed the atmosphere of good-hearted rivalry and especially the food and beds. During the afternoon we were again scrambled but did not intercept as the enemy formation had turned back at the coast. The four of us were told that we would be off the next afternoon.

That evening in the comfort of my room I was able to write to my wife and tell her of my visit to my parents and her parents and sister. I also told her about the Anderson air raid shelter and said it was a good job we never had to use the one we had before moving to Watermoor at South Cerney. I did not tell her about how many aircraft I had shot down or even about my own near misses, as long as I was well, that's all she need to know. I told her about Johnny and me in the pub in the East End and as she knew Johnny she was amused by it.

That evening we had a booze up with the sergeants from the other squadron at Biggin and also discussed a visit we were going to make to Bromley to buy an old car as we would certainly need one to get about in. There was an ample supply of cars among our rivals so we had to get something in order not to be outdone by them as far as the drinking stakes and even the girlie stakes were concerned. We decided that we would go to the pub first and that we would spend up to twenty pounds for the car; that was about as much as we could afford, nearly one week's pay each.

The next afternoon we got a lift into Bromley and were just in time to get into the pub and order a beer each. It turned out to be a most profitable pint because we found out that the barman was a friend of the garage where we were going for the car. He told us to ask the garage owner to let us have a Humber Essex 19HP car, which was in the garage and as it was heavy on petrol and insurance we would get it for a song.

We finished our drink and went to the garage to look at the cars on the forecourt and soon a man came up and asked us if we had seen anything of interest. We told him we had except that the price was too high.

'How much do you want to spend then?' he enquired.

'Nothing above twenty pounds,' said Stickey.

'You are sure you are looking for a car which goes under its own steam?'

It was a beautiful car, in almost perfect condition. The upholstery inside was luxurious. He started the engine and it went first time and purred like a kitten. I was almost wishing that he had not showed it to us as it was obviously worth a lot of money, more than we could afford.

He asked us how we liked it. There was no need, for our faces gave us away. We would have to have it and mortgage our pay for the next six months by the looks of it. He handed us the log book and a big volume instruction manual, and told us that it had been owned by an American lady and had been chauffeur-driven. I would well believe it because of its condition. We were waiting for him to tell us the prick.

'Well, let me have the twenty pounds then,' he said.

Stickey had been holding the money and took it out of his wallet. He kept it in his hand and said to the man, 'On one condition.' 'Oh, Stickey, for heaven's sake don't cock it up,' I was saying under my breath.

The man looked at Stickey somewhat puzzled as were we, 'And what might that be?' he asked.

'That you fill it up with petrol.'

'Do you realise that the petrol tank holds twenty gallons and even the autovac takes half a gallon before you can start it?' He then roared out laughing.' I thought I was doing you the favours, lads, but I will put three gallons in for free.'

'Done,' we all cried, and with that Stickey paid over the cash and was about to count out the last pound in change and the man said, 'Forget the other pound. Lets make it a pound a horsepower. Will that satisfy you?'

Thanks to a grand gentleman we had a car of our own. How we were going to tax and insure it none of us knew or cared and it was with great pride that Stickey drove the car back to the aerodrome. To our amazement the guard on the gate never said a word to us and let us proceed to the mess. We were now the proud possessors of a prestige limousine; no more would we have to rely on MT for trips from the mess to dispersal. The world of Kent was now our oyster, except for that one little item, petrol and insurance. We solved that the next day quite simply; we considered that as we were going to use it officially on the camp, then the RAF should pay for it, so we painted RAF roundels on each wing and RAF on the windscreen and filled up with petrol from the bowser. 100 octane petrol worked fine on that car.

On the morning of 14th September we were airborne and met the Me 109's and bombers going back across the channel but I had no claim.

In the late afternoon we were again intercepting 50 plus Me 109's west of Canterbury. (See combat report page 68.)

The other pilot who I had thought put a burst of fire into this aircraft as it was going down did not do so, and it was later confirmed that I had shot it down.

We soon found out the real value of having our own car. It saved the officers from having to deviate their car to pick us up and we were able to get to dispersal much quicker. It was even better when we stood down for the day because we could get away without having to wait for the officers. For the cost of the petrol the RAF were getting an extra transport vehide and it was a good booster for our morale.

We went in to Bromley that evening and found a nice club called the Country Club. Here we found some of the 92 Squadron sergeants who had found it days before and they were not too pleased that opposition had arrived, especially with those nice young ladies who used to dance there.

SECRET   FORMF
                          COMBAT REPORT

Sector Serial No.	(A)	
Serial No. of Order detailing Flight or Squadron to Patrol	(B)	
Date	(C)	14.9.40.
Flight, Squadron	(D)	Flight: 'B' Sqdn.: 72
Number of Enemy Aircraft	(E)	50 + Me 109s
Type of Enemy Aircraft	(F)	Me 109
Time Attack was delivered	(G)	18.25 approx.
Place Attack was delivered	(H)	West of Canterbury
Height of Enemy	(J)	20,000
Enemy Casualties	(K)	Me 109 damaged (confirmed crashed)
Our Casualties Aircraft	(L)	Nil
Personnel	(M)	Nil
Search Lights Was enemy illuminated. If not were they in front or behind target	(N)	

GENERAL REPORT   (R)

I took off from Biggin Hill at 18.00 as Blue 3 and we were told to patrol Canterbury at 20,000 ft. We met the enemy west of Canterbury and as we were about to get in line astern to attack a Me 109 dived down from behind and started to do a quarter attack on Blue 2 as he was going underneath Blue 1. He had fired a few rounds at Blue 2 and then I was in a position to do a quarter attack on the Me 109. I was at 150 yds range approx where I opened fire. I gave about 4 sec burst with full deflection and saw my bullets and tracer sweep down the side of the Me 109. It suddenly pulled back as though to do a loop and then spun down with what appeared to be glycol fumes coming from it. I watched it spin for about 6,000 feet then suddenly another Spitfire flew up to it so I left it to him in case it wanted finishing, while I went back to try and make contact again. The Me 109 eventually crashed in flames near Betherston after the other pilot had put another burst into it. Rounds Used 1,000 about.

Sgt W Rolls
72 Squadron
'B' Flight
Blue Section

When we returned late that night our car was more like a bus than a car. I forget how many we had rammed inside it; there were several WAAF and what appeared to be twice as many sergeants. I was driving and was having difficulty in getting my feet on the clutch pedal as half a dozen other feet were in the same spot. It was with great relief that we reached a large country house on the way to the airfield and I was asked to stop. The doors were opened and the sergeants from 92 Squadron and most of the WAAF disappeared before my very eyes. In the back were the two Johnnys with two nice WAAFs. One was a corporal. She was telling them about what had happened when the aerodrome had been bombed on 30th August. We thought we had been through it these past two weeks but after hearing what they had to say it was a wonder there were any WAAF left on the aerodrome. If the Johnnys had any thoughts of passionate embraces that night, they were soon dispelled.

We agreed that we would see them later that week and would call at their billet when we were next going to the Country Club.

Before going to bed we went to have a look at the next day's duty roster and we found that 'B' Flight were at Croydon and that we would be at readiness there by nine o'clock. It only applied to Johnny White and myself.

Early next morning John and I got our car and went to Croydon by road. We did not have to wait for anyone so we had plenty of time for a nice Sunday morning cross-country run. It was interesting to go through the small villages and to see the locals going to church. We seemed very far removed from the reality of what we would be doing later on that day, should we be ordered into the air. As we passed by a small crowd of people they waved to us and someone called out, 'Good luck, lads.' At that moment nothing could have brought back the horrible reality of this war more vividly than the contrast between this lovely country village and its inhabitants quietly going to church to give thanks to God, and our purpose for being in that village on the way to join 'B' Flight – to possibly kill enemy aircrew. I quietly said my own prayer for the day as we passed the old church gate.

When we finally arrived at Croydon we saw that John was on the board as Flying Officer Elsdon's number two and I was to lead Green Section as its number one behind them. This would be the second time I had led Green Section – that is if we got in the air-so I felt good and was actually hoping we would get the chance to become airborne.

At about ten o'clock we got word that there was a big build up of enemy aircraft across the Channel, one of the largest they had seen so far. We all knew that it would not be long before we would scramble so we went to our aircraft, strapping in ready for when we got the order to scramble. The airmen were there waiting to start the engines. I felt a terrific tension as I waited. I thought of my wife and baby, of the young lad at the tube station, of Edna and Emma from the pub at Rotherhithe and I knew that I had to get something or do something to help stop these people from being on the receiving end again.

At 10.30 approximately, we got the order to scramble our six aircraft and with Flying Officer Elsdon taking the lead we were all airborne in about two minutes, or even less, but who was counting anyway. We went into a steep climb and made for Maidstone, where it appeared that the first wave of enemy bombers and fighters were approaching. We swiftly climbed to 20,000 feet. At 11.05 precisely we were meeting them. There seemed to be hundreds of them in different groups supported by fighters all round and above them.

Flying Officer Elsdon turned us so that we were now head on to the nearest group and on our flank was 92 Squadron with our mates from Biggin.

Flying Officer Elsdon gave the order echelon port, and I immediately led my section under his and my number two went to the outside. Our flight was now in line abreast with six aircraft and in that way we went head-on to the formation which immediately started to break away and at the same time was met by the boys from 92 Squadron who were now in the ideal position. I got mixed up with the Me 109s (see combat report Jl5279, on this page)

I finished up well below the enemy aircraft and as I had been hit and I had oil all over my goggles, I decided to get back to base at Croydon.

Within ten minutes four of us had landed and all had some damage although not enough to put the aircraft out of action for long. Next, one of the officers came in wheels up but was not hurt. We heard from him that Flying Officer Elsdon had baled out. This was a shaker. His leadership of our flight had done what was intended of it, broken up the formation leaders of enemy bombers and by all accounts the other squadrons who were there had a field day.

We heard once we had landed that we would be put at 30 minutes' readiness as our full squadron at Biggin Hill were now at readiness. One hour later they were airborne and this time John Gilders and Stickey were with them. They had some successes but one of the fight commanders had been shot down but baled out.

SECRET   FORMF
COMBAT REPORT

Sector Serial No.	(A)
Serial No. of Order detailing Flight or Squadron to Patrol	(B)
Date	(C) 15.9.40.
Flight, Squadron	(D) Flight: 'B' Sydn.: /2
Number of Enemy Aircraft	(E) 30 + fighters
Type of Enemy Aircraft	(F) Me 109 and He 111's
Time Attack was delivered	(G) 11.05
Place Attack was delivered	(H) Brenchley
Height of Enemy	(J) 20,000
Enemy Casualties	(K) 1 Me 109 damaged
Our Casualties Aircraft	(L) Nil
Personnel	(M) Nil
Search Lights was enemy illuminated. If not were they in front or behind target	(N)

GENERAL REPORT   (R)

I took off from Croydon as Green 1 in the second section and we climbed to 24,000 feet and made contact with the enemy round about Brenchley. We saw some enemy machines coming in from the SW and we went flying at right angles from the SE. We saw another lot coming from SE to our starboard and as they were below us and an easy target we dived to do a head on attack after turning to starboard. I saw a Me 109 coming down and it passed well over my head and appeared to be firing at the one in front of me. As it climbed up again I climbed up after it and at about 200 yds I gave a burst of about 2 or 3 sees underneath it. I saw a big black patch appear and several small ones on the fuselage and I saw some tracer coming from behind me as well and in my mirror saw another Me 109 coming down on me. I evaded it and could not get round to fire at it because it climbed away and as there were about 20 more above with it I decided to leave it. I did not see what happened to the other Me 109 except that it was in a dive as I was in a steep turn. Rounds fired 900.

W. Rolls, Sgt
72 Squadron
'B' Flight

In the early afternoon we got word that Flying Officer Elsdon was in hospital with a very badly wounded leg and would be out of action for a long while. Johnny White and I were pleased to hear that Jimmy was safe but the fact that he would not be with us on future trips was indeed bad news; 72 Squadron without Jimmy as far as we were both concerned was like strawberries without cream, tolerable but not so interesting. Jimmy was not a big chap in stature, but in personality he was a giant in our eyes.

Later that day we had another scramble from Croydon. It was almost dark and although we did not see the enemy, he must have been worried knowing we were about.

It was dark when we arrived back at Biggin Hill and we did not have the floodlight to land by, only our landing lamp on the aircraft. But all four of us landed safely.

That night in the sergeants' mess there was a lot to talk about, especially with the other squadron's sergeants. They had several victories and agreed that we had broken up the main formation minutes before. They had been able to pick off the bombers who had lost their fighter escort in the initial attack by us.

We were talking about the yellow-nosed Me 109's which had dominated the German formations. We had never seen so many in the air at one time and so we guessed that they had put up everything that day to break our squadrons, but they had not bargained that after the first attack we still had many squadrons in reserve ready for their second attack and even then when they came the third time we still were able to put up a considerable force on the evening.

It was while we were discussing the subject that one of the 92 Squadron pilots asked if any of us had seen the other friendly aircraft coming from the north and hitting the bombers after they had done their bombing. Two or three had seen them and wondered why they had not attacked with us before the bombers had reached their targets.

Stickey came to the point: 'The bastards waited until the bombers had fired all their bloody ammo at us and then they had no opposition because the Me 109's did not go that far with the bombers.'

'Who the hell are they, and where do they come from? I have never seen any of them flying like that before?' queried another pilot.

'Perhaps we will hear tomorrow,' I said, and continued, 'If they had been with us on that initial attack, I don't think one of the bombers would ever have reached its target, it is bloody lonely with only five other aircraft with you.'

We did not bother to go out later that evening and settled for a drink or two in the bar. One of our ground sergeants told us that our passion wagon was being brought back by one of the airmen so we would have it for the next morning.

On 16th, 17th, 18th and 19th September we had several scrambles but very little success. We were either too far away, too high or even too low. Although during one of these trips I had fired over two thousand rounds at a formation of bombers I did not claim anything as I did not stay to see any of them going down.

On the 18th I had a very nasty experience. We had intercepted some Me 109's and had started to attack them at about 25,000 feet. I was about to set my sight when there was a puff of white smoke which seemed to come from my instrument panel and a smell of cordite. I thought I was on fire and turned quickly to take avoiding action, but I could not see because the smoke had partly blinded me. I felt my aircraft shudder and I went into a spin. I immediately pulled the hood back as the smoke was getting behind my oxygen mask. My first thought was to bale out but this can be dangerous in a spin and as I had plenty of height I decided to wait. My biggest fear was that one of the Me 109's would follow me down and get me as I pulled out of the spin, although I knew from experience that it would have to be a first dass pilot who could hit my aircraft while in a spin. All these thoughts ran through my mind as I lost height and I was now beginning to see where I was going as the smoke had almost gone. I decided that I was going to leave it to the last moment to pull out and if any fighter was on my tail waiting, he would be an easy target for the ack-ack guns. I looked round as best I could and at five thousand feet pulled out of spin. I remember thinking at the time, 'It's a good job I practised this so many times when I was up in Acklington.' I had another good look round and saw that I was on my own and made my way back to base and checked my instruments which all appeared to be OK. I made a good landing although in the last ten minutes I had never been so scared in all my life. My Mae West was covered in black oily dots like German measles, but I had no idea what had done it.

When I had landed, one of the ground crew came out to me and I saw him look underneath the port wing near the fuselage. He jumped up on the wing and told me that there was a big hole in my near gun ammo pan and it had gone into the cockpit.

I showed him the marks on the instrument panel and he took some cotton waste and wiped the panel. It was clean underneath and he asked me to let him get into the cockpit so that he could look at the hole which the missile, whatever it was, had made. While he was looking for it, I went round to the wing and the armourer took the ammunition box from out of the wing. It had a hole right through it and had damaged some of the links, but had not hit any of the bullets themselves, otherwise I would have been in real trouble. The hole was not very big and he took a block of lead and a hammer and in no time at all had almost sealed the hole. Another airman was getting a canvas patch doped ready to stick over the hole.

We were short of aircraft and this kind of service from the ground crew was no exception. We had got to the stage where to get an aircraft serviceable, they would take a part from an aircraft which was badly damaged and was unlikely to fly for a long time. The LAC fitter came over and told me that it would take ten minutes to check all the instruments and that he would test the engine and mags.

'You should have it back within the half hour, sergeant.'

As we were on thirty minutes' readiness for the others to refuel, this was fine and I would be ready for another flight if needed.

I went to dispersal and cleaned up my face and took my Mae West off to look more closely at the black marks on it. I found that some of the marks were actually very small holes and they were greasy. The Mac West was of no use because of the holes and I phoned the equipment section for a new replacement.

It was a sad moment parting with it, especially as I had not erased Sprog Three from the back of it. I would be the first of the Five Sprogs to graduate and was not what any of the five wanted. We were too proud of our reason for the Sprogs and I was always reminded of Jimmy Elsdon whenever I put mine on.

It was not long before I had a nice new Mae West on and this caused some ribald remarks from the others: they had no intention of erasing their numbers and I felt like an outsider. I still did not know what had caused the damage and the armourer said that he thought it must have been a dud cannon as there was no hole where it went out the other side of the cockpit. Someone suggested that the white smoke could have been glycol, but I knew different. I had smelt glycol too many times to mistake anything else for it. My aircraft was ready again so I had no reason to worry any more about the incident.

It's a good job my aircraft was serviceable so quickly as we had two more scrambles before the day was out and although I did not claim any victories, we did meet quite a formation of bombers and fighters on our second trip.

The next day we had only one sortie of two aircraft and we had to patrol a line near the coast, but the weather was bad and we didn't have any contact with the enemy that day. When I got back our flight commander was talking to the others about days off as we had been flat out for the last two weeks and with plenty of pilots and few machines it was possible to be able to let a couple go off at a time. I was told that Johnny Gilders and I would be off for two days from the 21st until 1pm on the 23rd. This was not long enough for me to go home to South Cerney by train and I asked my flight commander if I could borrow our Magister communications aircraft for the two days, so that I could fly home in about one hour. He told me to ask the CO first. While I was waiting for the CO to be free, I was talking to the engineer officer and told him I hoped to borrow the Magister to go to South Cerney for a couple of days.

'If I get some spares sent up from the MU at Gloucester, could you pick them up at Cerney? I can order them by phone and as there will be an aircraft waiting for them, they will make sure you get them. It will save us some time.'

Armed with this little piece of blackmail I told the CO that I was on two days' leave on the 21st and had offered to pick up some spares for the engineering officer, at South Cerney and could I borrow the Magister for the two days. I also told him that Sergeant Gilders was on two days' leave also and I could drop him off at Heston Aerodrome which was near his home.

'I suppose you have already got permission from your flight commander?'

'Yes, sir, he has agreed.'

'Would it be a coincidence that you live at South Cerney? Permission granted.'

I walked to our dispersal hut to tell Johnny Gilders that we had been given the aircraft and I would drop him off at Heston, which would save him a few hours of his leave.

'How did you wangle that?' he asked me and at the same time some of the other officers and sergeants were looking a bit puzzled, perhaps because I had had the nerve to make such a request at that particular time. I considered that I was lucky, that I had a new and sympathetic flight commander who had recently been promoted ' within the squadron, and who had the well-being of his men at heart. The CO was of the same calibre. Neither of them looked the part of the tough fighter pilot which was often portrayed in films. They were more like my masters at school. I could not imagine any other CO in Fighter Command at that time considering my request and granting it. Perhaps that's what made 72 Squadron so special.

Johnny Gilders and Stickey had been to the hospital to see Flying Officer Elsdon, and told Johnny White and myself that although Jimmy was looking cheerful enough, he was in great pain and there were fears that he might lose the leg that had been wounded a few days earlier. Johnny said that we would go over to see him when I got back from my days off.

Johnny White and myself had flown so many times with Flying Officer

Elsdon that it was a strange and horrible feeling to know that he would not be leading us into action again. It was unusual for me, a married man with a baby girl, to even consider any emotion for the male species and although we had lost some very fine officers and NCO's in the past weeks, I had accepted it unemotionally. It was a different kind of emotion that I and indeed all the Sprogs had for Jimmy. Our close relationship with him back at Acklington and his kindness in wanting to know about our families was something I had never known before except for my first instructor Flight Lieutenant Worger-Slade at Gatwick, on my EFTS course. Under Jimmy's leadership John White and I had made some successful kills with the enemy aircraft. The one consolation though was that all our officers were first class chaps and whoever was leading us in the future, we were bound to win.

That evening was spent quietly. Johnny Gilders and Stickey seemed too distressed at seeing Jimmy Elsdon. I was going to write a letter home telling my wife I would be home for a couple of days. I did not post it. I thought I would surprise her by flying over our house at Cerney; she would know who it was.

The next day I was on early readiness and about 11.15 we were scrambled to intercept 50 plus Me 109's at between 25,000 and 30,000 feet coming towards the coast of Kent. In the first place only Red Section of three aircraft took off to make a high speed climb to that altitude and having patrolled for a short while, we were told to rejoin our squadron which was climbing to our height. We met them and my combat report shows what happened from then on (page 78). We lost one of our nicest officers on this sortie.

I remember that sortie perhaps more than any of the previous ones. For one thing, I was going on leave the next day, so I had to win this one. The thoughts of that young lad at Holborn, which had haunted me for days, made me determined that someone was going to pay for that evening and it was not going to be me. I knew from the second I spotted that cross on the German aircraft that part-payment for the bombing I had seen that night was about to be paid.

I had forgotten all about how long I had been airborne and when I saw that my petrol gauge was off the clock, I thought I would have to force-land but as I had plenty of height I made for Biggin Hill and eventually landed with 3 gallons of petrol in my tank, according to my ground crew, and the glycol was leaking also. I had been airborne for 1 hour 40 minutes, which was ten minutes above the stated duration of the aircraft.

The next morning after an early start, I dropped Johnny Gilders at Heston and within the next half hour I was flying over my home. I landed at South Cerney and got in touch with the engineer officer about getting the magnetos. I was not going to see Flight Lieutenant Worger-Slade even though I would have liked to; but I thought of what he had said when I last saw him: 'Come and see me when you have the DFM.' I would wait as long as it took.

COMBAT REPORT

Sector Serial No.	(A)
Serial No. of Order detailing Flight or Squadron to Patrol	(B)
Date	(C) 20.9.40.
Flight, Squadron	(D) Flight: -B- Sqdn.: 72
No. of Enemy Aircraft	(E) 50 + Me 109
Type of Enemy Aircraft	(F) Me 109
Time Attack was delivered	(G) 12.10
Place Attack was delivered	(H) Ashford, Canterbury
Height of Enemy	(J) 25,000 to 30,000 feet
Enemy Casualties	(K) 1 Me 109 destroyed
Our Casualties Aircraft	(L) Nil
Personnel	(M) Nil
Search Lights, Was enemy illuminated. If not, were they in front or behind target	(N)

GENERAL REPORT   (R)

I was Red 2 in a section that was told to intercept the enemy fighters. We took off at 10.40 and after having done a patrol by ourselves we were told to rejoin the rest of the squadron as the leading section. We did this and met the enemy over Canterbury. We were climbing up towards one batch of Me 109's when we were told by our rearguard that another lot were diving down on us. We kept on climbing into the sun and the rest of the squadron had used evasive action to get rid of the Me 109's. I soon found myself by Ashford and could not see any of our squadron near me. I was flying along at 22,000 feet when I saw what appeared to be a Spitfire or Hurricane diving down to about 16,000 to 18,000 and then climbing up again. I decided to have a look at it, as I got into the position so that I had the sun behind me and could see the machine clearly. As it came up in the climb I saw plainly that it was a Me 109 with yellow nose and yellow fin. I let it climb up again and waited thinking perhaps it would dive again. It did so and then I dived out of the sun on to its tail and waited till it started to climb before I pressed the rit to fire. I let it have about 3 secs fire and the 109 did a stall turn to starboard and I followed it. I saw a large black piece break away from the side of the cockpit on the port side. I got it in my sights again as it turned and let it have another 4 sec burst. This time I saw the smoke and what appeared to be oil and water come from underneath it. It turned to dive and as it did I let him have a final burst when the whole lot of the cockpit dropped away and the rest dropped down towards the cloud. This was at 12,000 feet. I flew through the cloud and made for the aerodrome as I had only 10 gallons of petrol left. I marked the spot where the machine went in and it was near Wye between a wood and lake as far as I could make out from my own position. I landed back with 3 gallons of petrol and a leaky glycol rad.

Sgt W. Rolls
72 Squadron, 'B' Flight, Red 2

Words cannot explain how I felt on seeing my wife and baby again. After a few hours at home it was like being in another world. The dogfights of the previous days and scrambles were only a dream; it is surprising how quickly one's mind can react to a change of circumstances. I had even thought of that young lad without emotion; perhaps seeing my family again had made me see my future more positively.

All too soon came the next morning when I had to fly back and as the weather was good, I left as late as possible. I arrived back at Biggin Hill within forty-five minutes of leaving Cerney and had ten minutes to get changed into flying gear and check my Spitfire and I was back to the world of war, and fighting for my life.

We had two trips that day, Stickey had got an Me 109, and Johnny White a probable. Johnny Gilders damaged an Me 109,1 fired but did not hit anything. Unfortunately our commanding officer had been injured and was off flying for a long time. The next day we were scrambled to intercept thirty Do 17's escorted by about sixty Me 109's and when we met them, our CO placed us right astern of them and they were an easy target. I managed to get behind a Do 17 and opened fire at about 600 yards closing in quickly.

The rear gunners were firing at me and I felt something hit my wing.

Then suddenly I saw another Spitfire coming up in front of me and I stopped firing immediately and the other Spitfire finished off the Do1 7.1 had to break away sharply to avoid the Spitfire and doing so lost the formation and found in my mirror an Me 109 coming down on me. I did a barrel roll to avoid it and change position; as I was coming up from the roll and about to level out I saw on my port side an Me 109 almost flying in formation with me. At the same time I saw one of 92 Squadron firing at it and down it went. I don't know how I did not get hit at the same time as we were so close.

We had two further scrambles that day and I soon forgot about that inddent. On one of them we met up with yellow-nose Me 109's and with those you had no time for sentiment. One second's lapse and you were dead.

Before dinner that night, Johnny White suggested we go to *The Jail* pub again but I was not anxious. I told him I would let him know later if I felt like it but if he wanted to go with the others, I would not mind. I felt tired and wanted an early night.

When I had finished bathing and changing and was feeling much brighter, I thought perhaps it would be better to go out instead of moping on my own. I went to Johnny White's room where he was getting ready. The topic of girls came up and John asked me if I minded going out with them when they were going after girls. I told him that so far there had been very little time for girls and I had not seen many since we left Acklington. Even then it was a platonic friendship only, nothing sexual.

He then asked me why I had joined the RAFVR in April 1939, especially as I was then married and intent on having a family, knowing full well that a war was in the offing. He thought it odd that I could leave my young wife at home and be away for so long, and not want a woman in between times.

I told him that it was not a question of not desiring the company of women, but that my wife had enough to put up with, without her having to worry about mc having other women. She trusted me to play the game, but more important, she was there when I went on leave. I did not have to go out and find a girl on every leave, like he probably had to.

I had been sitting on the edge of John's bed while he was getting changed; he had just done his coat up and as I finished speaking, he came over and sat down beside me. He put his arm round my shoulder and said, very softly: 'Do you mind if I ask you a very personal question, Bill?'

I was embarrassed both by the arm round my shoulder and his question. I got up from the bed and went over to the table and put my cigarette out.

'Fire away, John. What is it you want to ask me?' I then sat down next to him.

'Do you ever feel lonely and want another woman to talk to, even though you are happily married? Do you ever feel that the way things are going, you should take all you can get from life and enjoy every moment of it, even to the point of making love to one of those lovely WAAFs we saw the other night?'

'Are you finished, John? If so and that is all you are worried about, well don't, because I am quite capable of looking after myself. Of course, I feel I could make love to another girl. It would have been easy on one or two occasions, as you already know, but I have one little insurance policy that stops me in time.'

I undid my top pocket and took out the photographs of my wife and baby. John had seen these before but he still took them both in his hand and looked at them.

This time it was me who put my arm round John's shoulder.

'My dear Johnny, don't you worry about that. I can assure you that nothing like that will happen. We will all enjoy the evening and forget for a while what this bloody war is doing to all of us.'

Johnny and I had flown so many times together in action and while we were at Acklington. We had a bond of friendship a bit closer than that of our other two pals. I had never had men friends before and absolutely detested any man putting his arm on me, but with Johnny I did not mind. He was like a young brother to me and had confided in me on many occasions when something was worrying him.

'Come on, John, let's go and join the others and discuss this party you have arranged.' We then went down to dinner.

After dinner we decided we would all go down to The Jail. Perhaps I would see the sergeant from 92 Squadron who had almost shot me down. It turned out to be a quiet night as there were only two of the other squadron's sergeants there and no sign of my old mate. I think someone must have told him that I was annoyed at him almost hitting me when he shot down the Me 109.

The next day was a bad one for our squadron. We had three scrambles and on the first one, met thirty Do 17's and Ju 88's with fighter cover. Once again we went in head-on, and it was a panic as the enemy were all round us. I saw one of our flight commanders get hit and another Spitfire go to pieces. I had no chance of getting a sight on any aircraft owing to the speed of the action. By the time you had got in a position to fire there were half a dozen Me 109's on your tail firing at you.

We returned to Biggin individually as about ten squadrons had now arrived to set into the broken formations. When I arrived back at flights I heard that Pilot Officer Males, our No 1 Sprog, had been killed in action; our Australian flight commander Des Sheen had baled out again but we had not heard how he was. There was some damage to three of us but the good news was that Johnny Gilders and Stickey had destroyed a Me 109 and a Do17 between them.

Later that day we had another scramble... with six aircraft as we were running short of serviceable machines. This time the bandits were only Me 109's and we could not get high enough before they turned back. Later in the afternoon we were scrambled again and got up in time to chase some Heinkel 111 's back across the Channel.

When we had all landed and were back at flights, our CO came in to us and he was holding a telegram. He looked over to Johnny and me and read out the telegram.

'Flying Officer Thomas Francis Elsdon, (Jimmy to his mates), has been awarded the Distinguished Flying Cross.'

There were some other words which were lost in the noise from the rest of us Sprogs and the other officers and NCO's. Our Jimmy had got the squadron's first DFC of this war; anyone looking in at that moment would have thought he was watching a party of homosexuals as we were hugging each other as the emotion of hearing this wonderful piece of news was so great–we sure loved that man. Who would have thought that a short time earlier those same sergeants were fighting and killing the enemy? Someone once told me that you had to be a schizophrenic or just plain mad, to be a successful fighter pilot. On this occasion I believe he was right.

We had not forgotten about our other Sprog, killed that morning. We would pay our respects to him later that evening in the pub.

Before we left the pub that evening we had heard that our flight commander was safe and this called for another round of drinks. We would celebrate Jimmy's DFC at a later date when we had visited him in hospital.

On the Saturday morning we escorted some Blenheims to France but did not meet up with the enemy. On Saturday evening we got prepared for our big night out with the WAAFs. We were not on duty until the Sunday afternoon as we had plenty of pilots and not enough machines for them to fly. We could enjoy a few beers and a dance at the Country Club.

At breakfast on the Sunday when I met John, we did not say a word about last night, but started to talk to Johnny Gilders and Stickey who had come to join us. We all agreed that it had been a smashing evening and that we should try it again in future, when we had some cash to spare. We settled up for the cost of the meal and drinks, what with the free bottle of wine from the manager and a bottle from a colonel who was near us with his wife, it was not very expensive. It had been a night to remember and it also let the WAAFs know that we appreciated what they were doing to keep us in the air. Considering how they had been bombed and losing some of their friends, I don't know how they could stick the pace they were working at. They were lovely girls and brought a sense of reality in a mad time. We owed them a lot.

Johnny White and I were on duty and at readiness when we got a call to scramble. We saw some Me 109's but they were too high and too far away from us and so after a short patrol we landed. They had been intercepted by other squadrons. In the afternoon we were again scrambled and this time to 25,000 feet.

We were to patrol a line between two points to stop any Me 109 bombers which had been coming over in place of the Ju 88s and Do 17's etc. These fighter bombers carried a bomb under each wing and were used for scatter-bombing by dropping their bombs directly they saw the Hurricanes and Spitfires approaching them. In many cases they would then turn tail back to France. It was not very encouraging to have to climb to these heights through cloud and bad weather just to see them turn tail.

On this second trip I was running out of petrol and had to land at White Waltham to refuel. I had been airborne for 1 hour 40 minutes. On arriving back at Biggin Hill I had to complain again about the state of the aircraft I had been using. It was appreciated that we were having to fly clapped-out Spitfires due to the shortage of replacements. In normal circumstances you would never have taken off with the state of some of them, some had not got any armour on the back of the seat.

The following ten days were the same: scramble, patrol, no action.

The nights were the same: passion wagon to pub and whatever came with it.

It was on 11th October that we saw some action. On the morning their bombs were dropped and turned for home. Some of us managed to hit them and we intercepted some Me 109 bombers who immediately dropped but did not claim any victories. Later towards evening we were scrambled and this time met some Me 109's and actually had combat. I fired but did not claim and I got hit myself.

It was dark when we returned to base. I was the last to land and was pretty fed up with waiting as each one had to land singly. It was my turn and I was on the downward run ready to turn on the runway when I decided I would do a slow roll. I had not made a hit so it was totally unnecessary because even victory rolls were banned because of the state of our aircraft. Before I commenced the roll I put my landing light on and rolled the aircraft. As I did a split-arse turn onto the runway, I put my undercart down. Nothing happened. I put my flaps down. Nothing happened. By this time I was too low to do much about it and belly-landed on the grass. Surprisingly I came to rest with very little damage to the aircraft. My hydraulics had been shot up and I had not noticed it in the dark of the cockpit.

I was soon back in dispersal to an angry flight commander who told me that the CO wished to see me back at the officers' mess. I went to the mess and waited in the hall. After a short time I saw the CO with some senior officers who were visiting Biggin. He left them and came up to me.

'Sergeant Rolls, that was a bloody stupid thing to do. I don't care that you have damaged a Me 109, one for one is not good enough. What is more important is that you endangered the aerodrome with your light and that you endangered yourself. At this stage pilots are more important.'

I stood at attention and was embarrassed by the way I was being told off in front of these other officers.

The CO continued, 'As a punishment you will do duty pilot for the next week.'

I could not believe my ears. That was for pilots who wanted a rest from operations. I stood there stunned while the CO returned to the other officers.

I walked towards the door and went out into the open. I knew I could not face the others. What a disgrace I had brought upon myself.

I had gone a few yards when I heard my name called and looked back to see the CO at the door. I went back expecting another telling off or perhaps another punishment and the CO said:

'Rolls, you can forget the duty pilot bit. Instead you had better take tomorrow off, when you have made out your report for the acddent.'

'Thank you, sir. Could I ask a special favour again?' I said, tongue in cheek.

He looked very surprised as I said, 'Sir, may I borrow the Magister so that I can go home to South Cerney for the day?'

He nodded and said, 'I will tell your flight commander.'

What a CO! What a squadron!

I walked back to the sergeants' mess where I went to my room to get changed.

I had hardly got my tunic off before the other three Sprogs came in.

'What the hell did you think you were doing, you clot?' said John, 'You could have killed yourself.'

Stickey was more to the point. 'I think the CO should ground you, obviously you are cracking up, to do a bloody stupid thing like that.'

Johnny Gilders did not say anything but just kept staring at me and I said to him:

'And what do you think?'

He laughed and replied, 'I would have loved to do the same thing myself. Anything to relieve the bloody monotony of this place. But unfortunately, I have not the guts to do it at night. The thing is what punishment has the CO given you?'

'A day off tomorrow and the use of the Magister to fly home and see my wife and baby,' I replied.

'You're kidding,' they replied, almost in unison.

'Perhaps he's hoping you won't come back,' said Stickey with a laugh.

'–' I replied to all of them, and proceeded to get dressed while they went down to the bar.

That evening we went to the Country Club to meet the girls as John had made the arrangements. This time there would be no dinner party, simply a dance and a few beers.

It turned out to be a most pleasant evening. We met a couple of our friends from 92 Squadron and I did not even mention the fact that one of them had almost shot me down. It was not important any longer.

The next morning I was down to flights early and saw my flight commander, who knew all about my trip home that day. I apologised for the stupid thing I had done the night before and asked him why the CO had changed his mind so quickly. One minute I was to be duty pilot for a week, the next I was having a day off with a bonus of an aircraft to fly home in.

'You will know in good time, but meanwhile make the most of the day off with your family but get back before dark this time.'

'Thank you, sir,' I replied. I then went to the Magister and within minutes I was on my way home. I reckoned that I would be home by nine o'clock and as it was Saturday we could go into Cirencester to get a belated birthday present for Rene and perhaps something for my young sister and my baby. I would leave at four o'clock and get back to Biggin by 5 pm. It did not sound a long time, but it was a bonus I had not expected.

I was soon flying over my house to let Rene know I was on my way and within thirty minutes I was indoors holding my baby Carole. The events of the past week had gone completely from my mind and even when I mentioned Rene's birthday present, I had no thoughts of that evening. My only thoughts were for her and baby. Rene was a bit puzzled as to how I had managed to get a day off, when every day the papers were telling about the air battles which were taking place daily. I did not tell her why but said that I had been doing a lot of flying and the CO thought I should have a day off; the less said the better. It was a lovely break from the kind of flying I had been doing lately and I enjoyed every second of it and we all walked to the aerodrome to prolong our time together.

I was soon airborne and had a wind behind me so I knew I would be back before dark. I felt so happy that I was singing my head off and suddenly found myself la-de-da-ing 'The Rustic of Spring' and I started waltzing the aircraft as Flight Lieutenant Worger-Slade had done on my first trip with him at Gatwick.

When I got back the two Johns were there to greet me. You would have thought that I had been away for ages or that the war was over. They were excited about something unusual and I knew it would not be long before I knew what it was. We were going up north for a rest. When I got to my room I found all my clothes packed and I panicked. Had I been posted to another squadron in my one day's absence. I had seen it happen to others; why not me?

It was not long before I found out that I was going to fly up to wherever the squadron was going to and that Johnny had packed my gear so that Johnny Gilders and Stickey could take it by road in our car. I breathed once more now that I knew the truth. Rumours were around that we were going back to Acklington and that suited me fine. I was looking forward to seeing the Hamiltons and *The Trap* again.

I later noticed that on the flight notice board Johnny White and I were with the flight commander on readiness the next day and this was rather upsetting because I thought we were supposed to be going back in the morning. Stickey and John had already been told they were going by road although they had not yet been told where to.

The next morning we had a scramble for Me 109 bombers escorted by Me 109 fighters and turned them back. This was getting a bore. Although we were doing a useful job, there was no satisfaction from it. My aircraft was almost clapped out and I dreaded the thought of flying it up to Acklington, if indeed that was where we were going.

When we got back to flights I looked at the notice board to see what the next order of flights was. I was surprised that I was still on duty and had been allocated a new Spitfire as were some of the others. My flight commander was busy with a large map and I noticed his flight track marked on the map. The line was nowhere near Acklington so I now knew that we would not be going there. This was disappointment number one as far as I was concerned, although the fact that I had a brand new Spitfire was more important.

We had an early lunch and then we were told that we were going for a rest somewhere in Yorkshire. That was disappointment number two, because we had heard from sergeant pilots in other squadrons that the RAF were not very popular there for some obscure reason – I think an enemy bomber had got through one night and it upset them. It was ridiculous to worry about such a little thing. We were not likely to be there long enough to meet the civilian population anyway. As long as there was a good local pub, we would be happy.

This time Johnny White and I were with the flight commander. It was like being back with Jimmy again, because he was every bit as nice with us as Jimmy had been. But he was not Jimmy, who was still in hospital and not likely to fly with us again.

WE ARRIVE AT LECONFIELD

After flying for almost an hour we heard the call for us to land in sections of three and we were soon down on an aerodrome called Leconfield. From its surrounding countryside it did not appear to be exciting and there was only one town, Beverley, about five miles away and it did not look as though there was much of interest there. We were on a rest and it looked as though that's what we would get. We finally arrived at our mess and got our rooms allocated and reserved rooms for the other two Sprogs. It was then tea time.

It was late evening when Stickey and John arrived in the passion wagon and we went and got our luggage. The back seat was full of empty five gallon petrol drums which had been used on the long journey. The car only did about 18 miles per gallon. The trouble was our luggage stank with petrol fumes and that night I had to sleep with all the windows open -1 even went outside the room to light a cigarette, because I was afraid something might explode.

I can summarise our stay at Leconfield in a few words: it was lousy.

We went into Beverley one night. It was raining hard when we eventually found a pub. We went into it and ordered our beers, but unlike Croydon and Bromley no one rushed to get our order or treat us to a round. I now understood what the other sergeants at Biggin had meant. We had been there about an hour when the sirens went and some of the people left the pub and went out. It was still pouring with rain and we wanted to go for a pee. John asked a man where the toilet was and he pointed to the door and said, 'In the courtyard.' We decided that we would get wet and looked out of the door and saw a little distance away, a building in the middle of the courtyard with an entrance like the 'Gents'.

Being anxious to get relieved as quickly as possible we ran to this door and as we did so started to undo our flies and get out the thing causing all the trouble. We opened the door and pulled back the blackout curtain, and, lo and behold, inside, sitting around the walls on forms, were men and women and kids and did they do the beholding! We realised immediately what had happened but unfortunately mother nature did not and so it was a very uncomfortable run out of the shelter to the back of it where in the pouring rain we finished that sortie. We did not bother to go back into the pub but went on to another one where the people were quite friendly.

Another incident was one day when we were going into Kingston-on-Hull for the day. It was a Saturday and as we were about to set off, I got a call from my flight commander.

'Rolls, I know you like low flying.' (I had been caught out at Acklington flying beside the express train). 'The army want some ack-ack co-operation with their Bofors gun and want you to simulate what would happen if they were attacked by enemy fighter bombers at low level.'

I could not refuse this offer and yet I wanted to go with the others to Hull.

'How long will it take, sir?' I enquired.

'For as long as they want the exercise,' he replied.

When the others heard, they were annoyed but decided to wait for me as I said I would finish the exercise as quickly as possible. They came over to flights with me and I did not wait to get into flying kit – I had my best blues on and shoes. I was airborne in a very short time. I had my new aircraft and was going to try it out under operational conditions.

I dived down on the battery and pulled up when I was almost hitting the gun barrel and I saw soldiers ducking for the ground. I spent the next ten minutes doing the lowest possible flying you could do without actually hitting the gun. I knew that my prop-wash would upset the soldiers and I was really enjoying myself when I heard on my RT my code number telling me to land. I did not answer, I knew what they were going to complain about. I was told that the Army would give me a red Very light when they had finished with me. This soon came and I landed immediately and was soon out of my aircraft and in the car with the lads. I told them to get off the station quickly as the telephone was ringing and I knew what it was about.

Tomorrow was another day and I intended to let it cool down a bit, before my flight commander saw me. Besides it was my day off, with the rest of the squadron.

I had now used the same aircraft on most flights and I was told that it would be mine while I was on flying duty or whenever I was on practice flying. That was why I was on duty – so that I would fly it to our new destination.

I packed my kit and John Gilders and Stickey would take the car by road. The next morning when I went to flights my flight commander was waiting for me.

'Rolls, what the hell do you think you were doing yesterday on your army cooperation flight?' Before I could answer he carried on, 'Do you know that the Station Commander gave the order for you to abort the exercise because you were flying so dangerously low?'

I stood still and was at a loss to answer back. I had never seen him in such a temper.

'Well? I am waiting for your excuse.'

Sir, my instructions were to simulate an attack by an Me 109 on the gun post. I carried it out as I knew any good German yellow-nose pilot would do. He would not come in high and give time for them to take aim; he would fly low and in front of the hangars and buildings so that the guns could not fire for fear of hitting their own buildings.'

I stopped for breath and was about to continue, but he waved his hand and went to his office. A while later we were told that we were going to Coltishall in Norfolk. This was better news because we might get more action from there with the odd German raids on the East Coast and perhaps if things got worse, protect London from the north.

COLLISHALL

It was a nice run to Coltishall and uneventful. You could see Norwich quite clearly and as I knew Norwich I felt that we would have more enjoyment than at Leconfield. It seemed a coincidence that the day after my low flying we were moved. I would love to think that I was partly responsible but I think there were other reasons.

For the next three weeks we did convoy patrols and air firing exercises and, having met some Merchant Navy men in Hull, I felt I knew every man on every ship we patrolled. What is more it made me more vigilant. I could not let a German come in low level and bomb the ships. The crew were probably having a rest now we were flying over them.

On 7th November 1940, Stickey and Johnny Gilders had received a posting notice and they were to leave the next morning for Kirton-in-Lindsey for another Spitfire squadron. This was a shaker to Johnny White and me. Somehow we had never thought of the four Sprogs being split up. We had seen others posted and had had a lot of new sergeants and officers come to us, but this was a real blow. We had been through so much together.

That evening we had intended to have a binge but none of us had any thoughts other than, tomorrow we lose two good mates.

The next day the CO let Johnny and me take them to Norwich for the train. While we were waiting very few words were said, I think we were too choked to say much. Finally we shook hands and wished each other best of luck and they were on the train and away.

That afternoon I was down at flights and was walking on the grass by myself when the CO came up to me. He handed me a telegram. I read it wondering what it was about and saw that it was from 12 Group and I assumed that it was a posting notice for me. I hardly dared read it.

To Sgt Pilot W T E Rolls. 72 Squadron R.A.F.
From 12 Group.
HEARTIEST CONGRATULATIONS ON YOUR WELL EARNED DFM
LEIGH MALLORY L6.30 5.11.40.

I did not know what to say to the CO. He said, holding out his hand, 'Let me be the first to congratulate you. You may keep the telegram.'

With difficulty I managed to stammer out a 'Thank you, sir' and I then asked him had Sergeant White received one as well. He answered, 'No'. What should have been the proudest moment of my time with the RAF was one of the most miserable. I dreaded seeing Johnny White. How would he take it, and what about some of the officers? Why had they not yet got DFC's? Many of them had earned one. I went to the mess for tea and some of our sergeants were there but I did not tell them about my DFM, as I wanted to tell Johnny personally first on his own.

I saw John come into the mess and he went straight to the toilet. He had been flying. I went to him and told him I had something to show him, I handed him the telegram; he read it and I was hardly prepared for what happened next.

He put his arms round me and lifted me off the floor the same as he had done in the pub in the East End of London.

'It couldn't have happened to a nicer guy. Bill.' He put me on my feet again.

'I am sorry, John. I had hoped that we would do it together. I am sure that your one is on the way,' I said.

We went to the mess where the others were and Johnny said, 'Bill has got something to tell you.' I then read out the telegram and received their good wishes and congratulations. Somehow I did not feel at all happy with the day's events.

Two weeks later when Johnny was on leave the CO asked me why I had not yet put up my medal ribbon and I made the excuse that I had ordered it but I was waiting to see if Sergeant White was going to receive a medal. He was very angry and told me:

'You will put up the ribbon immediately. That honour is for the squadron as well as you.'

'Yes, sir,' I answered. I had already been given the ribbon for my tunic. I was pleased in a way, I wanted so much to show it but I did not want to hurt John.

I was about to salute and walk away when the CO said: 'Another thing. Sergeant Rolls. That motor car of yours and White's. The passion wagon, as you call it. I want you to get rid of it. The Station Commander does not approve of the RAF roundels and its unauthorised use on the station.'

I told the CO that I would get rid of it as soon as I could. He then handed me a card which gave the name and address of a car dealer in Norwich so that I could make arrangements to have it towed away. I was not even allowed to drive it to Norwich myself. I then thanked him for his consideration in letting us have it at Biggin Hill and until now. He smiled, 'The less said of that, the better,' he said.

I got the garage man the next day and gave him the key, he offered me ten pounds for it, but I declined. He looked amazed and so I said to him,

'It has been a good friend to us these past few months and it is too good to sell as scrap. I am givmg it to you in all its glory. Besides it would be too much bother to split up the money between us.'

I watched it go out of the station under its own steam and I am sure there was an odd tear in my eyes. I was not happy with the patrols and monotonous training we were doing and I was getting restless. Without Johnny I was a loner. I did not mix much with the other sergeants who were all younger than me. I was not happy with some of the new officers either. We still had a nucleus of our old squadron but it was not the 72 Squadron I had joined earlier.

I went back to flights and repainted my mascot of Donald Duck on my Spitfire – one thing they were unlikely to take away from me. I was proud of my painting on the side of my cockpit. I had waited months to paint it on but because of the losses at Biggin Hill it would have been a waste of time. Now however it was safe.

Johnny was sorry about the car. He agreed with the way I had let it go. We would have to stay in the mess more and it was not so much fun nowadays without the other two Sprogs.

I went on leave on 6th December for two weeks and proudly showed my wife and family my medal ribbon and telegram. During my leave I received a telegram telling me to report to Acklington on completion of my leave. On 19th December I returned to Acklington to find Johnny wearing the DFM ribbon on his tunic. He had only just received notice of his award and was dying to tell me the good news.

We had a party that night up at *The Trap* and what a pleasure it was to see Mr and Mrs Hamilton and Nellie and Cissie again. We had only been away two months but after a few minutes with them it seemed as though we had never been away. We eventually spent our Christmas with them and tried to forget our absent friends, but it was impossible. It was a good job we had such good friends here at Acklington, otherwise life would have been very miserable. There were too many memories haunting us.

At the beginning of January, I was given the job of instructing our new pilots in instrument flying in a Magister and I knew it was time for a change as Johnny was getting restless and wanted to go back on operational flying which meant that he would be posted to another squadron down south or even abroad. For my wife and baby's sake I did not want to go back on operations until our baby was better as she was ill. I also knew that without John I would not want to stay in the squadron and I would have to ask for a posting with John.

In the meantime a notice arrived about a vacancy at a new Operational Training Unit at Grangemouth, Scotland. It was for a flight sergeant instructor with a DFM if possible and operational training experience, to teach Poles and other foreign students to fly combat in Spitfires.

This seemed to be an ideal posting for Johnny or myself and I spoke to him about it. He was not interested in it for himself but suggested that it would be ideal for me as the term of the posting was for six months and I could have Rene and the baby up there with me since I would be allowed to live out.

I spoke to my flight commander about it and he agreed it was a good idea and would recommend the CO to allow me to apply for the post. My CO agreed to my application and said that he would strongly recommend me for the post. It was not because he wanted to get rid of me, he said, but as I had been so well trained myself I could pass on this experience to younger pilots.

I was soon accepted for the post. I knew that it meant John and I splitting up and I knew that he was asking for a posting himself as he had now decided to make his move. At least both of us were still alive and well and who knew what the future had in store? We could meet up again when I went back on ops after my six months were up. I felt it was not goodbye.

There was a final farewell party at *The Trap* and I said my cheerios to Mr and Mrs Hamilton and those two lovely daughters, Nellie and Cissie. I would miss them and dear old Johnny. I thanked all the other officers and sergeants in the squadron and I knew that I would never forget such a grand bunch of officers and NCO's, pilots and ground crews and especially the three commanding officers I had been under during my stay with the squadron.

I felt very pleased with myself as I looked at my GO's signature on my last page of my log book. I had been a member of a famous fighter squadron with first class officers and ground staff. I had an idea I would never be so lucky in my future postings. Along with Flying Officer Elsdon who was our first DFC of this war, I had the honour of being the first DFM and was on the squadron's Roll of Honour.

It was now obvious the war was going to last a long time and as a matter of interest I counted up the number of pages of my log book that I had already filled; to my surprise it was forty – not bad really if I considered what my uncle had once told me. When he was in the Royal Flying Corps in 1917 each page of one's log book was a new life.

Award promulgated in the London Gazette dated
8th November 1940

Distinguished Flying Medal 745542 Sergeant William Thomas Edward ROLLS,
Royal Air Force Volunteer Reserve No 72 Squadron.
This airman, after very short experience of operational flying, has taken his place with the best war pilots in the squadron. In each of his first two engagements he shot down two enemy aircraft, and has in all destroyed at least six.

The Citation for my DFM

CHAPTER THREE

POSTED TO 58 OTU GRANGEMOUTH
INSTRUCTING

I had been only one hour at my new posting before I was regretting that I had ever set eyes on the place. It had only just opened as an operational training unit and I was allocated to 'B' Flight which consisted of myself. 'A' Flight had one officer and a sergeant. I was told by the Station Commander that for a while I would be collecting the aircraft in which the few pupils we had would be flying.

The sergeants' mess was a converted junior school off the aerodrome and the pupils would sleep in the old wooden huts but eat in the sergeants' mess. It was not a good arrangement and I did not intend to put up with it, if I could help it.

The wing commander CO of the unit was recently in command of a Battle of Britain fighter squadron and had got the DFC. My reaction to this was 'If it's good enough for him, then it's good enough for me.' I also thought that he would be like my other CO's in 72 Squadron, turning a blind eye now and again, but when I met him at first he did not look that type. There was not a lot of welcome from him, and I got the feeling that he was not happy himself at being at Grangemouth.

I picked myself a room in the mess and met some of the ground sergeants, most of whom had only recently arrived themselves. I was not going to like this posting one little bit.

The next day I went to flight test one of the Spitfires which was for 'B' Flight. I had flown some ropey Spits at Biggin and this was acceptable because of the circumstances, but when I got airborne in this machine I thought it was going to do aerobatics on its own; the trim on the elevators and tail unit were non-existent and the engine had seen better days. I dreaded to think what would have happened to a Sprog pilot had he flown it before I had. I landed and told the ground crew where and how much trim was required and made sure they did the job while I looked on. I then told the flight sergeant in charge of the ground crews not to make any aircraft serviceable that had not been air tested by me, or the other officer and sergeant pilots, available for flights.

I along with the other sergeant and officer; went to Burton Wood in an old Harrow and flew back some Spits. These were in better condition and the two I took for 'B' Flight, required only minor servicing.

The following day was a bit of a joke. I had a few pupils who were waiting for me to give them some instruction and a Master two seater training Aircraft which I had never flown, or even seen the inside of, before. The pupil got in his cockpit and I told him that we would try a bit of instrument flying on this first trip. I wanted his head under the hood so that he could not see what I was doing while getting height to do the instrument flying. I knew that the pupils had seen the cockpit before I arrived and that they had learned about the engine and cockpit in the classroom.

I asked the pupil to go over the cockpit drill with me so that I could see if he knew what to do; I dared not tell him I had never been in this type of aircraft before. He might have jumped out in a hurry, had I done so. He went over the cockpit drill very explicitly and I got in the rear cockpit and started up the engine according to how he had told me. There was no bother once I had the engine going and I soon took off and started to climb. On the Master was a large hood which came up in front of the instructor and when you closed it in flight you were likely to get a bang on the head if you did not lower your seat before closing it. I did not lower the seat and got a nice bang on the head instead.

I told the pupil to pull over his black-out and look at his instruments. I then did a turn to the right as perfectly as I could, I then asked him what rate of turn I had been doing and whether or not I had skidded in the turn. He was not sure so I told him to concentrate only on the instruments and ignore the feel of the aircraft. I did another rate two turn to the right and asked him what I had done.

'I think it was a rate two turn with a bit of right hand skid,' he told me.

'Correct,' I replied, 'I will now do another exercise and you will then tell me what I have been doing.'

I did exactly the same thing as before, even to the right hand skid and asked him for his opinion on that exercise.

'It was exactly the same as the last one,' he replied.

'Good show, laddie.' Why had I called him laddie? It's that little bit of Worger-Slade, I thought.

'Are you going to be my regular instructor?' he enquired.

'If that's what you wish,' I replied.

I had got my first pupil and, what was more, he had asked for me. I felt a bit happier. Perhaps I might make a good instructor like Jimmy and Flight Lieutenant Worger-Slade. It would be nice to have your pupils want to fly with you.

I had now done my first trip in a Master aircraft and rather liked the machine, but in no way could it match the Spitfire for handling.

Later that morning I took up two pupils for a spot of formation flying. This time it was in Spitfires as both pupils had already flown Spitfires but had been sent on the course for operational training. It was a nice trip and I managed to get them in nice and close in a Vic formation with me and then we flew over the aerodrome at one thousand feet so that everyone on the ground could get a good view of the tight formation, and see how good these two pupils were; I wanted to give them confidence and a little showing off was one of the best ways I knew to give them that. It was fifty minutes of fun. I felt better now I was flying the Spitfire, with two others in formation on me. It was like Biggin Hill again.

That afternoon I decided to do some more formation flying with them and this time go into the hills north of our base and look at the lakes and low flying area. Again in nice tight formation we flew over Falkirk, up the Firth of Forth to Stirling and then along the valley to Loch Leven. I then went into the low flying area and we did a spot of low flying formation. It was a nice way to spend an hour. As I pulled up from low flying, however, I noticed something wrong with my airspeed indicator; it had stopped working. I was not unduly worried as I could judge the airspeed by the rev counter and so I carried on towards the aerodrome. I then noticed that my hydraulics gauge was reading zero, I had no option but to tell my number three to return to base on his own. I then told my number two that I had no airspeed indicator or hydraulics and would have to land back at base as his number three. I then told him to take the lead and continue back to base and land as he normally would, but with a powered approach as I would not have any flaps or brakes.

On approaching the airfield I called up control and informed them that two aircraft would be making an emergency formation powered landing and to ensure the approach was clear for us. I told my pupil that I would fly two spans away from him and he was to carry out his usual approach and landing using his flaps. I let my wheels down at the same time as he did and asked him to confirm that they were both down. He said that they were. I then told him to put his flaps down and as he did so I started my engine controlled approach and kept in formation with him. He touched down about one third of the runway and I landed on the grass by the side of him but as I had no brakes I went past him and was now getting to the end of the airfield. I saw that I was going to overshoot possibly into the road, so I opened up the engine and turned towards one of the pens where we kept the aircraft as they were surrounded by earth mounds. I ran into the earth and as I expected my propeller hit the earth and the machine pulled up. I had a bent prop but not a lot of damage. It was only my pride that was hurt. We did not even have to use the fire engine which had been racing along by my side on the landing.

The Station Commander was furious and he did not want to listen to any excuses but told me to make out my report as quickly as possible. He never even asked me if I was hurt. I made out my report and let him have it.

Three days later I received a message from the adjutant that I was to go and see the CO and take my log book with me.

I gave my log book to the CO and he wrote in it by the side of the entry for the day I overshot: 'Overshot and crashed on landing due to Carelessness.' [81 G/C WO/5 trg refers].

It was so large you could read it a distance. I got a telling off at the same time and was told that the next day an officer was coming to take over 'B' Flight. I thought, 'Here it comes, I am going to be posted because of the accident.' I told him that I had had crashes at night and day when in 72 Squadron and I was surprised that I had this endorsement for such a minor accident.

His reply was surprising, especially from a CO who had only just come off operations himself.

'Flight Sergeant Rolls, you are not in an operational squadron now and as an instructor you are expected to set an example to the pupils and crashing an aircraft is not a good example.'

I did not have an answer for that one, but I sure appreciated more than ever the CO's and officers I had recently left behind in 72 Squadron. Had it been possible I would have willingly returned to Acklington.

I was about to leave when he said, 'Rolls, I know that you are a married man with a baby and would like to have your family with you. When you are settled in and when you have sorted out your programme and got the necessary aircraft, you have my permission to live out with them. I suggest that you look around for suitable accommodation bearing in mind that you will be entitled to ration allowance and lodging allowance.'

I could hardly believe it. One minute I thought he was trying to show his superiority over me and yet the next minute he was doing his best to help me. I was a puzzled man when I left the office thinking that his bark was worse than his bite.

The next morning when I had my pupils together in the crew room, we discussed my accident and landing without Airspeed indicator or brakes and flaps. They had all learned a valuable lesson as to what could happen to them one day and what to do if it did happen, so I think a bent prop was worth it. After all it was easily straightened out. I felt proud of my endorsement; the fact that I got down in one piece under those conditions was good enough for me. Had it been a pupil instead of me it might have been another story with not such a happy ending.

For the first couple of weeks I had not had a lot of contact with the sergeants from 'A' Flight, but one evening I heard one of them talking about my accident in an argument with another sergeant. It was real Cockney and flowery language and as it was about me I got two beers from the bar and went over to him and offered him one of them. He introduced himself as Sergeant Gooderham.

I could not help laughing at his cockney twang. I knew from that moment, Ron and I were going to be the best of friends, mates or pals as you wish to call it. We celebrated the evening with a few beers and in our discussions we talked about the sleeping and eating conditions for us instructors and while it might do for the pupils we thought that for operational pilots on a rest, the conditions were not good enough. I learned that Ron was a Hurricane pilot and wanted to fly Spitfires and had volunteered for the post so that he could get some hours in on Spits. About midnight we had decided that we would rent a flat or house near the mess for the bar and social evenings. We would have our food cooked by one of those nice landladies, who we were told, were in abundance.

The low flying area was a landscape east of Stirling and ran along a valley. There were some high trees in various parts of it and small hollows about thirty feet deep. There were also some telephone poles and electric pylons.

Before taking a pupil on a low flying exercise, I had gone there alone to inspect the terrain and to try out a pattern of flying so as to make the most exciting run possible. I measured the distances between pairs of trees where I could fly between them with only inches to spare. I saw other pairs of trees where by turning the aircraft on its side it was possible to scrape through them. The hollows were ideal to give one the impression you were flying below ground level. After two trips and familiarising myself with every bit of the area, I decided that I could now start training my pupils on real low flying.

My first pupil was a young Scottish pilot and officially the practice was instrument flying and low flying. He had not done either of these in Spitfires so it was going to be a good flight for him, although at the time we started out he was dreading it, as he had not liked instrument or low flying when he was on the Hart aircraft.

I took off and when I reached one thousand feet I told him to pull his hood over when he was ready (he could now only see his instruments and nothing outside) to take over the controls. He said he was in charge.

I told him that when he was straight and level he should climb at 140 knots up to 3,000 feet.

'OK. You are now ready so take over.' Which he did after a little bit of scenic railwaying. I then put him through a couple of turns and reminded him to keep on the same heading for three minutes. I then gave him another couple of turns and when he had completed them, I told him to open up his hood.

'What height did you start your first turn?' I asked over the RT.

'Three thousand feet, serge,' he replied.

'And what height are we now at?'

'Five hundred feet,' he replied.

'Do you know where we are by your map?' I then asked him.

'It looks like the low flying area marked in red.'

'It is the low flying area so I suppose we had better do the low flying bit now and finish your instrument flying on the way back.'

I then told him to tighten his straps and to take his hands and feet from off the controls and told him under no circumstances was he to attempt to touch the controls until I told him. With all this understood I did some normal low flying at two hundred feet and got him acclimatised to the height and contour of the ground.

I waited until I was in the correct position for my start of the low flying steeple chase and told the pupil to take his hands off the control column as he had taken hold of it while I was doing the flying. I then opened up the throttle and dived down as close to the ground as possible. This first stretch was flat and mostly small gorse bushes. At the end of it was a high hedge with a few small spaces in it. From a distance it looked the same and appeared to be impossible that there was room to fly between the gaps, but there was one and I knew where it was. So at the end of that speedy run over the ground I aimed straight for the hedge. I saw my pupil looking round at me as I went between the space and below the height of the hedge. I told him to keep his eyes in front all the time as he was missing the best part. I next flew down into one of the hollows and as close to the wall of it as I dared. It gave the appearance that you were flying below ground -a very peculiar sensation. At the end of this run I pulled up sharply and dead ahead were four large fir trees with very little space between them. I aimed straight at the far pair; as I got within feet of them I turned the aircraft on its side and went through them easily. I then levelled out and did the last lap of the course aiming at a bridge and level with it. I pulled up at the last moment and climbed steeply to two hundred feet.

'What did you think of that?' I asked the pupil.

'Smashing,' was his reply.

'Would you like to do it with me this time?'

'Yes, exactly the same as before.'

'Right, then take hold of the controls with me and use fingers only on the control column and lightly rest your feet on the rudder bar and left hand lightly on the throttle. Let me know when you are ready.'

I felt him do as I had told him and then he said he was ready.

I did exactly as I had done previously and I was feeling the reaction of the pupil on the controls. He was attempting to carry out the actions with me but very lightly. I knew that I had got a good pupil with me and one who would learn quickly.

The flying was now getting heavy going either in Masters or Spitfires. I had one pupil, a New Zealand pilot who was not yet twenty and who was a terrible pupil as far as flying was concerned. He could not do a thing right and he was trying my patience. I had given him so much dual on Masters, I felt it was a waste of time to continue with him. He had taken a couple of tests to see if he was fit for a Spitfire and failed each time. The only reason I kept going with him was that he had come a hell of a long way in order to fight in this war and I was determined that by hook or by crook he would make good eventually.

It was a few days after having the lad some more dual instruction that I took him up for another test. It was make or break as far as I was concerned. After an hour of test and instruction, I landed and told him to get out of the aircraft.

'How did I do, Flight?'

I did not answer him but went into the flight office to get the form 700 for my own Spitfire. I gave it to him and told him to sign for the aircraft as he was going to have to fly the bloody machine, reminding him that it was my own personal machine. I told him to get in the cockpit and prepare for his first flight in a Spitfire, the most important flight of his life. I gave him a few minutes to get familiar with the instrument panel and layout, and then I climbed on the wing by the side of him to explain take-off and landing procedure etc.

When I had finished I said to him, 'Now, sergeant, I am sick and tired of your bloody awful flying. I am sending you off in a Spit and should you crash in the hills, it will be your own bloody fault for being so stupid. Now go and do some flying in this machine and don't come back until you can fly it and land it safely.'

He started the engine and was ready for taxying out when I said to him, 'When you get back, the mess will be open and I will have a pint ready for you.' With that I jumped down and watched him take off. He made a good take-off and I watched him climb up to the cloud base and out of sight. He had about one hour before dusk and I was sitting on the tail of another machine when the ground crew of the aircraft said to me, 'Well, he has made it at last, but Flight, do you think he is going to make it back because the way you spoke to him could not have given him much confidence. Fancy telling him he could fly into the hills for all you cared.'

'Corporal, I have no fears of him not coming back, but I am worried about when he comes back. He has been airborne for 1 hour 10 minutes and control has told me he was not answering them since he went into the hills north of Falkirk.' It was now time for me to worry and the fact that all the airmen knew what I had said to him, made it worse. He had now been airborne for 1 hour 20 minutes. It was dusk and in another ten minutes would require the landing lights to be put on. I was getting ready to phone the CO for permission to put the floodlight on, when I heard the sound of the aircraft in the distance. It was soon on the circuit and he made a quick landing by short-cutting the approach. It was a good landing. I did not wait for him to taxi over to flights as I was in a temper and would have probably wrung his neck for the worry he had caused everyone.

When I saw Ron, I told him what had happened. He laughed and said, 'You scared the poor little sod when he took off and so he has had his own back. He has scared you stiff.' I had to agree with him, when you looked at it that way. But there was an added advantage; he had now done his solo on Spits and there would be no holding him back.

The sergeant came into the bar his face beaming and I handed him the pint of beer.

'Well, what have you got to say for yourself?' I asked him.

'When you let me have your own Spitfire, I knew that you had the confidence that I was going to make it in one piece and when you said you would have a pint ready for me on my return, that was more confirmation of your faith in me; the reason I was late getting back was because I was doing practice landings on some cloud north of Falkirk; I wanted to make sure that I could land properly when I got back to the aerodrome.'

'But what about your RT?' I enquired. 'Control could not get any reply from you after a while.'

'I think it got knocked off accidentally,' he said laughingly.

Towards the end of the month we had a batch of Polish pupils and we had a language difficulty. Fortunately they had an officer instructor with them who was allocated to our flight. He was a flight lieutenant and a first class pilot and one of the nicest people I had the pleasure of working with at Grangemouth. After a week he had taken over a new 'D' Flight mostly for Polish and Czechs and I was to be one of his instructors.

Jack, as I was told to call him, taught me the most important instructions in Polish like, I've got it. You've got it. Fine pitch. Flaps down, flaps up, undercart down (up), climb, descend, turn right (left) and many other words and phrases. I could speak French well and so could a lot of the Poles, so we soon got to understand each other.

They were a mixed bunch and unlike the Polish airmen who flew during the Battle of Britain as had Jack. Some of them were trying to live on the reputation of the earlier ones but some of them did not justify this attention. I soon got to know their capabilities as pilots and one trick I would do very early on the course, was to take the aircraft up to 8,000 feet, put it into a spin and switch off the engine. I would let go of the controls and say in Polish, 'You've got it.'

It was surprising sometimes what reaction you got and how you eventually finished up; on more than one occasion I had to fight for control because the pupil had frozen to the controls in panic. Before they had time to recover I would take them over the low flying ground and show them what real flying was like, by the time they had seen the trees just missing their wings and going under the pylons, they were ready to land.

When I had landed and got back in the flight office, I would tell them that I wanted them to fly like that before they left here. They soon realised that they had a lot to learn, before they came up to the standard of their fellow compatriots of 303 Polish Squadron. I will say this though, they were an eager bunch and were continually asking for extra flights. After a couple of weeks with them, I realised why they were so keen to get into action against the Germans. All of them had some tale of horror to tell about their families and even themselves. It made my own troubles I had been having seem insignificant.

The more I saw of Flight Lieutenant Jack Grezeszak the more I liked him. He was so different to our own officers and insisted that as an instructor I should call him Jack and he would call me Bill. He never shouted at a pupil but would take them aside and quietly talk to them, more like a father. He knew what these lads had already been through.

After I had got to know him better and he had been able to assess my qualities as a pilot, I asked him if I could go with him when he got his own squadron, even if I was the only Englishman in it. He told me that when that happened he would ask for me to be commissioned and take over one of his flights. What he meant was sections and as I had already led a section in the Battle of Britain period, I was dying to be able to lead one again. I would be impatient until that day arrived.

It was early May and I was on a low flying detail with a Polish pupil and I was to make an assessment of his reactions to unusual circumstances and the low flying I used to do with them was a good test of their nerve.

I started on my obstacle course and was coming to the last bit where I came out of the hollow, pulled up and went between two trees sideways below the level of the top of the trees. Everything had gone fine until I pulled up and aimed for the two trees. At 180 mph you don't have a lot of time to change your mind. I was horrified because between the trees was a cable which had only just been put up and was hardly visible. My reaction was that I had to carry on between the trees and that I had to go under the cable. I knew instinctively that if I hit it on top of the cable it would throw the machine into the ground whereas if I hit it going under it, I would be thrown in the air. With only a few yards to go, I went underneath and hit the cable with my propeller which was a three-bladed wooden one.

The impact threw us into the air and there was a loud bang and our hood had got torn off. The engine and aircraft were shaking themselves and I opened the throttle quickly as I knew that if I throttled back the aircraft would spin round the propeller shaft. I expected my pupil would be unconscious with fright in the front seat, but I saw a face pop up. He was smiling and saying something about we had lost the hood. I told him on the RT that I was going to attempt to fly the aircraft back and land it as the shaking did not stop me from handling it.

It was a long ten minute flight back and I had alerted the fire engines and ambulance as I was not sure what was going to happen when I tried to land

I had some hopeless advice from the control officer who suggested that we baled out as it would be impossible to land in that condition and it might plough into other aircraft or buildings.

I told the pupil to tighten up his harness and we would go straight in to land as we were flying at about three hundred feet only. Fortunately the wheels came down and I had decided that I could not use my flaps as I was unsure of what the increased descent altitude of the aircraft would do to the handling of the controls. I kept the engine going fully and came in to land. As I touched down I cut the magneto and the prop stopped. I bounced along the runway and kept the aircraft straight. At the same time the fire engine and ambulance were racing at the side of me. At last I pulled up. My pupil turned round to me and put both his thumbs up. He was not a bit worried about what had happened. In fact it seemed as though he had enjoyed it. My first thought was that he had passed this test with honours.

I had to see the CO again and explain what I had done. He was not at all pleased even though I had landed the aircraft in one piece. He told me that I had come in too fast. I could not accept that he was right and consequently I received an endorsement on my Log Book.

ENDORSEMENTS REGARDING AVOIDABLE
FLYING ACCIDENTS
AND ESTABLISHED BREACHES OF FLYING
DISCIPLINE NOT
NECESSARILY INVOLVING ACCIDENTS
2.5.41. Unauthorised low flying. Pilot hit electric cable.
Gross carelessness.
11.5.41.   Signed OC G/c

I wonder how long it took some ground wallah to compile a title which fitted so perfectly in two lines.

Perhaps I would now get a posting back into Fighter Command.

There the CO would first ask you whether you are all right after such a do. He did not worry about endorsements, they were the things you wrote on tombstones.

There were a lot of pints flying around the bar that evening. The Poles had seen the aircraft and the propeller which had lost a third of one blade and a half of another. They wondered why we had not been decapitated when the hood was torn off. I wished they would shut up – they were scaring the life out of me.

My prestige went sky high among the Polish pupils, especially the one who was with me. When I asked him how he felt when he saw the cable, all he could say was,

'I did not worry, you were flying the aircraft not me.'

At least this day was a bit of excitement and once again it showed the pupils that an aircraft would fly as long as the prop was turning.

The next day Flight Lieutenant Grezeszak had a chat with me and told me that I did the only thing possible when landing the machine. Had I throttled back, as had since been suggested to me, he said I would have crashed upside down.

'Do you still want me in your squadron after that episode?' I asked him.

'Bill, more than ever. You kept your head under exceptional circumstances, you must have had a fine instructor yourself for that kind of discipline.'

Good old Jimmy, good old Worger-Slade.

During the past few weeks our baby daughter had been very ill with heart trouble and was in Cirencester hospital. I was due leave to go and see her but I was too late as the CO received a telegram for me stating that Carole had died in hospital. He immediately sent me home on leave and suggested that I bring my wife back with me and live out.

It was a terrible journey home to Cirencester and I spent the most unhappy week of my life with my wife and I think it was only her courage that gave me the will to carry on. She told me that there was plenty of time for another baby and in time intended to have another one. At the end of the week I got the impression that my wife wished to go back to Enfield again; it was only for the baby's sake she had come to Cemey away from the bombs. She could see no reason for staying away from the parents and family and my young sister was wanting to go back to her friends.

Rene decided that she would not make a hasty decision as she knew I would have to have plenty of time to find a house back in Enfield and she knew my leave periods had to be taken at the RAF's convenience, not mine.

The journey back to Grangemouth was very miserable in more ways than one and I hated the thought of going back to instructing again. Ron met me at the station and had I wanted a shoulder to cry on, his was there. He suggested that as Rene was not coming back with me, we should go back in the mess and live on the station in future as some of the pupils were needing supervision on their time off. We heard some strange tales about what had been going on with some of the ladies of the night being invited back to the mess for social occasions.

He did not say much to me on the way to the mess and I was too worried for talking. When we arrived we went straight into the bar and Ron ordered a whisky for me which I thought unusual. 'Take this, mate,' he said, 'and sit down because I have something to tell you before anyone else does.'

I sat down and somehow I knew that I was going to get a shock as I had gone cold.

'What has happened, Ron, while I have been at home?'

'One of my pupils has been killed. He was low flying and broke his prop like you did but when he landed he throttled back and the machine turned over and went in upside down, he was killed immediately.' He was shaking as he was talking and I went to put my arm on him to say how sorry I was. But he said, 'Save it, pal. The worst is to come, better sit down again. Jack Grezeszak is dead. He was crashed into by a pupil who baled out. Jack could not make it and crashed and was killed.'

For a few minutes I froze, this was the last straw, my stomach could not take any more. Ron asked me if I would like another whisky, but I felt too ill. I had to run out to the toilets and I was violently sick. I had seen officers killed in my old squadron and even mates, but I could not take the fact the one of the nicest people I had ever met was now dead, because of a damned stupid pilot who had hit him. I could not eat my breakfast and told Ron I was going to walk over to flights.

My flight commander was already there and I asked him what had happened to Jack. I still could not believe it. The flight commander handed me a cardboard box and I took the lid off and saw that it was my flying helmet. If I was not flying I would often let Jack wear it because it was so much better than the new issues he had got. Mine had worn in lovely and soft and you hardly knew you had it on.

'He was wearing your helmet when he was killed, Bill. I suppose you will now want a new one.'

'No, thank you. I will keep this one. It will help me remember him if ever I get in a scrape. I am glad he was wearing it at the time.'

By now my pupils had arrived and I took up a pupil pilot officer to do some landings on grass. I had put my helmet on; I knew that I would never forget Jack and at the same time I had lost the chance of going with him to a new squadron and perhaps a commission also. I got no satisfaction at all from being proved right as to the way I had landed my aircraft with a broken prop. The price of that proof was a dead pupil.

The days went by and we were getting a mixture of pilots of all nationalities and it was becoming difficult to know what the nationality of each pupil was and this led to an amusing, but what could have been a very embarrassing, situation.

I had been taking pupils on a forced landing procedure. It involved taking the aircraft up to three thousand feet and switching off the engine. You would then tell the pupil to land on the largest field he could see, which was the selected landing area. The pupil had to be quick to spot the field and at the same time restart the engine, turn into wind and carry out normal landing with flaps and wheels down. It was a slick operation.

I had done about three trips doing the same thing with Poles and I went back for another pupil who climbed in and I told him it was to be a forced landing. I took off and flew to the area. At three thousand feet I said to the pupil, '*Ti, provargish*' and switched off the engine. The pupil looked round to me and I pointed to the ground. We were now commencing to dive with a dead engine. The next second I saw the pupil tugging at his straps and try to stand up to get out of the aircraft. I immediately switched on the ignition and at the same time pulled the stick back hard. The violent action of the nose coming up forced the pupil back in his seat. I tried talking to him in English, French, Polish, Czech and my own special curses but to no avail. He just sat in his cockpit and I flew back to Grangemouth.

After we had landed I taxied to flights and waved the next pupil away. There was some talking to be done first.

As I was walking by the pupil's side, I noticed on his sleeve, the Norwegian cross. I had never had a Norwegian pupil before and did not know a single word of the language. I had now got the message and had to laugh about it when I explained to the other instructors that I had almost lost a pupil. I could have imagined the pleasure they got from it.

When I got to the mess, I found that I had received a letter from Johnny White. He was on the way to the Middle East but could not say where. The other news was that Johnny Gilders had been killed in action. We had started with five Sprogs. How many of us would survive the war?

Ron had been away collecting another Spitfire. When I next saw him, he had seen the Master and its broken propeller and was waiting to tell me what he thought about that particular episode. He greeted me in his old style,

'You stupid bastard, what the hell did you have to fly that low for? You could have killed both your pupil and yourself. Have you no thought for Rene? The point is that none of your type of low flying is necessary. The other instructors don't do it. Why do you?'

I could not answer him immediately, he was right in some part but not entirely.

'Ron, when these lads leave here, they are going to an operational squadron and are likely to be doing sweeps over France and if they meet trouble, they are going to finish up at a pretty low altitude. They will be over enemy territory with enemy fighters between them and the coast. As you know, quite a few German fighters were shot down during last year's blitz because they were flying back at about 3,000 feet and we were able to come up underneath them in a blind spot. The only way to low fly is on the deck so that nothing can come up from below you. If you have the skill to fly at house-top level, not many German pilots will follow you and have time to get a bead on you. It's far too dangerous, as you well know. That is the reason I am giving my pupils the chance to fly as they might have to do in an emergency. I was taught this way and it has proved of great value to me. As for Rene, she is the incentive for me to come back.'

By now Ron had quietened down and readily saw my point, but he could not agree with me. 'Maybe it is good training and it might save a pilot's life but we are not here to make aces out of every Tom, Dick and Harry pupils. A lot of them are not worth the bother.'

I could not let him get away with that statement although I wanted to finish the discussion quickly, so I said:

'Ron, every pupil we have here is a volunteer and if they have the guts to want to be a fighter pilot, then we should have the guts to train them properly. I don't want any of them on my conscience when I read their obituaries. I want at least to say that I taught them to the best of my ability.'

I asked him how his trip to Digby had gone and he told me he had found out that the wife of one of the pilots whom we knew had just had a baby girl, thanks to me, according to the husband.

I laughed because it sounded as though I had been up to mischief but when we first met Monica it was at a dance and while I was dancing with her, she told me that she wanted a baby, but her husband who like us was a pilot did not wish her to have one in case he got killed.

I asked her what colour nightdress she wore, which rather shook her, and also did her husband use Durex to ensure she did not get pregnant? She said she had better sit down for a bit. While her husband was busy dancing with another woman she answered my question. She said she wore a blue one and her husband did use Durex.

I then said to her, 'If you really want a baby – and it will be your responsibility – I suggest you buy a nice pink satin nightie and hide the Durex one night. Make a fuss of Bert and I don't think he will worry about the Durex. If you do have a baby he will be the first to congratulate you.'

I was glad to hear that my suggestion had been taken up as they were so happy now, according to what they told Ron.

BLIND TAKE-OFFS AND LIVE FIRING

At the beginning of July I was told that all the pupils had to do blind take-offs. This was one of the most dangerous of operations, both for the pupil and instructor. It meant that the instructor would line up the Master aircraft on the runway; he would set the trimmers and ensure that the gyro compass in the pupil's cockpit was unlocked. He would then check both artificial horizons. When ready, he would tell the pupil to pull the hood over his cockpit, thereby blocking out any outside view. He would then put on the cockpit panel lights and glim lamp. The pupil was now under a night condition, but worse as he could not see anything outside his cockpit. The feeling gave most pupils a kind of claustrophobia; it was a horrible feeling. The pupil would then open up his throttle and take off, using his gyro compass and artificial horizon only. He had to make sure that he was perfectly in line with the centre mark of his gyro and that his artificial horizon was level and central. At the correct speed for take-off, he would ease back his control column and apply a little right rudder and lift the aircraft off the deck. He would climb steadily at the correct speed and level out at 500 feet.

The instructor would have his hands on the controls but only lightly so that the pupil could not feel them. It was essential that the instructor would only take over in the split second that the pupil made a mistake, either by veering off course or climbing too steeply. If the instructor took over too quickly – a split second was enough -the whole exercise was wasted for the pupil. On the other hand if he left it a split second too late you were both in the deck. It was most nerve-racking for both pupil and instructor.

If at 500 feet the pupil was straight and level and climbing at the right angle, the instructor would take over and do a split arse turn to the left and with wheels still down, land as fast as possible. He would then re-position the aircraft and the pupil would have another go. It was usual to do three take-offs on each sortie. By the time you had finished you were both saturated in sweat.

If anything did go wrong, which it did on two out of three tries by the pupil, it needed a speedy reaction from the instructor to open the throttle and get the aircraft in a safe attitude.

It was absolutely essential that you gave your pupil every second you dared and if necessary a split second to correct his mistake, before you took over. Some of the other instructors dreaded this exercise and, as much as I hated it, on the first day I did five different sorties of three trips each. This means fifteen take-offs and landings; this was to be the pattern for the future.

Another exercise the pupils had to do was to fire into the sea target. This meant flying in Spitfires to Leuchars on the north-east coast where the range was situated. On one occasion I was taking two pupils for practice to fire at a sea marker. This was a packet of aluminium powder which exploded on hitting the water making a large silver circle at which we would fire. It was approximately the same area as the cone of fire from the eight guns in the Spitfire wings. I had to open my hood and toss the packet out of the side. I had done this successfully on numerous occasions, but on this day, before it got to the open side window, it exploded into the cockpit covering my face and the cockpit in silver powder. I was temporary blinded and I pushed my goggles up so that I could see. Some of the powder went on my face and I took my silk scarf and tried to get the powder out of my eyes as it was burning and they were watering. I called up my two pupils and told them that we would have to abort the exercise and number three was to return to base on his own. My instruments were covered and I tried to wipe them but the powder seemed to be more like paint.

I was going to have to fly formation on my number two so I told him on the RT to come up on my right hand side and take the lead, keeping at least a couple of spans from me, so that I could see him from the side of the cockpit as the front view was obscured. He did this and I told him to head for home giving him the course to fly. I did not want to land at Leuchars because the aircraft would have been unserviceable for a long time. Anyway I had full confidence in my pupil to get me back to Grangemouth. At Grangemouth he was perfect in his approach and we both landed with plenty of room to spare. I felt proud of my pupil, there was no sign of

South Cerney, March 1940. Some of No 1 Course. Myself centre, front row.

Squadron Leader R Lees (right) visits the sergeants' mess.

Spitfire Mk IIA-P7985 of 'B' Flight, 72 Squadron, Acklington.

Hornchurch Dispersal. Self, with Pilot Officers Van de Poel, Bland and Muller.

Farewell display for departure of Squadron Leader Lees, DFC. Squadron Leader Lees, Flight Lieutenant Smith, Flying Officer Elsdon, Flying Officer Wilcox, Pilots Officers Robson, Pigg and Winter, Flight Sergeant Steere, Sergeant Norfolk, Gray, Plant, White, Rolls, Pocock, Glew and Staples.

72 Squadron, Acklington, June 1940. Back row: Sergeant J Gilders, Pilot Office Males, self; front row: Sergeant J White, Sergeant N Glew

We meet again, Jimmy (Group Captain T A F Elsdon, DFC) 47 years on.

Scorton, November 1941. We say goobye to our last Spitfire II.

Hornchurch dispersal. Left to right: Pilot Officer Van de Poel, Pilot Officer Prest, Sergeant Barratt, myself, Pilot Officer Bland, Pilot Officer Maynard and Pilot Officer Giddings.

Rene. My lucky mascot – better than a rabbit's foot.

I get my commission, 10th January 1942.

122 (City of Bombay) Squadron, Hornchurch, June 1942.

No 64 and 122 Squadron, Hornchurch, July 1942.

Some of the ground crews. Your life was in their hands.

'B' Flight take a gamble. Left to right: Sergeant Mortimer, Sergeant Barrat, Sergeant Nadon, Flight Lieutenant Griffith, DFC, myself, Pilot Officer Van de Poel. Back to camera: Pilot Officer Muller.

Teatime outside old dispersal bus in Malta. Self in right foreground.

My last view of dispersal, Malta.

'A' Flight take it easy. Left to right: Flight Lieutenant Hallowes, DFM and Bar, Sergeant Hubbard, Sergeant Park, unknown, Pilot Officer Mulliner, unknown.

Wings of Victory, Belfast. AC Alf Linstead, myself, Corporal Tony Meadows. The photograph was taken by the other member, LAC Victor Cummings.

I take over my first flight and mascot. 'B' Flight, 126 Squadron, Malta, Auugust 1942.

The author presenting a silver trophy 'Swift' to Wing Commander Colin Reineck, of 72 Squadron 'Wessex' at Odiham in 1975.

nerves when he took over.

On another occasion at Leuchars I had taken a flight lieutenant and another pupil for air firing and as we started the exercise the flight lieutenant told me on the RT that he did not like the sound of his engine. The other pupil was about to make his run at the target and I told him to finish his exercise and return to base on his own. I then told the flight lieutenant that we would land at Leuchars to see what was wrong with his engine. I had no intention of taking him back to Grangemouth if he was worried about his engine.

After we had landed I asked one of the ground crew to look at the officer's engine and he went over and ran up the engine and then took the cowling off. I sat in my aircraft and if it could not be done in a few minutes the officer would have to stay the night until it had been properly serviced the next day. After a few minutes the officer came over to me and told me that the crew would have to do a full service on the aircraft now that it had been reported to them. It would not be ready until the next morning.

His next remark took me by surprise. 'Flight Sergeant, I want your aircraft and you can wait here for mine until it has been serviced. I have to be at Grangemouth tonight.'

I quickly replied, 'I am sorry, sir, but I am the instructor and you are the pupil and I have to be in Grangemouth early tomorrow to look after my pupils. I am afraid it was you who put the aircraft unserviceable and you will have to wait for it.'

I told him to get in touch with my flight commander at Grangemouth and ask him what he should do. He went off to the control tower and within minutes I had a call from the controller that I had permission from Grangemouth to return to base.

On landing at Grangemouth I told my flight commander what had happened and he told me I was correct in what I had told the officer as I was more important to him than any... pupil. I felt, though, that for the first time in my dealings with many nationalities, I had upset one of my pupils.

POSTING TO 61 OTU HESTON

I was now getting tired of instructing and I asked for a posting to an operational squadron and Ron did the same. We waited patiently for a posting, especially as Ron had asked for a posting to a Spitfire squadron. We hoped we would be posted to the same squadron. Our posting notice came through at the end of the month and I was horrified when I saw it- we had both been posted to Heston OTU as there was a shortage of experienced instructors. It was no different to what we had been doing except that now that Rene was living at Enfield both of us could get home on days off.

Another shock I got was the news that poor old Johnny White had been killed in action in the Middle East. Two more Sprogs to go, I thought.

When Ron and I arrived at Heston we were not at all happy. We were received by the group captain with very little enthusiasm. We had to live out in lodgings and I was glad when I eventually got my posting to an operational squadron again.

I was going to a newly formed squadron of mostly Canadians at a place called Scorton in Yorkshire, once again flying Spitfires. Ron had not yet got his posting notice and it was a sad farewell to a grand mate. As I packed my log book, I noticed that the next entry would be on a new page. I remembered what my uncle had said, 'A new page of your log book is a new life.' I had turned many pages since I left my old squadron. I hoped this new life was going to be worthwhile.

The best sight I have had was leaving the gates at Heston and going home for a couple of days. I had the satisfaction that the time I spent as an instructor was going to prove very valuable in the future. I had done a lot of cloud flying, leading sections to 28,000 feet, and quite a lot of low flying; showing pupils deflection shooting and firing on the range was very valuable as I could readily assess deflection under almost any conditions. Flying in bad weather conditions was another asset and the need to be quick thinking in formation with new pupils had made me faster in my own reactions.

In all I would say that I was lucky to have had all this extra training and as the war was going to last for a long time yet, I could face operational flying without fear as I was a much better flier now than I was during the Battle of Britain.

Perhaps in future I would get a chance for a commission. That would be the cream on the cake and a realisation of a dream.

My big regret was that I was going to lose another good pal. Once I got to my new squadron I was going to ask the CO to get Ron posted to his squadron. I would strongly recommend him.

CHAPTER FOUR

I Go Back on an Operational Squadron

When I first read my posting notice, I had no idea where the place was. It was with difficulty that I found marked on the map a village called Scorton and I assumed that the airfield was there. I knew it was really a landing ground as it had only been recently taken over. The village was about ten miles south of Doncaster, about three miles east of Richmond and was bounded on the east coast by the range of North York Moors which stretched between Scarborough and Redcar. My first reaction was that the squadron would almost certainly be doing convoy patrols for that area. It was not going to be so good in the coming winter when the moors would be covered in snow and low cloud.

I was to be reporting for duty on the morning of 23rd October 1941. I did not have a lot of time to spend at home, as I would catch the night train on the 22nd so that I could have a night at home with my wife, who was now nicely settled in at our new home in Enfield, North London. The time passed all too quickly but even a night off at the time was a bonus I did not expect.

On the train I had time to think of what I might be going into as I was not over-enthusiastic about the posting, as much as I wanted to get back on operational flying. I would have preferred to have gone down south in 11 Group where the action was taking place with sweeps as bomber support over France. After my meeting some merchant seamen at Hull, however, I looked on convoy patrols with a new interest. If our presence over the convoy gave them so much confidence, then it was worthwhile. There was the added incentive that you were keeping enemy bombers away from the convoy which was better than shooting them down when they had made an attack on the ships.

I had misgivings about going to a newly formed squadron only a few months old. It looked as though I might have to do some more instructing. After a somewhat boring train journey I had come to the conclusion that as I had asked for a posting I had to make the best of it.

On the morning of the 23rd, I arrived at Doncaster, not a pretty sight to greet a hungry passenger so early in the morning. I had to go into the Hotel to get a proper breakfast at a very inflated price. I found the bus I had to catch after asking many people what number it was for Scorton. Most of them had never heard of it. A good encouraging start, I thought.

After a nice bumpy uncomfortable ride I was there in the Valhalla of the Yorkshire Moors, RAF Scorton. As I watched the bus pull away I wondered if I would ever see civilisation again. Here I was, in the middle of nowhere with a village square with two pubs and a shop. Behind me was a small school which was evidently the sergeants' mess or that is what the sign said. Further along the road was a conglomeration of nissen huts one of which said Headquarters. I picked up my cases and made my way to the building. No! I don't think I am going to like this place one bit, I thought, but beggars can't be choosers, so put on a smile, go and find the jolly old adjutant – that will wipe the smile off your face!

I went inside the hut and saw a door marked Adjutant and made for it. The adjutant was expecting me, which itself was unusual. On all the other postings I had had, the adjutant had generally asked me what I was doing there. His first words were encouraging,

'Welcome to 122 Squadron, Flight Sergeant Rolls. First things first, have you had any breakfast yet?'

'Yes, sir, thank you very much,' I answered, thinking at the same time, well, at least he is considerate.

In no time at all he had put me at ease and had explained all about the squadron, its officers and sergeants and even the ground crew. This man knew his job and each minute with him took away some of my anxiety about my posting. He told me that the commanding officer. Squadron Leader Miller, wished to see me after he had finished with me and as he said it, the squadron leader came into the room. I stood up as he came across the room.

'You are obviously Flight Sergeant Rolls?' He held out his hand which I took.

'Yes, sir, and I am very pleased to be joining your squadron.' The things some people say when standing in front of your CO. He looked a kind chap and if the others were like him and the adjutant, it could not be bad.

'Come and see me when you have finished here and I will put you in the picture.' I began to wonder whether I had three rings on my arm instead of three stripes and a crown, especially after the kind of treatment Ron and I had received at Heston from some of the officers.

The adjutant impressed on me that the accommodation was not yet up to standard but he assured me that it would not be long before I had better rooms. He mentioned that transport was sometimes a problem, but you had to push if you wanted it.

I then went into the CO's office and was told to sit down. He asked me if I wished to smoke, but I said no, although I would have loved to. I believe in first impressions and I was not going to cock this one up. I would probably be here a long time.

'I have received a copy of your records and your experience as an instructor and although I do not intend to use you in this capacity, I will expect you to help train the new pilots in operational tactics, but more in terms of conversation, than as lessons. You see, most of the squadron are Canadians and I would not like them to get the impression they are trainees still. In their opinion they are operational pilots.'

'I understand, sir.' I grinned a bit and continued, 'I am pleased for that information, sir. I want also to be an operational pilot and not an instructor, but the fact that I am a few years older than most of these chaps might help, especially as they are all strangers to this country.'

He asked me about my family and I told him about Rene and our losing our baby at South Cemey. I showed him Rene's photograph which I took out of my top pocket, it was a little dog-eared with the continual taking it out and putting it back in my pocket.

'I am sorry to hear about the baby but I am sure when the time is right, your wife will want another one. She has plenty of time ahead of her.' He was looking at the photo still and continued, 'My wife is here with me and we live just down the road. When you are settled in she will be in touch with you because she helps look after the chaps' welfare.'

When the CO had finished with me the adjutant called for a van to take me up to my billets which were further along the road. Yes, you've guessed right, they were also nissen huts, which on a winter's morning looked more like igloos.

The nissen hut was divided into four parts, making separate rooms or should I say cells. The room contained an old iron bedstead, a wardrobe and a chest of drawers. There was a small window and what looked like net curtains, until I looked closer and saw it was grime. After a few phone calls I told the accommodation officer that I wanted something better than what I had got. I was a flight sergeant and expected treatment as such.

What a relief it was to see my new flight commander. He was an old hand and made me welcome, as he might have done a long lost friend. His first words after I had introduced myself were, 'How the hell did you get transport to bring you here?'

'I just rang up for it and told them I wanted it. The Adj told me I would have to push to get transport and so I pushed.'

'Jolly good show, Flight.' He then introduced me to the other pilots who were mainly Canadians and some Belgians. I knew that I would like working with them, they seemed a happy crowd. I went with the Flight Commander to see 'A' Flight chaps who were just down the perimeter track. I received the same kind of welcome.

It was quite a nice afternoon when I did my first trip and I decided I would fly round the area and make for Redcar, along the coast to Scarborough and then fly over the North York Moors and pick out some landmarks. It was handy to know the terrain over which we had to fly so that in bad weather you could assess your position in relation to the airfield. I had a good look at the highest point on the moors called Stony Ridge about 1422 feet high. That was well worth remembering as on most trips you were doing convoy patrols; the quickest way to base was over the moors, but in bad weather it was dangerous. The Great North Road was a good landmark and would be easy to fly low over if the weather really closed down. In all I was happy with the location and landed after 1 hour 5 minutes. It was my first trip with my new squadron and if all my other trips were to be as pleasant as this one, then I was going to be a happy man.

It was late afternoon when the CO came to our flights. He came up to me and asked me how I was fitting in. At the same time he handed me an envelope and said, 'This will keep your wife's photograph in good condition.'

I thanked him and opened the envelope and inside was a thin perspex double-sided cover in which the photograph just fitted. It may have been a small gesture on his part, but to me it showed what kind of a CO he was, to be so concerned on my first day. Shades of 72 Squadron. How much different were the officers to some of those in the training schools.

When the day was over and we returned to the billets, I was not sure what I was going to see. Whether my linen had been changed or the windows and curtains had been cleaned and changed did not seem so important now that I had met the chaps I was going to fly with.

One of the Canadians asked me what my room was like so I told him to come and see for himself. When I opened the door, I thought I was in the wrong room because there was a carpet on the floor, curtains at the cleaned windows and what seemed to be new bed linen and on the wall under the window was an electric fire.

Larry exclaimed, 'They must have thought you were an officer. What are these?' He went over to the chest of drawers and picked up a jam jar with some lovely chrysanthymums in. If this was that airman's idea of a joke he would know it when I next saw him.

That evening I went to the local hop with some of the others and we first went into the local pub and had a few beers and from there went to the village dance. It was very enjoyable. It seemed that all the locals knew that I was a new arrival and did their best to make me welcome. During the dance I noticed a young WAF there and in an excuse-me dance one of them came up to me and asked me to dance with her. As I was dancing with her, she said:

'Did you like the flowers in your room?' She was laughing as she said it.

I immediately thought that the joke had got round and I was beginning to get angry with her, when she said, 'I heard about you wanting your room cleaned out and I thought I would make it a bit like home for you. I hope you did not mind?'

I replied, 'No not now that I know you put them there in all sincerity, but I thought the airman was taking the mickey and if he had it would have been a different story.'

After the dance had finished we sat down and talked about the station. Suddenly she said, 'May I see your wife's photograph. I know you are married and that you have the photo because I gave the CO a cover for it when he told me what he wanted one for.'

That established it once and for all, I was an old married man and all the girls knew it.

I was on duty the next morning so I did not stay late and I walked back to my billet in the sharp evening breeze wondering what the future now held for me. It was not going to be dangerous flying like it was at Biggin Hill but it could be exciting and worthwhile being back on operations once more.

The weather was too bad for flying the next day and I spent most of the time in the photographic department looking at camera gun practice air firing. I was not impressed either with the quality of the picture or the angles of deflection used by the pilot in the various attacks on the target aircraft.

All the camera guns I had met were most unreliable, as I found out when I was with 72 Squadron. As an instructor I had found it easier and more reliable to teach deflection shooting on a cinema screen using a picture of the target aircraft at various angles which could easily be calculated; then by superimposing a ring and bead sight over the picture you could get the exact deflection. What you learned after lots of practice was a mental picture of what you had to do in the air, under those conditions.

For my interest in this field the CO made me the Camera Gun Looker After. It was not easy because most of the pilots did not seem to want to know about angles of deflection and converging speeds. They preferred to aim the aircraft at the target and hope to hit it.

The following day was a bit better and in the morning I took Blue Section up for some formation practice. On landing we were sent to forward base at Hartlepool. This was where we would usually stay for convoy patrols or readiness. We did one scramble over the sea for a reported German aircraft but it went off the board and after 30 minutes we landed. Later towards the evening we returned to Scorton. If this was going to be the pattern of flying in future it did not seem too bad as it was always nice to see the seaside, even in winter.

It did not take long to get to know the other chaps in each flight as the Canadians were a friendly bunch. Although we had other English chaps I seemed to get on easier with the Canadians. I had made my mind up that I was not going to make any special friends as I had done in my last two postings. I would try to be friendly with them all but after flying was over, I did not want to get in with any small clique which was the way things went in all squadrons. They nearly all went out in groups of three or four. This was understandable with the younger men as their pastime was pretty girls. With the older ones amongst us it was generally beer and the pretty girls' mums. There were not many of them in such a small village and as the surrounding land was farming, most of the husbands were home anyway.

One night about a week later, I had to do an operational patrol between Hartlepool and Skegness. It was a black and cloudy night and I was to patrol about thirty miles out to sea. There were supposed to be enemy aircraft approaching but it would have been impossible to see them unless you were right on top of them. Sometimes in this situation, the enemy could see you first and the first thing you knew was when you saw red tracers coming at you. Your immediate reaction was that the crew were learners as a skilled crew would never give away their position, by firing at a Spitfire. Still, even the bullets from a learner feel the same if they hit you or the aircraft. The patrol lasted for 1 hour 15 minutes, which is a long while on your own in a dark cockpit, in a cloudy dirty black sky. Landing at night then seems fun.

The days passed and nothing much exciting occurred. The weather was not good for flying. Even convoy patrols were a bit risky but we had to do them; that was the only reason we were there. When we went to Thornaby for convoy work we generally stayed there for a couple or three days depending on the weather. As there was always something going on in the cinema it made a nice break, and there was the added incentive that you were helping the Merchant Navy. When we were doing convoy patrol we were not allowed to use our RT in case German intruder aircraft could home in on our signal. We had to use our morse lamp beneath the aircraft to tap out the code of the day and as this was changed every few hours you had to make sure you had the right code otherwise you might get shot down by the ships' guns. Some of them had been bombed by German aircraft with British markings so it was a question of 'shoot first, ask questions after' if you had not got the correct code. I remember one occasion when I was flying very low over some ships and was almost at mast height because of very low cloud. This was the only way you could see any distance beneath the cloud. After passing over the convoy several times Willie and I saw the morse lamp from one of the boats and I could not help laughing. It was obvious Willie had read the message correctly. It was short and sharp and translated into basic English meant FUCK OFF.

It was obvious that they were getting disturbed by our low flying, but we had a job to do so on our next run I tapped out a reply which translated into whatever language you choose means BALLS.

On our next run over the ship which had sent and received these coded messages we saw some of the crew and they were waving at us and looking quite friendly.

When we had finished our time we returned to Thomaby. I went to the duty pilot to report on the weather and I asked him if he was in touch with the convoy and he said he was. I told him what had happened and asked him if he would pass them a message, 'Are we still friends?' He called up the Signals. Whether it was the same boat I did not know but after he had sent the message, a reply came back: 'Yes, dear.'

Only a little incident it may seem but at times of danger like these men had to endure every day we were in convoy, those little gestures kept you human.

When we got back to Scorton the next day we were told that the next day we would be getting our new Spitfires Mark Vs. With two cannon and four Browning machine-guns. This is what we had been waiting for and the squadron was being stood down for a few days so that we could align the guns and cannons to our own satisfaction.

The next day I did a test in one of the new machines and I found it a better machine than the Spit II because although the airframe was almost the same it had a better engine and a higher rate of climb. I thought at first the two cannon would upset the aircraft balance in aerobatics but there was no trouble at all. I was going to like this aeroplane and with its armament you could attack anything on the ground or in the air. It meant that I was going to be busy assessing camera gun firing and aligning up the new armament.

I had only just got to know my flight commander when he was posted to another squadron of his own. It was good news for him but who were we to get in his place? It was not long before we were told that one of our Belgian officers was going to take over 'B' Flight. This was good news because Boudwan as we called him was popular with all of us and we knew he would be as easy to get on with as our first one was.

There was a party in the officers' mess to say farewell to our former flight commander and we were all invited. The less said about that party the better. A minor event during it was that someone started up a steam roller and ran it into the village green: someone let the water out of the storage tank on the unit and everyone was gloriously tipsy.

It was just before Christmas that I was given a big surprise by our CO. He told me that I had been recommended for a commission and along with three Canadian sergeants was to attend 12 Group Headquarters to be interviewed by the Air Officer Commanding Air Marshal Sholto Douglas, CB, MC, DFC. I did not have any idea about what the interview would cover and neither had the others so you can imagine our feelings on the great day.

We were to be interviewed in alphabetical order and I was the third to go. When the first one came out from the interview after about twenty minutes he looked worried and was not allowed to talk to the rest of us. There was no chance of finding out what questions he had been asked. The second chap came out after about the same time and I was called in.

I had seen photographs of the AOC so I was not surprised that he seemed to take up the whole table. It was not his size, it was his air of authority and I had never been interviewed by an officer above wing commander before. To say I was nervous was an understatement. I was expecting a twenty minute grilling. His first question almost knocked me for six:

'Flight Sergeant, imagine you are the CO of a squadron in the desert and you are confronted with the army who are in retreat. They ask for your help. What would you do?' He paused and then added, 'Take a few moments to think over the question.'

A few moments, I thought, I would want hours to answer that one. I already had visions of 'failed' on my report.

Then it occurred to me. It was simple.

'Sir, as the CO of that squadron I would already have available to me all the information regarding the enemy dispositions, our own army's availabilities and my own squadron's aircraft serviceability, armament and stores. I would also know where our rear base was and what hope we could expect from them.'

He was looking hard at me and I thought to myself, now what?

'Sir, if I could be given all that information from you, I could readily assess my best plan of action.'

I waited for the bomb to burst, but the AOC continued to write on his form. He had not said a word or asked me another question and I was getting worried.

At last he looked up and smiled at me, not much but I read into it a lot: 'Thank you. Flight Sergeant, that will be all.'

I saluted and turned round and walked out of his office and joined the other two. They both seemed reluctant to tell me what questions they had been asked and both remarked that I had not been in there as long as they had.

I had noticed this myself, hence the gloom and it was even worse when Willie came out after twenty minutes looking pleased with himself. I could already imagine him in an officer's uniform. On the journey back little was said about the questions which had been asked us and so I did not bother to tell them what I had been asked. I think we were all afraid that one of us would be told by the others that the answer was silly or wrong. We knew from other Canadian sergeants who had recently been commissioned that we would hear nothing for at least three weeks so we were going to be on tenterhooks and best behaviour just in case.

It was getting on for Christmas and we were off flying owing to the bad weather. I decided I would go back to my billet to write some letters after lunch. I walked up the road from the mess towards the billet and about halfway up I saw an elderly lady with a large brown and white collie dog on a leash. I was watching the approach of the lady because I thought she was pulling the dog when it obviously wanted to relieve itself. As I approached her and the dog I felt that I must say something to her about the dog, but I did not know her and so I did not want to upset her by saying anything that might distress her.

I came level with her and said, 'Good afternoon, madam, what a lovely dog you have. What do you call him?' By this time the dog had started his relieving. The lady looked at it and said, 'Naughty boy, Ruff.' She turned to me and said, 'You did that deliberately, you did not want to tell me about it, so you talked about the dog instead, knowing that I would stop and the dog could carry on doing what he wanted.'

'Madam, you are correct in your assumption, but I cannot understand why this should have arisen.' I was a bit worried because she had one of those malacca canes in her hand.

She laughed and said, 'Are you in a hurry to get where you are going?'

'No, madam, I have all the afternoon.'

'Come with me for a minute and you will see why I did not stop with Ruff.'

I walked by her side and we went slowly along the road to a little passage which led to a gate of a large field. She unleashed the dog and he ran down this passage and again relieved himself.

'Now you see why I did not stop, for years the dog has done this walk to the same place and never once has it stopped until you came along.'

It was my turn to feel small now and I asked her to accept my sincere apology.

She smiled and put her arm through mine and we walked back along the road towards the church. She told me that she owned the aerodrome land and the large field where the dog had gone. She told me she had a son John who was very keen on the RAF but being a farmer had to stay on the farm. She told me that she would like me to meet John and as it was getting near tea time, would I join her and John for some tea?

I felt as though I had known her for years; she reminded me of someone in my childhood but I could not think who it was. As we neared the farmhouse which was right opposite this lovely church she said something that really puzzled me. 'You are a fatalist, William, and our meeting was arranged many moons ago.'

We were now inside this lovely old farmhouse in a very big living room with a big fire in a fireplace that took up half the wall. It was a lived-in room, solid and comfortable and I took no time in getting in a chair near the fire, while the lady went to the back of the house. It was only a minute or so before a young woman whom I recognised immediately came in. I had seen her at the dance when I first arrived; she was the maid called Nancy. 'Hello,' she said. 'Have you got settled in yet? I am pleased to know that you have now met Aunt Fran.'

I now knew who the lady was or so I thought, but I soon learned that she liked to be called aunt by her young men friends from the aerodrome.

Nancy smiled as she said it and added, 'We have had some of the young pilots here for tea and they all call her Aunt Fran and she loves it.'

'How did she know my name?' I asked.

'I told her the other day that we had a new flight sergeant who was a Battle of Britain pilot with a DFM. It was easy to know who you were once she saw you. She has been out several times hoping she would see you at the camp. She likes to know what is going on. So does her son John who is mad keen on the RAF and likes to meet the pilots whenever possible.' She added quietly, 'By the way, she owns the land the airfield is built on.'

It was not long before another young woman came in to join us. I was told that she was a companion housekeeper called Madge. I liked her immediately. Madge picked up the tray to take out and as she opened the door in rushed the dog and behind him was a young man who I knew must be John. It was obvious at first acquaintance that he was mad keen on the RAF and in spite of my promises to myself that I was not going to have any more special friends I knew that John and I were going to get on well together. My first invitation to tea turned out to be a late night and I felt happier than I had done for months as I walked to my billet.

Most of December was spent doing air to ground firing and camera gun exercises on air to air firing. I had rigged up a nice room at flights for assessing the results of the camera gun test and I had rigged up a miniature ring and bead sight which could be placed over the gate in the lens and on the screen on which the film was shown and by using different size ring and bead sights I could very accurately tell the pilot what he had done wrong and the fact that the ring and bead on the screen gave the correct picture of what should have been seen in the cockpit. This soon improved the standard of air to air camera gun practice.

For the next few days there was not much excitement and it was mostly trips to forward base and back. It was on 10th January 1942 that the CO sent for the four of us who had been interviewed for a commission. He told us that we had all been successful and as from 8th January we had become officers. There were, however, a few formalities we had to adhere to and these would be explained to us by the adjutant. He congratulated all of us on our success. It was a marvellous feeling to know that your service to date had been appreciated and I had now got the cream on my cake which I had tried so hard to get.

Ten minutes with the adjutant and we found that we had all been discharged from the RAF and would be entitled to our accumulated leave. We signed another document and we were back in the RAF this time as pilot officers. We were given twenty pounds for our new uniforms, shoes, shirts and ties. Our battledress we would keep, but take off the stripes and put pilot officer stripes on the shoulders, and of course buy the officer's ceremonial hat. We would also receive a rise in pay and I would receive a higher marriage allowance for my wife. You can imagine that we all came out of that office very happy men. I was more concerned that I was going to have two weeks' leave, especially as my wife had been ill.

The CO agreed that we could start our leave at once and go to London and get measured for our uniforms. When we went to collect our railway warrants we found they were for first class travel and realised that from now on it would always be first class.

The adjutant had also told us that we would have new billets and a WAF bat-woman between two of us and naturally we would use the officers' mess from then on. By the time we got back, it would all be arranged.

On arrival in London the next day, Rex and I went to Gieves to buy our uniform. Willie and Larry went somewhere else for their Canadian uniforms. I was to collect mine the following week. I had not been able to let my wife know that I was coming home on leave for two weeks and it was a lovely surprise for her especially when I told her that I was now an officer, or rather when I picked up my new uniform I would look like one. I picked up my uniform the next week and naturally went to see my parents and in-laws to show them how I looked as an officer. The rest of the leave was great and it was hard when I had to return to Scorton.

My first day back at Scorton seemed rather odd as I was now in officer's uniform and instead of being spoken to as flight sergeant, I was now called sir, and received a salute. There was also the introduction to the officers' mess, and although I had been a visitor there on many an occasion, this time I was a member and could buy drinks at the bar. What was more important was that you were now called by your Christian name, although most of the officers had done this when I was a flight sergeant. I had a change of bedroom and of course a proper bed, but most surprising was that Willie and I shared a bat-woman who looked after our rooms and did other little tasks, like looking after your laundry, keeping your uniform pressed and, above all, adding those little feminine touches like the odd vase of flowers in our room.

When flying, there was no difference as I had always led a section as a flight sergeant. With the ground crews, they were the same, I knew them all by their Christian names and that was the way it was going to stay, friendly. Your life depended on their skill and this was a special relationship which both sides respected.

When flying recommenced it was the usual scramble to the coast for a suspected German intruder aircraft, or on a convoy patrol. These trips meant one night at our forward base at Thornaby. There were only two of us and we only had an overnight bag with us. There was not room in a Spitfire cockpit for anything else so we would fly in our best blues and shoes instead of flying boots. We never flew very high on convoy patrols and it was necessary to dress for dinner at Thornaby. That is why we did not fly in our battle dress.

It was on one of these trips on 28th February that we took off from Thornaby, Willie being my number two, to patrol a convoy off Whitby. It was early morning and low cloud and very cold. The intention was to see what the weather was like over the convoy and then go back to Scorton. When we arrived over the convoy we were in very low mist and low cloud and it would have been too dangerous to stay too long as the weather was getting worse.

I was not happy with the sound of my engine and I noticed that there was fluctuation on the rev counter although the temperature and oil pressure seemed normal. I did not worry too much and after we had been airborne for twenty minutes I decided to return to base as it was obvious no German plane could get through to the convoy. I informed control and received permission to pancake.

We were now about five miles south of Whitby near Robin Hood's Bay and I knew the route back over the moors. The cloud base was about two thousand feet but misty underneath. I knew that the highest point on my route was about 1,100 feet so I was not unduly worried either about the weather or my engine. We had been flying in close formation for about five minutes when it happened. My engine stopped dead and a cloud of black smoke came from the engine. I instinctively knew that I had to make an immediate decision to land as I was too low to bail out; there was only 600 feet and I was dropping fast. I could only glide for a few seconds. I had switched on my RT and was telling Willie to circle me and inform base what had happened. I also managed to ask him to get some food dropped to me. I saw a large snowdrift to my left and decided that I was going to side-slip my aircraft into it. If I carried straight on I would go down a very steep slope full of boulders which I knew would be under the snow. That would be the finish of me and my aircraft. I side-slipped into the snow drift and hardly felt the impact as the snow was so deep. There was a little forward movement but it was smooth. Clouds of snow were tossed up over the windscreen and I could not see a thing.

My wireless was still working and I could hear Willie asking how I was. I could hear him on the RT telling Control what had happened. I climbed out of the cockpit onto the wing and waved to Willie to let him know I was all right. I then switched off my radio as I smelt petrol. Willie waggled his wings and made off for Scorton.

I struggled with the hood and managed to climb on the wing and fell into the snow. It was bitterly cold and I had got my trousers and shoes wet with snow as I got out of the aircraft. I was not worried about a rescue team coming out for me as I knew Willie had given my exact position to them, but I was worried about the cold and wet. The knowledge that one of our chaps had been missing on the moors in his crashed aircraft for five weeks before he was found frozen to death did not help me. I also knew that I was a long way from the small road that led to the top of the moors so it was no good my thinking of walking to a road for help, I would obey the golden rule, STAY PUT, and wait.

I could not sit in the cockpit because of the fumes and I was afraid of sitting under one of the wings in case the warmth of the engine melted the snow packed up in front of the nose. It was possible the whole lot would go down the slope and over the top with a nice 800 feet drop.

I saw only one possible place I could get out of the wind and that was under the rear edge of the starboard wing which was sticking out about 45 degrees making a good roof if I scraped the snow from under it. This I did and it looked good. I did not notice the time go by as it had taken me some time due to the continual efforts to keep warm. Its a good job I had my gloves on.

I was about to climb up to get my parachute out of the cockpit when I saw coming towards me a Magister aircraft. It flew low over me and I saw Willie and someone in the backseat who was holding something in his arms and standing up in the cockpit. Willie made another run and this time the parcel came down and a small parachute broke its fall. It landed only yards away from me and I went to run and get it and in my haste I fell forward face down into the snow. Fortunately I managed to brush most of it off and I waved to Willie that I was all right and on his run over he put his hand up showing his fingers, I counted eight I think but I did not know what he meant. Perhaps he meant eight hours to rescue time, which was a long while to wait in this cold.

The thermos contained some real hot coffee and hot bacon sandwiches and there was a small bottle of whisky. This must be Willie's contribution, I thought. There was a note telling me that the rescue teams were on the way. I had some coffee, a couple of sandwiches and a swig of the whisky and I now felt like a boy scout on his first camping trip, cold, wet but bloody happy.

This mood quickly wore off as I started to feel the cold of my feet and my chest was getting tight with the cold so I took my silk scarf (good old Emma) off and tied it round my chest. This was much better. If I was going to be here for eight hours then I had to do something about survival so I climbed up to the cockpit and took out my parachute pack and unrolled it, without letting the wind spill it out. I wanted it as it was rolled as it gave a very thick blanket of silk about one foot by twelve feet which I wrapped round and round my body from top to toe. I then put the seat of it under the wing and went and sat on it. The thermos and sandwiches were at hand so I was content to sit and wait for my rescuers. I never want to spend another day like that one.

For the first two or three hours I did not notice anything to worry me but as time went on I thought I was hearing things. It was a peculiar sensation. I could hear these noises but could see nothing. I was getting a bit nervy and started to imagine I was not alone. I wanted to unwrap myself and run, but I did not know where to go to; I wanted to put a radio on and talk to control but I knew they would not hear me with the hills between. I was also saving the battery in case I was still there on the night, I could use my cockpit lights for illumination to guide them to me.

I got fed up with thinking about things and hearing these strange noises or sometimes I thought voices. I sang my old school song:

> Forty Years On
> When afar and asunder
> Parted are those
> Who are singing today,
> When you look back
> And forgetfully wonder
> What you were like
> In your work and your play.

I thought, what will I be like in forty years' time? Will I have anything to look back on? Will I have anything to look back on in four years' time was more my worry! I sang other songs, I said all the prayers I knew, I sang all the hymns I knew, anything to stop those bloody noises. Then suddenly I put my thumb and finger on my nose and pinched hard and at the same time popped my ears and on the second attempt, hey presto! the noises stopped. What a bloody clot I was! It had happened so many times when climbing to a high altitude that I did it automatically. On the ground I had not even thought of it.

In the far distance I could just make out one of the larger roads and I thought I could see some RAF vehicles coming down it and assumed that in two more hours I would be in one of them. It was about two hours later when I heard a shout and saw some men tramping over the snow towards me and I knew then that I was home if not dry.

I was soon given a change of clothing and sitting on a nice dry bed. I was given some hot tea and someone stuck a needle in my arm, I don't know why but I was hoping it was not going to have the same effect as the other inoculations. The RAF team were soon at work on the Spitfire with cowlings off and they stripped quite a bit of it and dismantled the radio etc. They took good care of the Very pistol and colours of the day.

The medic did not wait for the others to finish and we started off to walk to the vehicles. I could have lain on the bed but I did not want to. It was hard enough going for the team and I was in a good state of health even if I was tired.

It was almost two hours before I was back at Scorton and I got quite a welcome from the lads. Willie told me he thought I had had it, when he saw the smoke come from the engine and the propeller stop. He told me he could hardly bear to look as I sideslipped into the snowdrift; from the air, he said, it looked impossible.

I asked the CO if I could leave my report till tomorrow as I was feeling tired. He told me not to worry as Willie had already made out a full report as to what had happened on that sortie.

That evening when I met John at the farm, he asked me if I had done much flying that day. I replied, 'Only twenty minutes, John.'

He laughed and said, 'What an easy job you chaps have. Only twenty minutes in one day.' If only he had known the truth.

We heard a rumour that we were going to be posted to Madagascar and it did not sound good. All jungle and bad food. We received all the inoculations which put us all out of action for a few days.

There was very little excitement as far as flying was concerned and most of the others had been taking leave as it was obvious we were soon going to be posted somewhere. We had new pilots posted to us and that meant training them in formation and gunnery. We also had some of our older officers posted to other squadrons. This did not help to keep a good team together as no one knew who was going to be posted next.

It was nearing the end of March and by then we had two of our mates killed on the moors and a couple of good flight commanders had been posted also. These are very important positions in a squadron and it takes time to get used to new ones, as in most cases they have only just been promoted from other squadrons.

In a pilot's log book, the entry, 'Scramble, Convoy patrol,' does not sound much, but in actuality it involves a lot of nervous tension in most cases, especially in bad weather and it was nearly always bad weather at that time of the year at Scorton.

Before the actual scramble you would be at readiness in the crew room, dressed in flying kit and Mae West. The ground crew would be by their Spitfire, ready to start the engine the minute they got the Scramble on the tannoy. The pilot would rush out to his aircraft and get in the cockpit and assisted by a member of the ground crew would get strapped in. The engine would be running, then the aircraft -perhaps one or two or even the whole squadron – would take off as fast as possible, start climbing and at the same time get into proper formation.

The ground control would tell you on the RT to climb to Angels 10,20 or 30 (thousand feet). He would then give you the course to fly and inform you what you were going after. It could be a formation of enemy bombers or as with most convoy patrols that the aircraft bogey was about 50 miles away from the convoy.

The tension built up during the climb, especially if you had to go through a few thousand feet of cloud first. This made it harder because you had to fly solely on instruments and if one of your section could not keep up with you, you wondered whether he was going to come and look for you instead of turning away and making his own way up. Too many pilots had been killed in this way. As leader of the section, you had to make sure that you kept climbing at the right altitude and speed that would allow your number two and three to keep in formation with you. All this was building up tension on all of you and it was with relief you broke cloud, even if there were enemy aircraft about, and you were a good target for them against the white cloud.

On many occasions you would patrol up and down the coast waiting for the next instruction from control. You would watch all of your instruments very carefully especially your oxygen supply, as above 12,000 feet you were likely to pass out without oxygen. If you had been up for over an hour or more you would have to watch your fuel and calculate how much you required to get back to base. There was another hazard at Scorton and that was the moors, with the continual cloud cover, they were not friendly as I knew to my cost.

Eventually you would hear the voice of the controller,

'Hello, Bluebell one, you may pancake, over.' These were the best words of all, it meant you could now return to base and land.

On 28th March, we were told that we were going to move to Hornchurch the next day and I went up to the farm to say my farewells to Aunt Fran and John, Madge and Nancy. It was a nice evening and during some talk about fortune-telling Aunt Fran took my hand and looked at it. 'Rene is going to have a baby boy sooner than you think and you will survive this war safely.' She said that I would soon be leading a squadron over water. This part I could not believe as I had only been a pilot officer since January. She told me many things that did come true and her prophecies helped me considerably especially the one about the baby. This would make Rene happy.

I had wanted to give Aunt Fran something for what she had done for me. An ordinary present did not seem enough, it had to be something special. John had told me once that his mother would like a pair of RAF wings some time as a memento. After all the aerodrome was on her land.

I had something I treasured most and that was my original pair of wings I was given at South Cerney. I had these in a box lined with velvet to keep in case I had a son or grandson to leave them to. I had taken them with me on this day for this reason, to give them to her.

I handed her the box which she opened and I told her that I treasured them so much but that I treasured her more. She was in tears as she looked at them and I got a lovely wet kiss and hug from her which I would never forget. (John returned the box and wings many years later, when his mother died. They are more important than ever to me as they are a constant reminder to me of a lovely lady).

I said my goodbyes to John, Madge and Nancy and thanked them all for the wonderful time I had had with them and it was with very sad feelings that I went back to the mess that night. The next day we flew down to Hornchurch.

The officers' mess at Hornchurch was a long-established mess with first class sleeping quarters, dining rooms and bars. It was a nice change from Scorton. Willie Prest and I shared a large bedroom-cum-lounge. We also shared a nice WAF batwoman, a well-endowed young lady at that. Directly I arrived at Hornchurch I knew I had to get a car to be able to enjoy any of the outside amenities and as I lived only 18 miles from Hornchurch in Enfield, I could get home for days off quite easily. As there was nothing for us to do until 1st April I went off for a couple of days to get a car and to see my wife and tell her what Aunt Fran had said about the baby.

A friend of my father's whose son had moved us to and from South Cerney also dealt in second-hand cars. The one I wanted, however, was too dear and I was not able to ask for it until the man's wife, who knew me from a baby and who had in the past given me my first gramophone and bicycle, told her husband to let me have it for what I had offered. It was a Wolseley 14, in excellent condition and worth at least twice what I paid for it.

Soon I was driving up outside my house to show Rene what I had got. We did not mention costs as she knew my father's friends had something worked out for me. The next day I was on my way back to Hornchurch and I registered the car with the adjutant so as to get petrol coupons. I also got a lock-up garage behind the officers' mess. I was not worried about petrol as I had a cousin whose father-in-law owned a garage in Ilford and I could fill up when I liked.

That evening Willie and I discussed what we would be doing from Hornchurch. We were both convinced we were here for a long time and would be doing sweeps over France and cover for bombers on daylight raids over France. It was certainly going to mean a lot more action than at Scorton, but the compensation for the Canadians was that they were nearer to London and could spend their days off there.

For me, I was more than content. Days off at home, just think of it. Sweeps over France shooting up every German army vehicle you could see on the road and all those aircraft, if you were lucky, in the sky.

WE MOVE TO HORNCHURCH

The next day was 1st April and I went up to do a sector recco. I flew down the river to Southend and had a good look at the pier from the air. I had been there so many times as a youngster and knew every part of that coast to Shoeburyness. In those days it took hours to go all along the beach, but from the air it was only a minute or so. I went out in the estuary to look at Reculver Towers, did a spot of low flying and saw the men on them waving back at me. I went over to Whitstable and round the coast to Margate and then back to Hornchurch. I was going to enjoy flying from Hornchurch over places that I was familiar with. There would be no chance of getting lost in bad weather, as you could low fly along the river to the Towers, and a couple of minutes later you were over Hornchurch.

The aerodrome did not have any runway as such; it was all grass. It had a peculiar shape because when the aerodrome had been extended only a part of it was made into a landing area. Consequently you had one short run and one long one and at times in strong winds the short run could be difficult. For single take-offs and landings there was no trouble at all. I landed and taxied to flights where most of the others were inside, looking at the flight readiness board.

I went to my locker and put my flying gear away and took out my log book. This would be my first entry on a new page. A new page, a new life. Well, I hope it is a better one than the others. Only time will tell.

The next day at breakfast I noticed that all the aircrew were at the top tables which I thought unusual. They were mostly the other squadron pilots who shared Hornchurch with us and I recognised some of the old Biggin Hill chaps who had also been commissioned. I noticed when I was seated that all the pilots were having eggs and bacon and sausage and plenty of it, while the other ground officers were having chopped kidney on toast, not an appetising breakfast as I well knew from the days at Grangemouth. On asking why the two different kinds of breakfast, I was told by the WAF waitress that aircrew had special meals.

I found out why after breakfast. It was because the squadrons were flying over the English Channel two or three times each day and many of the pilots had come down in the sea. They had to wait sometimes hours to be picked up by the Air Sea Rescue launches and in the winter months a pilot could die through exertion, hence the reason that each meal might have to last a long while. It sounded good common sense to me, but had I been on the ground all the time I might have felt there was something wrong with the idea.

That evening we went out in the car to sample one of the local pubs and went to one of the locals in Romford. I was surprised by the number of young girls who were there, but we were soon told that there was a dance on just along the road so after a couple of drinks we went along to the dance. There was quite a crowd enjoying themselves and some WAF, Land Army girls and Army girls. I was told that word had soon got round that a new squadron had arrived and they wanted to see what the chaps were like. It was so easy to make friends and it was hard to believe that there was even a war on, everyone was so blasted happy.

Towards the end of the evening I thought I had better round up those who had come in the car with me and, not to my surprise when I saw the girls on their arms, four of the five said they would make their own way back. Tony came back with me. I had not known him much as he had only just arrived with us. He was not a big drinker and was engaged and did not want to go with other girls, so he preferred to look on. Him and me both, I thought. I will make sure he comes next time, then I will have someone to talk to other than these lovely girls. I had too much on my mind for them and it was not far away either.

The next day we had a wing formation or Balbo and it was led by the station wing commander. I was his Red three and I liked the idea. Should we meet up with enemy fighters I would have a good chance to have a go at them. On the other hand if they attacked us head-on I would have the best chance of getting hit. I would take that chance. It was worth it to be able to fly with an experienced leader, for you could learn a lot from them.

We were going over the English Channel at 25,000 feet. From that height it did not look very wide and you could see the coast of France for miles along it. It looked so peaceful and quiet that it was hard to believe that we were going over there with the intention of enticing the German fighters up for a scrap. It was of a nuisance value only and the Germans did not rise to the bait. We went inland for some way and saw a couple of aerodromes with aircraft on them, but there was no action and we returned to Hornchurch and landed.

When we were assembled in the flights our CO told us that it was a practice flight to get us used to flying in formation with another two squadrons. Entry in log book: 'Balbo. 1.40m.' In the Squadron Operations Record Book would be entered every movement from the time we took off until we landed with descriptions of where we had flown and at what height and what the weather was like. Add that all up and it makes the word: 'Balbo. 1.40m.'

As we were on early dawn readiness the next day, we did not go out that night.

The first offensive sweep was by our squadron only. It was to Ostend to support some bombers who were going to bomb the docks. It was a bad day for us as we were jumped by Me 109's and our CO went down almost immediately. There was no hope for him it had all happened so quickly. It was impossible for the bombers to remain on the target now that the cover had been broken and petrol was getting low and we still had a long way to go to get home. It was not an easy ride back and we knew that this was going to be the pattern of things to come.

We got back with very little fuel to spare and to our surprise we found that we were to do another sweep over France in the afternoon and that this time the station wing commander would lead us and the other two squadrons. Once again I was his number three.

At lunch our flight commander told us that he would take over for a few days while we got a new CO. We could not understand this as we thought he would be our CO now. He was a good leader and we all liked him.

There was nothing spectacular about the afternoon sweep and so in the log book went entry 'Offensive sweep. 1.40 m.' I had just made my entry into the log book when I was told that my wife had called and I was to ring her at her mother's home. I could not understand why, unless she was not well, yet she had looked fine a couple of days before when I was at home. I also heard that my dear old mate Ron had been killed on Hurricane bombers. I wondered if Kay had phoned Rene about it.

It was a very personal conversation and it looked as though Aunt Fran's prediction about us having a baby boy sooner than we thought had come true and that I should think of having a day or so off, in three or four weeks time. So I should save up my days off until then, and keep my leave for the christening,

As much as I wished to tell the others, I decided to say nothing, because there were going to be some changes in the squadron and if our present flight commander was promoted to CO I was going to ask for some consideration for the position of 'B' Flight commander. After all I was the most experienced pilot in the squadron and I knew I would make a better flight commander than some I had met. This was one of the reasons I did not want to talk about the new baby. Someone might think that I might be too worried in the air and not do the job properly. It was because of my family that I made sure I did do my job properly; it was the safest way to stay alive.

For the next few days it was mostly practice flying in formation getting some of the new sergeants used to formation. In between there was the odd Balbo.

On the 9th we did a sweep over France and were stood down in the afternoon; some of us went on the tennis courts to bang some of the aggro out of us. During the next few days during the day we did some convoy patrols in the Thames Estuary and as the weather was better it made a nice change. On one occasion we saw a Ju 88 going towards Southend but he saw us at the same time and about turned quickly and was out to sea flat out and eventually went into cloud.

Towards the end of the month we were doing two sweeps each day over France and although we had contact with enemy fights we did not get the chance to shoot any of them down. These Me 109's were a match for us.

We had now got our new CO who I think was a Czech. He was a quiet chap and not very talkative – perhaps the language was the trouble – but he had his own ideas on the way we should fly our formations. I had seen these formations in my old squadron and was not impressed by them. If they had been any good the RAF would have been using that pattern in all the squadrons.

At this time we had two more of our Canadian officers posted and a few of us went to London with them to celebrate because they were being promoted. That was a night to remember, had we been sober enough to remember. We got mixed up with some other Canadians who were friends of our two pals and the sky was the limit. If you have never tried Canadian hospitality, I suggest that before you do you take the following week off.

On the last night of the month we had a concert by the Windmill Girls and they were to come to the officers' mess afterwards for drinks.

Our station commander was Group Captain Harry Broadhurst, DSO, DFC and Bar, one of the most popular station commanders in the RAF. Because I was a married man he made me responsible for seeing that all the girls were put back on the bus and that no officer would be allowed to show the girls their rooms. What an impossible task to give anyone, I would think I was lucky if I got half the girls back in the coach by 10 pm., the witching hour. The party in the mess was better than the one on the stage and everyone knew that if there was any monkey business, there would be no more concerts in the officers' mess in future.

On 1st May I was on a sweep over France and we were jumped by Me 109's. My starboard exhaust was partly shot off. Fortunately they did not stop for combat but flew off. I was glad because I did not know what other damage had been done to my aircraft and I was relieved when the wing commander turned for England and home.

Later that day there was another sweep and we lost one of our Canadian officers.

SECRET   Personal
INTELLIGENCE FORM T

STATISTICAL

Date	(a)	5/5/42
Unit	(b)	122 (Bombay) Squadron
Type and mark of our aircraft	(c)	Spitfire VB
Time attack was delivered	(d)	1535
Place of attack and/or target	(e)	Lille vicinity
Weather	(f)	Hazy
Our casualties, a/c	(g)	Nil
Our casualdes, personnel	(h)	Nil
Enemy casualties in air combat (In confirmation)	(j)	1 Fw 190 by P/0 Bland
Enemy casualties – ground or sea targets	(k)	N/A

GENERAL

I was Red 3, and when I heard the warning of bandits attacking I saw a Fw 190 on my tail who opened fire. I did a steep turn to the right, and saw the e/a dive away. I started to follow, but saw Blue 3 (P/0 Bland) doing a quarter attack on the same a/c. I continued my dive and saw both the e/a and Blue 3 break away. As I was still in my dive, and dosing in range, I still followed and saw the e/a, which appeared to have its tail shot off, execute a 'flick roll' at about 400 mph!! It continued on its downward course, upside down and practically tail first. Seeing this e/a was definitely finished, I saved my ammunition, as I imagined it would be needed pretty soon.

Four days later on a sweep over France we had a clash with many Fw 190s. This was a far superior aircraft to the Me 109 and we were hopelessly outnumbered and outmanoeuvered. Although I fired all my ammo I had no time to see what I had hit. It was a battle right up to the coast and most of us made our way back on our own. It was a sad evening in the mess that night. We had lost four of our mates in one go. Some had been shotup,but managed to get back to base after a hectic twenty minute flight not knowing when their engines were going to pack up. These new German machines were better than ours and our only hope was that the pilots flying them had not got a lot of experience, but it was false hopes after today's results.

We were told that we were going to have a new CO who was a Belgian and this did not please me because I recognised a name from my Grangemouth days. Of course it might not be the same chap I was thinking of, so not to worry for the time being anyway.

We had another tragedy that week, one of our Belgian officers was coming in to land after a sweep and another Spitfire landed on top of him and he was killed instantly. I am glad I was not at flights when it happened, I had seen it happen at Grangemouth. The pilot had been decapitated and I was the first to reach him. He was a Polish pilot who had been through hell to get to England and fight against the killers of his entire family.

A few days later we lost our 'B' Flight Belgian officer and things were looking black and the other squadron with us was suffering just as much.

The day came when we were told that our new CO was going to arrive and we would all be at flights to greet him. I had intended to ask him outright if I could have the 'B' Flight commander vacancy. I desperately wanted to have it as I felt I could do something with it. Having been in a first rate squadron to start off in and having been an instructor I knew that I could do better than some of the leaders we had been having. Moreover the Canadians were a great lot of chaps to have behind you; you knew they would not run away when you went into an attack. I had so much to gain by asking the new CO to recommend me for 'B' Flight, but there was one snag.

The pilots were gathered in the flight room and the CO's car drew up at the door. Before he even got out of the car, I knew I now had no chance of getting 'B' Flight. He was the same man who I had clashed with at

Grangemouth. The same one who had been told by me when I was an instructor there that he would have to stay overnight until his aircraft was ready and that no way was I going to let him have mine even though he was a flight lieutenant and I was a flight sergeant. This was at the Air firing range at Leuchars in 1941.

The adjutant did the introductions and it came to my turn. When I was introduced to him, he had a smile on his face, but to me it seemed to say, 'It's my turn now.'

'Oh yes, I have already met Pilot Officer Rolls.'

A couple of days later we got a new 'B' Flight Commander. He was an Australian who had just been promoted to flight lieutenant and he held the DFC. His main experience was in sweeps over France. He was too easy-going at first and although this suited some of the chaps I did not think it was a good thing. Pilots were picking their own sections to be with their mates and this was not good. Each section depended on close cooperation with each other, it's true, but it was experience that had to be shared among the whole squadron equally.

A few days after he arrived we were scrambled to meet up with another squadron for a sweep over France and he was to lead the squadron, I was to take 'B' Flight. It was a bad day and the cloud base started at 3,000 feet and was solid for at least 15,000 feet according to control. This meant that the leader of the squadron had to fly and climb in such a way that the rear section of the formation could keep up with him and bearing in mind that the rest of the squadron would be looking at the aircraft at his side only and not at his instruments. It was a situation that could not be learned in a few weeks.

The squadron was in good formation when we hit the cloud base and the order was given to close up which it did immediately. I watched 'A' Flight go into cloud and I looked at my air speed and rate of climb; I instinctively knew that there would be trouble for the leading section to keep formation for long at that rate of climb and speed. For the safety of my own flight I turned slightly to starboard and ignored 'A' Flight. I continued climbing at my own rate and saw that I still had all my flight with me and so I continued flying at the same rate until we hit the top of the cloud at 15,000 feet. In the distance on my port side I saw the flight commander who was on his own. None of the others had kept up with him in the climb up.

I flew over to him and suggested we wait a few minutes to see if any more of his flight were coming up and after a short while we knew that we would have to carry out the sweep and meet up with the other squadrons. They had not waited for us and so we continued the sweep on our own. We had not been told what our target was and as there was RT silence we could not ask. We continued our sweep over France on our own. We did not see any other aircraft and so we returned to Hornchurch having achieved nothing.

What with a new CO and a new flight commander and the fact that I had not been given 'B' Flight, I was glad when we had a few days' rest from sweeps over France and did some convoy work and squadron formation to get the newcomers used to formation flying.

It was on 17th May that we had another big operation and this time it was to be led by the wing commander, and again I was his number two. It was a Ramrod, a diversionary sweep. We made landfall at Hardelot at 20,000 feet and saw fire and intense flak coming up over Boulogne.

SECRET   Personal
                    INTELLIGENCE FORM 'F'

STATISTICAL

Date	(a)	17/5/42
Unit	(b)	122 (Bombay) Squadron
Type and mark of our aircraft	(c)	Spitfire VB
Time attack was delivered	(d)	1135
Place of attack and/or target	(e)	St Omer/Audruick and SE of Guines
Weather	(f)	Fine, slight haze, 5/10ths cloud
Our casualties aircraft	(g)	Nil Our casualties –
personnel	(h)	Nil
Enemy casualties in air combat	(j)	1 Fw 190 Destroyed; 1 Fw 190
Probable Enemy casualties – ground or sea targets	(k)	N/A

GENERAL

I was Red 3, flying No 2 to the W/Cdr., and went down with him when he attacked the Fw 190's. I got in a 2 secs burst at one Fw 190 which came past me from port to starboard, and saw white smoke issuing from it. I followed it in a dive down to approx. 11,000 feet, the range closing from 200 to 50 yards, giving it another 2 secs. burst of m/g and cannon. Very shortly after the e/a exploded in mid-air, and an undercarriage leg and wheel came hurtling past my port wing. I claim this e/a as destroyed.

I pulled out of my dive at 3,000 feet and started to climb, reaching 10,000 feet, approx. south-east of Guines, but shortly after saw another Fw 190 very close on my tail. I did a steep turn, and after about a turn and a half got on to the tail of the e/a, managing to get in a 2 secs. burst (m/g only) from about 15° port. I saw white smoke coming from what appeared to be the port wing root, but could not observe further as I was overshooting. This combat, however, was seen by F/Lt Thomas of 64 Sqdn, who stated that the e/a was completely out of control, going down over and over 'very sloppily', obviously finished and not worth while going after to make sure. In view of his confirmation I claim this e/a as a 'probable'.

After overshooting, I half-rolled down to 0 feet, joining up with Blue 1 and 2 (122 Sqdn.) I saw Blue 1 (F/Lt Griffith) make his attack on the gun post, and a number of Boches strewn over the ground. I crossed back over the Channel, landing safely at Hornchurch by 1215 hours.

[Signed] W Rolls
Red 2, 122 Sqdn.

SECRET   Personal
INTELLIGENCE FORM F

STATISTICAL

Date	(a)	2/6/42
Unit	(b)	122 (Bombay) Squadron
Type and mark of our aircraft	(c)	Spitfire VB
Time attack was delivered	(d)	0720
Place of attack	(e)	Le Crotoy
Weather	(f)	Bright. Visibility Good
Our Casualties, a/c	(g)	Nil
Our Casualties, personnel	(h)	Nil
Enemy Casualties in air combat	(j)	1 Probable★. 1 Destroyed. (Halved with Sgt Nadon) ★ Admitted Damaged
Enemy Casualties ground or sea targets	(k)	Nil

GENERAL

I was flying Blue 3. Shortly after crossing the French coast at Le Crotoy, I saw 4 x Fw 190's diving towards Blue section (port). I turned with my No 2 – Sgt Barratt – towards them in a head-on attack firing a 1 and a half– 2 second burst at range of 150-100 yards. My height was under 1,000 feet.

I saw strikes on the engine cowling, and on ceasing fire and drawing away, I saw the engine cowling fly off. I then lost sight of the E/A but claim it as a 'Probable' in view of the supporting evidence of my cine-gun film.

I then turned starboard out to sea with the rest of the Beehive, and immediately saw a Fw 190 (camouflaged black) diving on two Spits on my port side. I did a tight turn, but could not get deflection in time to stop the E/A shooting down one of the Spits, but when he broke off his attack,

I was 15° astern and gave him a 2 sec burst at 250 yards. The burst caused the E/A to slow up and go into a gentle turn with white smoke issuing from his engine. I then saw Blue 2 – Sgt Nadon – come on to the E/A from starboard and fire a burst before breaking away. Going into a 360° turn at about 600 feet, I saw the Fw 190 go down in a shallow dive and strike marshland at the Somme estuary. With Sgt Nadon, I claim this E/A as destroyed.

[Signed] W Rolls P/O

We were moving towards St Omer when we met up with some Fw 190's. The wing commander gave the order to attack them. I got in a two second burst of cannon and machine-gun at an Fw 190 which came past me from port to starboard. I followed it down in a dive to 11,000 feet, my range closing from about two hundred yards to fifty yards, and I gave it another two second burst. This time I knew I had hit it and a second or so afterwards, it blew up and its undercarriage wheel and leg came over my port wing. I pulled out of my dive at 3,000 feet and climbed again to 10,000 feet; but shortly afterwards I saw another Fw 190 on my tail. I managed to out-manoeuvre it and got on its tail, fired a two-second burst of machine-guns only and saw white smoke come from its engine.

I did not wait to see what happened to it but one of the flight lieutenants of 64 Squadron saw it go down completely out of control and he did not waste any ammo on it. After overshooting this aircraft I half rolled down to house top level and set course for home. I was just east of Dunkirk when I spotted my own flight commander and his number two. I joined up with them and after shooting up a gun post on the beach we flew at wave top level back to Hornchurch.

Back home I made out my combat report, claiming one Fw 190 destroyed and one probable, as no one saw it actually crash. (See combat report page 145.) Our losses were two officers but one was safe. The rest of May was uneventful with some convoy patrols and sweeps to keep us in trim.

Summing up, it had been a good month for me and as we now had our new flight commander I felt I could now tell the lads that I was the proud possessor of a baby boy and that mother and baby were doing well. Some of them could not understand why I had kept it quiet for so long but when I explained my reason about wanting 'B' Flight commander post, they understood but insisted that the baby's head still wanted wetting, which we did that night. This time we went to the local over at Suttons Farm entrance and a very nice time was had by all without having to worry about transport.

The new CO had not mentioned a word to me about the episode at Grangemouth and I had no intention of reminding him. Leave well alone was my motto.

It was on 2nd June that we again had some action on a sweep over France and I was the wing commander's number three. It was a low flying intrusion east of Le Crotoy.

When I saw four Fw 190's diving towards Blue section port, I turned with my number two with the wing commander towards them in a head on attack firing a two second burst at a range of 150 to 100 yards. I was under 1,000 feet. I saw strikes on the engine and the engine cowling flying off. I had my camera gun on as I went past it. I caught up with the other members of the Beehive and as I did so I saw a Fw 190 camouflaged black diving on two Spitfires on my port side. I turned into them but could not stop one of the Spitfires getting shot down. I hit his attacker as he broke off his attack and with white smoke pouring from his engine he went down in a glide. I then saw number two fire at it and the Fw 190 went into marshland at the Somme Estuary. (See combat report, page 143). By this time the wing had broken up and the two of us made our way back to base without further trouble.

On 8th June the squadron moved to Fairlop which was really an extension of Hornchurch, as we were still part of the Hornchurch wing. It meant that the wing could airborne much quicker as formation take-offs at Hornchurch were difficult. It was nice and cosy being on our own and the airfield was large and formation take-offs were easy. It was easy for getting to London on days off and at night there was a lot of entertainment going on. The quarters were good and it was so near to my home, by air that is, that I often flew over my house on the way back from a sweep, if I was on my own. There was a golf course at Hainault which was quite handy.

We went to Martlesham for air firing practice and did the odd convoy patrol. It gave us time to train newcomers to the squadron and to practice squadron formation take-offs. On 15th June I took some days off to have the baby christened. He was now growing into a bonny baby and did not make a sound as he was christened Derek William Rolls.

The days went all too quickly and I had to return to Hornchurch as the squadron had returned there on the 18th. Willie and I still shared our old room and I arrived late at night ready for work the next morning. Willie was out and so I went straight to bed.

'Good morning, sir, time to wake up. Would you like a nice cup of tea?'

I felt a light touch on my shoulder just as I was wondering what a female voice was doing in my bedroom at this time in the morning. I knew that I was not dreaming because I saw that the electric light was on and I could hear tfie rain teeming down. I had only returned from leave the night before, so I knew it was not my wife talking to me. So I took no notice and pulled the bedclothes up over my shoulders ready for another sleep, I must have been imagining things: I thought I had seen a beautiful blonde leaning over me.

The next thing I remembered was someone was pulling at my bedclothes.

'Hey, Bill, wake up.' It was my room mate's voice, 'Had a good leave?' he enquired.

By this rime I was awake and looked up to see instead of a beautiful blonde, my room mate standing there in his 'Y' fronts and his dark curly hair all over his face; he had just come from his bath.

'What did you want to wake me up for, Willie? I was dreaming of a beautiful blonde who was offering me a cup of tea.'

That was no dream, mate. That was a reality,' he replied. 'Her name is Betty and she only came here last week and I met her two days ago. She is a blonde so keep your hands off her because she already knows that you are married and have just come back from having your baby christened.'

I started to drink the cup of tea by the side of my bed. 'She makes a nice cup of tea anyway,' I said.

'There have been a lot of changes this last few days,' said Willie.

'We are on stand down today, but are on dawn readiness tomorrow instead. A couple of sergeants have been posted to Malta and have invited us to drop in for a drink with them in the *White Hart* for a farewell drink.

I have said we will be there at about eleven-thirty.'

We then went to breakfast where we discussed what had taken place in my absence. The main topic of conversation was Malta. The intelligence officer told us that a second bunch of Spitfires had reached the island but the first lot had been bombed on landing at Malta and now they urgently wanted more Spitfires in case of a threatened German invasion, before the big push in North Africa. The second batch had flown off the *Wasp,* an American Aircraft Carrier in the Mediteranean.

There was a lot of discussion as to how a Spitfire could take off on such a short run as a carrier deck although we knew that Hurricanes had done it easily. It was a prospect that none of us would wish to do. Our sympathy was with the two sergeants who were being posted there.

It was agreed that things looked very black for Malta and unless we could hold the island, the Middle East War could not be won. The fact that our entire squadron had been inoculated for all tropical diseases led us to believe that it would not be long before we were all posted abroad, perhaps even to the Far East. Malta was preferable to that.

I happened to mention that I would not mind going to Malta, except that I had no desire to go on an aircraft carrier and fly six hundred miles over enemy territory with no loaded guns. Willie turned to me and said:

'Don't worry. Bill, the chances of your getting to Malta are not much in your favour. They only want young good-looking chaps out there so as to satisfy all those beautiful young Maltese girls. You're far too old.'

'OK, Willie, when my posting comes through for Malta, you can take my place, I'd hate to deprive all those lovely young girls of the chance to meet such a big Canadian Don Juan as you.'

Breakfast over, I went back to our room and sat down to read the morning paper.

A few minutes later the batwoman came in to make the beds and tidy up the room. She was carrying my best blues which she had pressed and I noticed that she had tidied up my wardrobe and had put my clean shirt ready on the bed.

I said, 'You know we have not been used to this kind of service at our previous stations and I hope you don't spoil us in your efforts to please.'

'Don't worry about that, sir,' she replied, 'you only get what you deserve. When I saw the squadron take off for France yesterday, I could not rest until I had seen them all land safely. Heaven only knows what I will be like in a few weeks' time.'

Willie came in and we got changed while the young lady carried on doing her work.

'Don't worry about me, sir, I have four brothers at home so I am not shy.'

It did not take us long to finish dressing and we decided we would go to Romford a bit earlier as I wanted to go to the garage and Willie wanted to get some shopping.

We then put on our raincoats and went to the garage for the car. Larry and another officer were waiting for us. We were soon on our way to Romford and it started to pour down.

'I hope we are not going to get wet,' said Larry.

'Don't worry,' I replied, 'the garage is only a little way from the pub so we should not get wet.'

We soon arrived at the garage and I told Joe the mechanic what was wrong with the clutch and he said he would have it ready by the time we had finished in the pub. He asked if I had enough petrol and I told him I would leave it to him. Nice chap Joe, always ready to oblige the RAF.

The four of us then walked down the road to the shops where Willie went to buy some socks and handkerchiefs. We went into the shop and got the items and as we came out it poured down again and we ran into a doorway of what looked like an empty shop full of old junk. The window was full of old pots and pans, and pieces of aircraft and a few Union Jacks.

We saw some of our sergeants inside the shop looking at the exhibits, so we went inside. It was evidently one of those places where people could take their old pots, pans and railings etc to be melted down to make Spitfires. Round the walls were small items from a Spitfire. You could buy stamps and help to pay for a particular part of the Spitfire.

It all looked very interesting and the fact that you could buy an aircraft in bits and pieces was certainly a novelty. We had to wait for the rain to stop so we all decided to have a look round the small exhibition of photographs etc.

We had been in the shop for a few minutes and I happened to look towards the door to see if it had stopped raining and saw an elderly lady with a walking stick come into the shop. I was struck by her appearance as she looked exactly like a picture of Queen Victoria I had seen so many times when a child at my grandmother's. I knew every detail of it.

The old lady was well over seventy by the looks of her and she wore a black lace shawl round her shoulders, had on a small black bonnet with a black veil tied round it. Her black lace-up boots just protruded from under her long black skirt; her face was round and what I thought was most remarkable for a woman other age was that her skin was perfect. It seemed impossible that in just a few seconds I had seen so much character in an elderly lady and although she was wet with the rain, she did not seem to worry about it. I noticed her walking stick which was a malacca cane and very strong.

She had been looking at some of the items and came over to the counter where I was standing, she said, pointing to a clock from a Spitfire, 'What is that, young man?'

I replied, 'It is a clock from a Spitfire, madam.'

'Why do you have clocks in the aircraft when you can only fly for a short time?'

'Well, ma'am!' I explained, 'it's because we have so little time that we have to have such an accurate clock and it is a very important part of the Spitfire as far as we are concerned.'

At this stage one of the New Zealand sergeants. Sergeant Park, came over with a clock in his hand. He held up the clock in front of the lady and pointed to the hands which were on eleven o'clock.

'This clock has another very important use for us, ma'am. Now if you were a pilot and you heard someone say on your wireless while up against the enemy that bandits were at eleven o'clock, you would look for the enemy fighters out here,' and he pointed outside the clock to the extended eleven o'clock angle. 'If the bandits were at three o'clock you would look for them here,' and with that he pointed to the extended arm of the three o'clock. 'In other words, the sky is one big clock, when we are flying.'

I was surprised for two reasons; one, the kindness of the sergeant; and two, the look on the lady's face, as all this was being explained to her; she seemed very excited and was fiddling with her large black bag which she had on her arm. Out of the bag she took a small red purse which she carefully opened. She took out a ten shilling note which she unfolded. Turning to us she said, 'Would this buy that clock for one of your Spitfires, if it is as important as you say?'

As the question seemed to be directed to me I replied, 'Yes, madam, that will buy the clock in your name.'

She put the ten shillings on the counter and said to the man behind it: 'I want to buy that clock. Will you see to it for me?'

The man looked puzzled because the price on the clock was for some reason £5. Whether or not this was the correct price was of no importance. It was a gimmick to get people to give five pounds away.

He was about to say something to her when I waved my hand to him not to say anything, so he just said, 'Thank you, madam. I will see that your name goes on it.'

The lady thanked us for being so kind and she took my hand which I had offered.

We all watched her as she went out of the door. What a lovely old lady she was. She had hardly got out of the door when she came back again saying to us, 'God bless you, boys. If that clock goes for as long as I do, it will be worth the ten shillings.' With that she now went out and away.

The sergeant who had been explaining the clock to the lady came over to me.

'Sir, you know very well that the clock was more than ten bob. Why did you kid her it was only ten bob and not a fiver?'

'It's obvious. Parky, that's all she could afford. What does it matter if she only had that amount. It's the principle that counts, not the money.'

He took out his wallet saying, 'I am going to make sure that she has bought that clock.' He walked over to the counter and gave the man four pounds ten shillings and told him to enter in the book: 'One Spitfire clock from a grand old lady.'

The man entered it in the book in which he kept a record of what people had paid and towards what. Willie and I looked at the entry he had made which was as requested.

I looked at the sergeant and said, 'You New Zealanders are certainly a sentimental lot.'

'No!' Parky retorted. 'Ten bob is probably her week's pension but the other is not my week's pay, so she still gave more than I did.' He laughed out loud. 'Anyway I can now say I have helped buy a Spitfire. I've broken up enough.'

That statement made us all laugh and Willie told us that it had stopped raining so off we all went to the pub; here we spent the next couple of hours wishing the best of health to the two sergeants who we knew were going to Malta. During the conversation I told Parky that I was going to miss him as my number two and that I hoped to meet up with him again after his Malta tour.

He remarked to me in all seriousness, 'Why don't you volunteer to come out with us? You are bound to be posted soon anyway and better Malta than Russia, where they are screaming out for flight commanders, so I have heard.

'No bloody fear,' I replied. 'I'm quite happy here, besides I am not likely to get a posting as a flight commander yet, I'm still a pilot officer and not likely to get promotion for a long time yet.'

I gave him a bit of advice on what he was likely to meet up with in Malta as conditions of flying were similar to those of the Battle of Britain period. Too many against too few; the same applies to girls – lay off them as it's a Catholic population and anti-copulation.

I explained to him what he could expect with the hot weather on the ground and how it was just as cold at 20,000 feet in Malta as it was in England, so 'make sure you don't fly in shorts because if there is a fire you want some protection!'

It was time for us to say our goodbyes so we did just that and made our way back to the garage to pick up the car. Before leaving us Parky said,

'I have a strong feeling that this is not goodbye. I think we will be meeting again very soon.'

I replied, 'Not in Malta, if I can help it. Anywhere but that place. I don't like flying over the English Channel. It is twenty miles too wide as far as I am concerned.'

With that we went our different ways and Willie and I went back to Hornchurch as I wanted to do my calibration test before readiness the next day.

For the next two days we did sweeps over France and were so busy that I did not get a chance to see our new batwoman, Betty. It was the next day when we had a later start that I was able to see her. She asked me how we had enjoyed the day seeing the sergeants off, and I remembered an earlier conversation I had had with her.

'You remember you told me it would be a lucky day for me, well there was not much luck about it as far as I was concerned. In fact a couple of drinks and getting soaked in the rain. Nothing at all happened. By the way, I have had some thoughts on your number eleven, several things have happened to me on the eleventh day or month, you could be right.'

She stopped what she was doing and put her hands on her hips in a very provocative way and with a hint of a smile on her face she said, 'Don't tell me you are beginning to believe in the stars after all? Believe me they are going to play a very important part in your life and as you have a very long lifeline on your hand, it will not do you any harm if you learn a bit more about them.'

With that she started carrying on with her work and I did not say anything further as I was not all that keen on knowing what the future held for me, except that I felt good about the bit that I had a nice long lifeline.

The next week we did more sweeps over France and had a couple more losses and we were going farther inland over France and it was not a good feeling at all.

On 20th July we were over France with another two squadrons going to Paris, and on the way back we were jumped by Fw 190's. It was just one big running fight to the coast. I was very low, having dived on a Fw 190, and I stopped firing at it because it was flying over a school playground and I could see the children running across it. Intent on keeping the Fw 190 in my sights and waiting that second or so to clear the school, I had completely forgotten about my rear mirror, when I felt something hit my engine at the side and I saw cannon fire going past me. I was almost mesmerised by the aircraft in front of me when the control column came back into my stomach and I felt my throttle going forward against the pressure of my hand, the Spitfire seemed to take over from me and I heard this voice shouting at me:

'Look out, you bloody clot'.

I went cold as I saw two Fw 190's go just under my wing and I took immediate evasive action. But something was wrong. I was turning the wrong way and I could do nothing about it. Then I saw on my right about five Fw 190's which I would have gone smack into. I dived down to tree level and flew to the coast and joined up with another squadron till I reached the English coast. It was a terrible journey back, what with a shortage of fuel and this voice still in my ear, 'Look out, you bloody clot.' I knew whose voice it was. It was my old pal Johnny White's and I knew at that moment that although my best pal was dead, without doubt he had been with me on that trip. Two of the other squadron with me told me afterwards that they saw the Fw 190's coming at me and thought I had been shot down.

That night I did not go out with the others, I wanted to be alone with my thoughts and to go over in my mind what had happened to my controls on that flight. The more I thought about it the more I was certain that but for Johnny I would not be on my bed thinking about him. I would probably be up there with him. Thanks, Johnny, I love you, mate.

A few days later I had returned from a sweep near Paris and when I had landed after a trying 1 hour 40 minute flight, I was told to go and see the adjutant as quickly as possible. When I went in his room he had a signal in his hand which he read out to me. It told me that I had been posted to RAF Debden the following day. It was Top Secret and Urgent and I knew it was not good for me. 'It is a Command Posting. You are to report to RAF Debden 28th July,' said the adjutant.

That night I had a drink in the mess with the lads and I was off home to see my wife and baby before going to Debden the next day.

I can't say I was sorry to leave Hornchurch or even my squadron as I had never been happy with some senior officers but Willie was an exception and I would miss him. The next day as I left for Debden, I had to go by train according to instructions so I knew that I was going somewhere overseas as we had heard that pilots for Russia went from Debden. It all sounded ominous to me.

I said to my wife when I said my cheerios to her and the baby, 'Don't worry about me, dear. I will see you in time for Christmas.'

CHAPTER FIVE

I Am Going Overseas. But Where?

I arrived at Debden fully expecting the worst and was told that I was not going to Russia but I was going on a special operation. I was to leave my camp kit and only take with me my flying battle dress, flying helmet and goggles and flying boots and one change of clothing. I was to wear my best blue tunic on the journey, which I always did anyhow. I was given a first class ticket from Euston with no arrival station marked in. I was given the train and reserved seat number. I felt like a VIP but was most concerned about where I was going to and why all the secrecy.

I arrived at Euston Station and got on the train as instructed. I noticed that there were two other names on the reserved lists although all the seats had been marked with reserved labels.

It was a good ten minutes before two young naval officers came into the carriage and soon introduced themselves to me. They obviously knew my name from someone as it was not on the ticket or reserved label and (his got me wondering until they explained that they were my escorts and I would not be allowed to talk to any passengers on the train and I should not talk about what I was or what I had been doing; any subject but my flying. This seemed rather way out to me and I decided the less said the better. They knew their job and they intended to do it.

My meals were brought to the compartment and plenty of drink but I did not feel like drinking much. I felt like a prisoner under arrest, though I knew that I was not.

Eventually we arrived at Glasgow Station and it was dark. We were met immediately by a large black car and I was almost bundled inside and we were away.

AIRCRAFT CARRIER *FURIOUS*

After a while I recognised the docks and could see the Navy vessels in the middle of the channel. In no time at all I was in a motor launch and I could see this huge vessel we were going out to and soon I was going up a ladder on board. I still could not see what kind of vessel it was except that it was very large. I climbed some more ladders and knew that I was on the captain's bridge. I was ushered into the captain's cabin and saw two other RAF officers at a table. I was introduced to the captain and to Group Captain Walter Myers Churchill, DSO, DFC, and then to Flight Lieutenant Eric Norman Woods DFC. I also saw the name of the vessel I was on and it was *Furious*, one of our older aircraft carriers. I knew now that I was going to have to fly off the carrier to some far distant shore, but at that moment I did not know where to.

It was the early hours in the morning and it was suggested that we had some sleep first and we had the beds in the captain's second cabin and before we had even got to sleep I heard the engines start up and felt the movement of the vessel. We were off to somewhere but I still did not know where to.

The noise of the engines grew louder but I was tired and went to sleep easily enough, there was very little movement of the vessel.

We were awakened early and had breakfast and were briefed on the purpose of our being on the carrier. We were to try and fly a Spitfire off the deck and to estimate how many could be lined up on deck at one time to enable as many as possible to get off in the shortest possible time. We were told that there were forty Spitfire Vb's in the hangars.

When we went up on deck I saw we were in the middle of the Irish sea and no sight of land. We were being escorted by some other vessels but I did not notice what they were. My eyes were on the landing deck. That was the first shock. About one third of the way along the deck was a ramp which was used to help pull up the Swordfish, when they landed, and the thought of a Spitfire having to get over that ramp and then take off was not pleasant. Nor was the fact that the deck did not finish at the prow of the boat but stopped short enough to allow a gun emplacement on the lower deck. The situation looked impossible from my experience and it looked as though the flight lieutenant and myself were to be the guinea pigs and probably baked ones at that if we hit that gun turret on take-off.

On deck was a Spitfire Vb and the three of us RAF officers knew that it was going to be impossible to get more than one Spit at a time off the deck and only then if it was a pilot with a lot of experience.

After a confab we asked the captain what the maximum speed over the deck we could hope to get wherever we were going to take off from.

'Twenty-nine knots maximum,' he replied. We now knew that it was impossible to get even one Spitfire off unless we put it almost over the stem of the ship. We made some wooden chocks of about forty-five degrees so that we could put one under each flap thereby increasing lift. With chocks under the wheels and two sailors sitting on the tail planes tied to a rope and winch, which would pull the men and the chocks away leaving the aircraft to catapult a little.

The idea was to see how soon the Spitfire got off and then we would put a second one a bit further ahead, that way we could calculate how many could take off on one run of the carrier.

The flight lieutenant won the toss. He would go first. He soon climbed in his cockpit, the carrier put on steam and reached the 29 knots, everything was ready and the engine had been run up, the batman waved the off signal and the pilot opened up his throttle fully. The aircraft shook and the signal was given by the pilot for chocks away. They were pulled away immediately, the aircraft lurched forward and had hardly got up speed when it touched the ramp. It seemed to pull up and then it was over and on its way, the flight lieutenant had to bounce it off the end of the deck and my heart nearly stopped, as I thought it was going to drop on the gun turrets below. It missed by inches only and was soon climbing away to land at Prestwick where the pilot would be picked up and brought back to the carrier later.

It was fortunate that the captain and group captain realised that it would be impossible to do another take-off farther up the deck and I must say I was in full agreement. As I pointed out, both the flight lieutenant and myself had over 680 hours flying. What would happen to a pilot with only a hundred or so hours experience? It was decided to abort my flight and we made our way back to our berth near Glasgow.

When we arrived back the flight lieutenant was waiting for us in the captain's cabin and we got down to discussing what was going to happen next. There seemed to be no way we were going to get these Spitfires off, other than by crane and from what we were told where we were going, that would be impossible.

It suddenly came to me that there was a solution if we had the time. When I was at Hornchurch one of my friends from another squadron had flown in to see me and he told me that he was doing a test with a new hydromatic propeller and he suggested that I have a go in the aircraft and see the difference in its take-off and climbing speed. Naturally I was only too pleased to have a go. I found it great, the take-off was about half our normal and the climb was much better than our own machines. I did two take-offs to make sure how good it was and I was only waiting for the day we had them for ourselves.

I told the captain and the group captain that if we could change the props on the aircraft in the hold we would get at least eight off on each run. They accepted my word for it. It was all we had to hope for anyway.

The forty airscrews were ordered quickly and were soon loaded on the carrier along with about a hundred airmen who were going to put them on in the hangars.

No sooner had they been taken on board than we sailed again. This time all our pilots were on board and the first aircraft was ready. I had suggested that one of the sergeants on board should be given the chance to stay behind, as we had one aircraft too many on board. We quickly got a volunteer. We were now in convoy with battleships *Rodney* and *Nelson* and plenty of destroyers protecting our carrier. I lined the Spitfire up on the mark where we already knew the first of eight aircraft would have to be placed in order to get the eight off as fast as possible.

This time we did not use the flaps nor did we put a sailor on each tail plane. It was chocks only, like a normal take-off.

I was on the bridge with the group captain and flight lieutenant and the signal was given for take-off. I held my breath. If I was wrong I would be responsible for killing a pilot and wasting all this valuable rime. If I was right it would change at least one theatre of war in our favour.

The Spitfire went forward and over the ramp. There was no sign of it pulling up and it sailed off the deck of the carrier like a bird and was up in the air in no time.

We had won the day, thanks to an old pal of mine coming to visit me and letting me have a go on his Spitfire with the new prop.

My biggest shock was yet to come. We were in with the captain and we were toasting our success, or rather the RAF were, when the group captain told the flight lieutenant and myself that we were all going to Malta. We would be taking eight aircraft each off from the carrier just off Algiers and would fly with long range tanks to Malta. We would have no armour in our guns and we could store cigarettes etc in the drums instead. We were to try to retain our long range tanks as they were urgently wanted in Malta for escort duty. So now we knew at least where we were going and my worst fears were over. It was not to be Russia. We were also told that our kit would be sent on to us, but it never was.

We sailed in this great convoy called 'Pedestal', one of the biggest convoys of the war up till then and it was a few days of lying in the sun on the flight deck, plenty of any kind of drinks you chose, plenty to eat and very good company from the Naval officers and ratings. The RAF mechanics worked day and night to change all the airscrews and one of my old squadron's sergeant fitter was one of the NCO's doing the job. Every one of those airmen deserved a medal for the way they worked, but they did not get one naturally; they always seemed to be the forgotten ones when medals were dished out. On 20th August we checked that all the aircraft were now serviceable and ready for take-off. A note was made of the numbers on each aircraft and what position it would occupy when coming up from the hangar to the flight deck. We had decided that as we could only get eight Spitfires off in one batch that we would have four sections of eight and one of seven as we now had 39 Spitfires on board. One had been sent off un the first day to test the take-off run.

Group Captain Churchill was to lead the first section and Flight Lieutenant Woods would lead the second section. I would lead the fourth section. Two other officers would lead the other two sections.

The route we were to fly was over the Mediterranean to a place called Skerki Bank, north-east of Tunis, turn south-east and fly north of the island of Pantellaria and continue on course for Malta. From the point north of Tunis we could expect the enemy to try and intercept us as he would have aircraft in Tunis and on Pantellaria and Northern Sicily. The height would depend on the cloud base. Each leader of the sections would make his own decisions as to the best way of getting to Malta as much depended on what happened on the way. In the event of an attack the RT could be used but RT silence was the order of the day. We could not afford to give our position away to the Germans.

Each pilot was given his aircraft number so that he could put some cigarettes in his gun magazines, and stack his personal kit behind the radio behind his seat. He was also told which section he would be in and what position he was to fly in the section; at readiness time he would be strapped in his aircraft in the hangar ready to take off directly the eight aircraft were lined up on the deck.

On the morning of 11th August we were off Algiers and the first batch of eight aircraft were lined up for take-off. The carrier, supported by the battleships and destroyers and the *Eagle* on the other side of us, was now at the take-off speed.

I was on the bridge with the captain and watched as the first aircraft took off. It was quickly followed by the other seven. There was no bother at all from even the least experienced pilot. The mechanics had done their job thoroughly.

The next batch of eight were now coming up the lift and the carrier had now slowed down until they were all on deck and ready for take-off. The carrier then got up speed again and the pattern was repeated again. No trouble at all. It was while we were getting up the next batch from the hangar, that the siren sounded, the alarm was given and the convoy was under attack. It was now about one o'clock and I remained on the bridge as take-offs were suspended. It was about one fifteen when I saw on my right the aircraft carrier *Eagle*, I saw some explosions on its side and in no time at all it had turned over and gone down. It was a terrible sight with all those men in the water and the destroyers racing about to sink the submarine which had sunk her.

The captain after discussing with the rest of the escort decided that he was going to restart operations again and the next batch of eight was brought up on deck. I got the latest weather report and went into the bridge toilet before going down to get ready for the second batch that afternoon.

While I was in the toilet I heard some other officers come in. By their voices and what they were saying I knew they were Naval officers. It was what they said that worried me.

One of them said to the other, 'I would not be in the second batch off. They don't stand an earthly chance of getting to Malta. Jerry will know by reports of this batch going off in a few minutes that operations have restarted and by now he will have his aircraft waiting. If he doesn't get the first lot, he is bound to get the next batch and the one after.'

I did not dare go out while they were there and so I waited. I heard the other officer say in reply. 'Fancy all that way on one engine and if anything happens you are either drowned or blown to pieces. I feel sorry for the poor bastards.'

They then went out to the bridge and I went down to the hangar to make sure all my section were getting ready for the take-off, once this batch which were now lined up on deck had got off.

I went up on deck to watch the take-off. Three aircraft got off safely. The fourth hit the ramp, swerved smack into the bridge and folded up. In seconds the pilot was pulled out and the machine tossed over the side and the rest of the section took off only a few minutes late and joined the leader who was circling round waiting for them.

I then climbed into my own aircraft which was now up on the lift and was pushed into the first spot; the other aircraft were soon up on deck and we got the signal for take-off.

INTO THE UNKNOWN

I took off and climbed to one thousand feet turning round the carrier as the others took off and by the time I was on course all of them had joined me. Within seconds there was trouble. One of the pilots had jettisoned his long range tank and without it could not possibly make it. I was told to proceed with the seven aircraft and I then started to climb.

I saw on my right that there was a nice cloud at about twelve thousand feet and it was over the land I made a quick decision. I was not going to fly the same course as the others. I would fly over Cape Bougaroni, then south of Tunis and over Hammamet; from here I would change course to take me well south of Pantellaria; this would take me on a direct course to about five miles south-west of Malta; I would then call up Malta on the RT and ask for landing permission. They would have no idea that I would be coming in from the south of the Island until I was quite near as I intended to dive down over Hammamet almost to sea level, so the German radar would have no idea where I was making for. It could be North Africa for all they knew.

I also thought that a change of tactics might confuse them when the batch following me was airborne. They would not know whether it was going north or south of Pantellaria.

I had to guess the courses to set as I had nothing in the aircraft to calculate them but I knew I could not miss the Gulf of Hammamet and I could take another bearing from wherever we came out from the land.

One other thing I had in mind was my other pilots. If anything happened to the aircraft such as engine trouble they could bale out and would be PoW's, but this would be better than shark bait. I think they all knew that because they looked so bloody happy every time I looked at them and they were keeping a nice formation. After a couple of hours, they still looked the same and I was pleased that they were coming to the same squadron as I was. They could trust their leader and that was most important.

During those two hours I had been thinking about the events leading up to today; I had noticed that it was 11th August and I remembered Betty telling me eleven was my lucky day so that helped a bit. I remembered her saying I was going to lead a squadron in a very short time. Well, it was not a full squadron and I had not been promoted so she was only half right. All these things were going through my mind and she was dead right about the sea and so was Aunt Fran. They had both said that I was going to be surrounded by sea and flying over it.

Back to reality, as we approached south of Tunis, the cloud broke and I could see plainly the airfield at Tunis with German and French aircraft on it. It's a good job we were not bombers or they would have been blown to pieces.

I pointed to my number two and three and pointed to their long range tanks and I saw them point to the other aircraft the same way. This was the signal to go onto your reserve tank of petrol in the Spitfire. We did not jettison the tanks although they were dangerous being empty. When I thought that all the tanks had been changed over I went into a shallow dive. When I saw all the rest were with me I dived down as fast as possible and out over the sea in the Gulf of Hammamet, or rather a couple of miles north of it. I expected some flak of some kind. That is why I had gone out at speed. But none came, neither did we see any aircraft. We had taken them completely by surprise.

About ten minutes later I looked up and saw some contrails which must have been at about 20,000 feet. They were north of Pantellaria. I knew that they would have eventually to land to refuel and that might help the last batch who would probably be taking the other route. Only time would tell.

We were about fifty miles in my estimation from Malta and the cloud was thickening up and so I climbed to get over it; visibility was poor and I began to get worried. I did not want the last ten minutes of our three-hour flight to mess things up. It was essential we hit the island first go as there was no fuel for overshooting or getting lost, so I waited till I thought I was about five miles south-west and climbed to 8,000 feet and called Malta, with all this cloud I had to take the boys down through it and I did not know how they were on instrument flying.

I heard a calm voice answering me and telling me to vector NE for eight miles and land at Luqa.

CHAPTER SIX

MALTA! WE'VE ARRIVED!

I will never forget the first sight I had of Malta. It was from about 8,000 feet and a mile away. I saw it through a hole in the cloud and it was as though it was saying welcome.

I had been praying enough during my flight but on seeing Malta perhaps it was its religious aura which came up into the clouds – I said one big prayer of thanks on behalf of all my flight. I know they would have approved. The cloud seemed to disappear as we went down and made easy landings. It looked as though God had opened up the sky in order to let us land safely.

I taxied to the point where the crew were waiting to arm our guns and refuel the aircraft and as I switched off I took my wife's photo out of my top pocket and kissed it. The airman who was undoing my cockpit door said, 'Rabbit's foot, sir?'

I remembered what Betty had said and I replied, 'No, it's luckier than a rabbit's foot.'

In no time at all the magazines were opened and all the cigarettes were on the wing. The flight sergeant in charge of the ground crews came up to me as I got out of the cockpit, he held out his hand. 'Glad you made it, sir, I am Flight Sergeant Cagby.' I introduced myself and I knew that he was a man who was to be respected. Even under these terrible conditions he was still a flight sergeant and acted the part. That's what I liked. Even amongst the sand and dirt, he was smart and clean and, what is more, polite.

I told him the cigarettes were for the lads. Some of them were a present from the captain of the aircraft carrier *Furious* who had given every pilot who took off from his carrier several hundred cigarettes for the lads on the island. With four gun magazines and two cannon bays there were a lot of cigarettes on our seven aircraft.

I had a little time to talk to the CO who was there to greet us but his main concern was to get us back to our hotel and for us to have a bath and something to eat. He had done the trip himself and knew what it was like when you had landed after over three hours in a cramped Spitfire cockpit.

The journey to the mess took quite a while and we went through several villages and small towns to get almost on the other side of the island near a bay. During the ride I had a chance to look at the lovely churches and houses which had been bombed and I could understand why it had been awarded the George Cross, and was now called 'George Cross Island.' I imagined that once it must have looked like Jerusalem and for a moment I could envisage the Holy Land and the Crusaders. After all, we were like the Crusaders coming to rid the Maltese of the Germans. There was a terrific religious fervour about the place. I knew that I was not going to like conditions here, but I knew that I could tolerate it because of this feeling you got from the place.

It was not long before the sentimentality was knocked out of me and after the bombing and food shortage, plus the dogfights, things were not so rosy as that first impression.

On 13th August I was on readiness and our squadron, Number 126, was to escort the tanker the *Ohio* which was limping into Malta. We had our long range tanks on and I took off as the CO's number two.

Our section of three met the *Ohio* and saw some Ju 88's about to bomb it. We were at 5,000 feet and the CO dived down and fired at one of them. I saw smoke coming from it and went in and fired a 2-second burst of machine-gun.I saw another Spitfire dive in front of me so I broke away and dived on a Ju 88 from above, firing about three or four seconds of cannon and machine-gun. I saw strikes on the port engine and a cloud of black smoke come from it. The aircraft went into a gentle dive and I broke away. I made another attack from about 15 degrees to line astern and saw a pattern of strikes zig zag along the fuselage. I ran out of ammo. By this time the Ju 88 was pouring black smoke at 1,800 feet from both engines and it dived nearly vertically into the sea. I saw another aircraft diving down on me from astern so I broke away immediately to port and up sun but did not see the aircraft again. Number three had shot down the other Ju 88 and the other two had long since gone after having dropped their bombs but missing the tanker *Ohio*.

The *Ohio* was escorted all the way to Malta by relays of Spitfires because without the tanker we had no more fuel left and the island would have had to surrender.

This epic of the *Ohio* was probably the most brave action of a merchant ship crew to have taken place in the war to date.

When we returned to Malta and I arrived at dispersal which was an old bus, I saw a familiar face grinning at me. It was Flight Sergeant Park. 'So they have got you at last, Bill,' he said, slapping me on the back. 'I am in 126 Squadron and perhaps I can be your number two again. It will be like old times, except that I have a lot more experience now.'

'Don't worry, I'll fix it straight away.' I replied.

There was no need to worry because I was promoted in the next day or so to Flight Commander 'B' Flight. Because of the scarcity of aircraft at that time each squadron was broken up into two flights; in other words each flight was twelve aircraft. It was arranged so that one flight came on at lunch time till the following morning and the other flight would take over until lunch time. In this way we covered from dawn to dusk each day without undue strain on the pilots because flying in conditions of heat and sand and hunger, that's all a pilot could endure safely. The CO would fly with each flight whenever he felt like it. This was a good way of running a squadron as each flight commander was actually the squadron leader with twelve aircraft.

On 14th August, I was at flights when I suddenly felt hot and sickly, my stomach started to bubble and in a short time I was rushing to the lavatory. I had suddenly got a bout of dysentery and the pain was horrible. Parky saw me running and he came over to me and asked me how I was. I told him what was happening to me and he laughed. I thought it no joke, but he said, 'You have got a dose of the Malta Dog. We all get it some time or other. It's to do with the food and the human excrement on the bloody stuff. You probably got it from an orange or vegetable. It will last for about four days and you have to see the MO to get some tablets.'

When I had finished, I felt really ill and I was taken over to the station medical section. I thought I was going to see an RAF doctor but it was an Army one.

He took my pulse and temperature and said, 'Ah, you have the Dog, man.' He went to the cupboard and got some tablets which he gave to me. 'These will help. What you really want is some paragoric tablets, but we have not got any. Come and see me tomorrow some time.' End of surgery.

I went back to flights and took a couple of the tablets and decided to wait until the rest of the lads went back to our hotel. How I was going to last the journey back in a ramshackle old bus, without a toilet, I had no idea and at that moment could not have cared less.

The next day I was feeling very ill but I managed to get to the MO and as I pulled my gun holster belt tight I realised I had lost a lot of weight. I went into the outer office where sat an army soldier behind a desk. I told him that I had come to see the MO as ordered the day before.

'Oh, you are the one with LMF, the doc thinks.'

I was so shocked by the use of the those most hated initials in the RAF. They meant Lack of Moral Fibre, and it was the excuse for taking fatigued pilots out of action, which in a lot of cases was not justified.

My mind went immediately to my flight off the carrier and the trip to Malta and what I had done since. I was in a rage when I went to the captain's office and as I entered I pulled out my revolver. If he had been there and if he had told me that he thought I had LMF, I think I would have shot him. I went to the toilet to calm down.

I then went back to the army corporal and said to him, 'I should be careful what you say when you open your mouth, corporal.' I then went back to my own flight.

It was late afternoon when I arrived back at the hotel and I saw the Army MO come in the door and I was ready to challenge him about what the orderly had said. When he saw me he was smiling and came up to me, 'Glad to have caught you in flight. I have been all over the bloody island to get you some of the tablets I was telling you about yesterday. These should do the trick.'

The friendliness of him rather surprised me and I knew then that the corporal had made some stupid mistake and so I told the MO about what he had said to me about LMF. He was furious and told me that he had been expecting an RAF officer that morning who was being posted home on his recommendation. Poor chap, he was suffering from nerves and who could blame him.

He was about to leave and turned to me and said, 'I will give that corporal something to think about when I get back. LMF is a term only us doctors talk about and that is in confidence with his CO.' He told me to take a couple of days off and I should be all right then.

Was I glad that he had not been in his office that morning! I hate to think what might have happened.

Within two days I was back on duty and the days were hectic. We were being bombed on the ground and a slit trench was our only shelter. Trouble was, it was in the middle of the Beaufighter pens which the enemy were always trying to bomb.

The days went by and we received some new Spitfires and pilots but they were inexperienced, and their first flight was against the more experienced German and Italian pilots.

On 19th September, I took one of my Australian pilots with me on anti-E-boat patrol. He was one of my old squadron lads whom we had been seeing off to Malta a few weeks earlier. The aim was to get to Sicily before dusk and back to Malta as it was getting dark.

I made landfall east of Scalambria and flew along the coast towards Syracuse which was a German seaplane base and was heavily defended. I had just passed Cape Passero when I saw in the distance two white wakes on the sea. It was an easy target if I could get out to sea and come in head-on to both of them. I turned out to sea as though we were going to return to Malta and when about a mile or so away I turned steeply to the left and we levelled out head-on to the two wakes. I was coming in at about 1,500 yards when I saw the wake of one stop and then saw that it was a Dornier 24 Flying boat about fifteen feet above the water. I opened fire with cannon and machine-guns and at the same time my number two opened up on the other one which was a Dornier 18. Both machines were now in pieces on the water and so we swiftly made for home. According to our Intelligence Officer, there was a lot of activity in the area all night with rescue launches and aircraft.

At this time our Wing Commander Flying had been experimenting trying out a Spitfire with a bomb under each wing. It was a bit of a Heath Robinson arrangement and it was a 250 Ib bomb which was hooked onto a Beaufighter bomb rack. It operated by pulling a piece of string in the cockpit which pulled out two pins holding the bombs in the rack. The danger was if the bomb got caught hooked up on one pin only because the bomb was likely to hit the ground when you landed and as the bombs were fused live you can imagine the risks we took when trying out the bombs.

It seemed worth the risks just to go over to Sicily and drop a few bombs on the Germans and Italians for what they had been doing to us for a long while. We were all behind the wing commander who took the first risks in trying it out himself first. The idea was that one squadron would fly with the bombs and two or three squadrons would fly round us and that way the Germans would not suspect that there were twenty-four bombs ready for them. We would fly in formation over Comiso aerodrome and since sometimes the German fighters did not waste their reserves just to go after fighters, we would then bomb the buildings, escorted by the fighters who shot up the aircraft on the ground with cannon. It worked successfully as it took the Germans by surprise, but they soon got to know which Spitfires were carrying the bombs and went straight for them ignoring the other Spitfires. It soon got too dangerous for us and most of us were glad when we finished bombing. After all we were fighter pilots not bomber pilots.

On one occasion we were on a scramble and met up with fifty plus Me 109's about 40 miles from Malta. Behind them were some Reggiane 2001's and I was anxious to have a go at these Italian planes. They had radial engines and looked quite ugly compared to the Spitfire. I had heard some tales about the Italian pilots being easier to shoot down than the Me 109's but I ignored that. A pilot was only as good as his machine and these Reggianes looked very manoeuvrable to me. I soon found out because we went straight in to the whole gaggle with the aid of two other squadrons who had come up on either side of us and some on the side of the enemy. A huge dog fight started, and it was every man for himself. I went for the leading section of Reggianes and was almost head-on to the one left of the leader. I opened fire before he even had the chance to break away and I had never seen anything like it. His engine started to smoke immediately. By then I was pulling up and over, coming up underneath another one. I was about to open fire when another one came up behind and to one side of me and I knew I had to get out of the way quickly and so I pulled up and climbed as fast as I could to get above the main battle. Then I saw that this same aircraft had come up behind me again and I went into a steep turn to shake him off. It took a few turns before I could lose him from my tail and I flicked over to get him to follow me so that I could do a stall turn and come down on him. He did not fall for it and I then knew that I was up against a very good and resolute pilot. I then started to do a roll, hoping he would think I was going to do a half roll down into a dive. He came down after me and I immediately completed my full roll. By that time he had overshot and I was on his tail.

The rest was easy, I put a two second burst in his aircraft from above at about 300 yards and I saw his engine start to smoke. By this time we were on our own at about 4,000 feet. He did a steep turn to get away and as he had just started to turn, I opened fire again. This time I saw that his engine was on fire. I stopped firing and watched as he kept in the turn. There was no point in my firing anymore. Then I saw him flip the aircraft over. He came out and eventually his parachute opened. We were at 750 feet by then.

I circled round him as I saw him get in his dinghy. I knew that I was silly letting him get away with it, especially as we had lost some of our own pilots who had been shot up on the end of their parachute. Somehow I respected the man who had given me a good fight and was not afraid to continue combat after he had been hit. He waved to me as I circled him, but I did not wave back.

I saw two Me 109's coming at me firing their guns. I went down as low as I could when suddenly I heard my engine start to run rough and oil come on the windscreen. I was about 30 miles from Malta and thought it was all up when I saw the two Me 109's fly off. They were probably short of fuel or out of ammunition or did not like such low flying.

I immediately thought of my crash landing on the moors with a dead engine and I was now really worried. It would be impossible for me to climb or land with my engine like it was.

I called up 'Mayday' on the RT, the SOS of the air, and prayed that I would make it back to Malta and not meet any more enemy aircraft. I did not know how long my engine would keep going and I thought of Johnny and how he had crashed when he returned to base. What had gone wrong for him?

'Dear God, look after me. Dear John, help.' Every second seemed an age but almost immediately I saw three of my own flight coming over to me and Parky came up beside me.

I knew that I was now protected from enemy fighters but how about my engine? As I was approaching Luqa I kept thinking, 'Don't throttle back when you land. You will spin in like Johnny.' I managed to motor in just above stalling speed. By now my temperature gauge had gone berserk and I was afraid I would not make it. As I touched down I switched off the magnetos and as the aircraft came to rest I flung myself out of the cockpit and ran away from it. I sat on my parachute waiting for the van to pick me up. All I could think of was: 'Dear God, thanks. Dear John, thanks, mate.'

I was soon in the flight office and we all made out our combat reports. We had claimed seven fighters in all and the Reggiane which I first attacked I claimed as a possible until Parky told me he had seen it hit the sea.

On the morning of 12th October we were told that there was a build-up of bombers over Sicily and that this was going to be the start of a new blitz as new squadrons of German bombers and fighters had flown in to the Sicily bases. Evidently Hitler had ordered that Malta must be captured at all costs. It was not long before we were scrambled to meet the first wave of bombers.

This time our CO was going to lead my flight and I would take the other flight. We agreed beforehand that in the event of bombers being supported by fighters, he would take on the fighters and me the bombers. We heard on the RT that there were thirty Ju 88's supported by fifty fighters in the first wave and they were now 30 miles at 18,000 feet from Malta.

Both the Luqa Squadrons and one of the Takali Squadrons were scrambled and the others were kept ready for the next wave which was sure to come. We were vectored onto either side of the enemy formations. The enemy would not know who was going to make the initial attack. To me it was the Battle of Britain all over again except this time I was the flight commander making my own decision as to how I was going to make my attack.

As we approached the enemy, the CO called 'Tally Ho' and started his attack on the top cover fighters. As I approached the bombers I noticed that the other squadron had taken on the top cover as well and left the second wave of bombers uncovered. I then gave the order for echelon port and we flew over the first wave of bombers and dived down to the second wave head-on. In seconds all hell was let loose as six aircraft opened up with cannon and machine-gun and I saw Ju 88's burning and going down all over the place. Bombs were being dropped into the sea and some enemy aircraft were turning round and heading back for Sicily. It was taking all my efforts to avoid crashing into other aircraft. I saw one of the Ju 88's I had fired at diving down and I put a final burst into it and it almost fell to pieces. I did not see what had happened to the others I had hit, I was too busy getting out of the mass of aircraft flying around. I saw another squadron of Spits coming in to have a go and I thought it was time to get out of it. I had run out of ammunition anyway.

I had reached the outside of the melee when I saw a Spitfire going down and the pilot trying to get out. I flew up to it and saw that it was my CO. He was injured by the looks of it. I watched him bale out and saw his chute open. I stayed with him all the way down in case any German fighter tried to shoot him down. After what seemed ages he hit the water and his Mae West was supporting him, but there was no sign of life. I circled round at wave top level but got no response from him and reluctantly I made my way back at low level feeling very depressed at losing such a good CO. He had given me my big chance to lead a squadron. I owed him a lot.

After having landed and given the intelligence officer all the combat forms, we found that we had shot down four Ju 88's and five Me 109's. The other squadrons had done as well. So much for Jerry's Blitz.

The elation did not last long because within an hour we were again airborne and I was leading the squadron again. This time they were Ju 88's, supported by Macchi 202's. I was to take on the fighters and the other squadron would take the bombers.

Soon we were approaching the enemy formation and I was annoyed that I was going to take on the fighters because the Ju 88's were in tight formation and the fighters were much too high to be able to stop a head-on attack, but as the other squadron were behind me I had to carry on climbing to get to the Macchi's.

At first I thought they had not seen me because they made no attempt to take avoiding action, or so I thought and when we were in range to open fire they suddenly pulled up in the steepest climb I had ever seen an aircraft do from a straight and level flight. I knew that when they had the height they would half roll down on us which they did, but before they started to turn over for the roll, I did a steep turn and as they came down we were behind them.

It was easy. We were nicely in position and I fired at one of a pair and it blew up. I followed the other one who had turned round by now and was trying to get on my tail. I saw Parky come up behind it and he blew it out of the sky. I was surprised to see another four of them still in formation and that the Ju 88's were being chased by the other squadron. Parky was still with me and we went in again to this formation and hit one each but ran out of ammo. We then made for home and on landing were told that two Macchi's had gone down off the island of Gozo and they could only have been Parky's and mine. So we had got two each.

In the afternoon 'A' Flight came on duty and I had a word with the chaps about our morning combats. I told them that they were to take no notice of what they had heard about the Italian planes and their pilots, because it was not true. They were better pilots than a lot of the Germans and they did not run away even when the odds were against them. I would respect them next time I met them in the air.

At this stage it would be only fair to say something about our ground crews. They were RAF and Army lads who had worked for weeks without a day off and who had performed miracles in getting aircraft serviceable and taking parts from one aircraft to get another one serviceable.

The flight sergeant in charge of them was one of the unsung heroes and nothing I could say about him would be good enough. During the bombing of the airfield he would still be pushing aircraft to safety pens and like his men he was responsible for saving some Beaufighters which were loaded with torpedoes from blowing up.

One of them was burning fiercely when he and his men pushed it away from the other aircraft before it went up.

When I went to help his reaction was swift. 'Get in the trench, sir. We want you for the Spitfires to stop these bastards tomorrow.' I went in the trench and watched them from a safe vantage.

We now had no CO and as each flight commander was virtually a CO in his own flight it was not important but it did give both of us a bit more authority and I decided to use it to some good. I had a word with the flight sergeant and told him that the men should start a roster to have days off in the week. I was prepared to go short of the odd aircraft if it could not be made serviceable because of the shortage of a crew. What did he think of the idea?

'Smashing, sir, just what they need.' Within minutes he was sending off his first crew for the 24 hours off. It was well appreciated by the men and nothing suffered because of it; we never had any unserviceable aircraft except when it was impossible to repair.

On the morning of 13th October I had just finished putting the names of the pilots on our readiness board. Parky came up and pointed to my number two position and then to his own name which was leading the second section of three.

'Can I change with your number two, Bill? I would like to fly that position this morning.'

I agreed and changed the names round. I had no objection to him letting one of the new lads lead a section.

At 10.30 am we were ordered to take off to intercept some fighters which were coming from Sicily. They were supposed to be at 18,000 feet and about sixty miles away.

This sounded like an easy interception and we would have plenty of time to get up to that height before they reached Malta. We got airborne very quickly and were soon given an interception course by operations control. They also warned me that there was another plot building up over Sicily and that they were probably bombers.

There was quite a lot of cloud about and so I continued to climb the squadron away from the nearest bunch of enemy aircraft, taking care to keep the clouds between the highest batch of fighters and myself. In this way the sun was on our port side. I knew that the enemy had all the advantage of height, but I imagined that they were rendezvousing for the bombers so I had time to get more height by making a turn to starboard still climbing. I also knew that our controllers were well aware of our situation. We had been airborne for about twenty minutes when I was informed by control that the Me 109's and Macchi's had now split up into two formations and that friends were on the way.

The situation was beginning to get tricky as I now had to watch the two lots of fighters and the bombers which were to our starboard side about 20 miles ahead and below us, and at the same time I had to watch for the other Spitfire squadron which was being vectored to the fighters. By this time we were in a clear section of the sky, so I decided to do a 180 degree turn to starboard, keeping my eyes on the top layer of enemy fighters. I had no intention of going up through the clouds where I knew they could easily dive down on us.

I was about to straighten out from the turn when I happened to look at

Parky's aircraft which was on my starboard wing tip. He was waving at me and pointing towards his instrument panel or thereabouts. I did not understand what he was getting at and I took another look at the enemy formation above the cloud. I then heard Parky say:

'Hello, Red Leader, the old lady's clock's stopped!'

I thought what the bloody hell is he talking about and I called over the RT,'What?'

'Eleven o'clock,' was the reply which made me instinctively look up to the sky at the eleven o'clock position and as I did I saw a glint of the sun on a wing. The enemy were coming off the top of the cloud in a steep dive above and ahead of us.

I called over the RT, 'Through the gate and up', at the same time pushing my throttle right forward and the control column back making a very steep climb towards the enemy aircraft. I knew that the chances of their being able to pull out of their dive or get sufficient deflection on us to get in a good shot were almost impossible and in no time at all we were up and past them and then I did a powered stall turn to port followed closely by the rest of the squadron. We were now in a dive and I saw the bombers which had now appeared about three miles ahead of us.

There was only one thing I could do and I gave the order to close formation and form line abreast for a head-on attack. The fighters which had dived on us in the first place were now forming up over the Ju 88's of which there were about thirty in a wide vie formation.

In seconds we were head on to the bombers and as I took aim on the leader I called over the RT, 'Fire.' I saw my cannon shells hit the leading aircraft; its port engine blew up and the aircraft went down. The others had also opened up at the other bombers and although it was only a couple of seconds firing, several of the bombers had been hit and the formation had broken up in chaos.

We pulled up above the broken formation and attacked the fighters which were in a turn and broken formation. I soon ran out of ammunition and went down on the deck to see what had happened and I saw a Spitfire hit the water and a couple of Ju 88's were floating half submerged. I could see above me two other Ju 88's smoking and coming down.

I then heard Parky call 'Mayday' and I looked round for him but could not see him. Bombs were being jettisoned into the sea and there were aircraft all over the sky and it was a while before I got my bearing, as my gyro compass had toppled. I was most surprised when I saw ack-ack fire coming up although it was well above me. It was from the Malta-based guns and they had obviously waited for us to get clear before they started firing. The enemy had turned and were making for Sicily and I soon saw the reason, a new squadron of Spitfires was approaching the scene.

I heard nothing from Parky over the RT and I was now worried that he had been injured. When I landed I was told by one of the ground crew that Flight Sergeant Park had been taken to hospital and that one of our aircraft had not come back.

In the crew room they were talking to the Intelligence Officer and someone asked: 'What was that about the old lady's clock?'

'Whatever it was, it saved us from being jumped. If I had not heard the eleven o'clock at that moment, a lot of us would not be here now.' We finished making out our combat reports and our total claim was five Ju 88's destroyed, two Me 109's destroyed and some probables and damaged. Our losses were one missing believed killed, one injured, two aircraft repairable and one lost.

I confirmed that Parky had shot down a Ju 88 at the same time as me. These were both seen by the rest of the squadron as they were behind us when we first went into the attack.

I found out that Park's injury was not serious. A couple of days off would put him right. I then went to look at his aircraft to see what was wrong with the clock he had been talking about on the RT. I spoke to one of his ground crew and they said that the clock had stopped at eleven o'clock but as far as they could tell, there was nothing wrong with it now. I took no more notice of the incident as there were too many other things to worry about.

We were scrambled again before lunch and were recalled. My engine started to give trouble and I had to make an emergency landing. As I was on the approach my engine packed up but I was able to land safely. Another couple of seconds earlier and I would not have made it. I was rather shaken and was glad when we took the bus to our hotel for the afternoon off.

It was a nice day and I went to the beach for a lie in the sun and a swim. I had not been sleeping much and I had lost a lot of weight. For the first time I felt rather depressed about the bloody war, all this heat and then the food shortage. Flying under these conditions was becoming unbearable. I felt too tired to go to the hospital to see Parky. I would ring in the morning.

The next day Parky was back to work. He was OK for flying and he put his name down as my number two. I did not say a word to him; if this is what he wanted, it was all right by me. I told him that I had supported his claim for a Ju 88 and the squadron was put at thirty minutes' readiness. The 'A' Flight commander told me that we were getting a new CO posted to us– Neither of us knew the chap; in fact we both thought that one of us would get the squadron; after all we had both led it enough times and both of us would have liked the promotion to squadron leader,

I then went to the pen where my aircraft was parked and I sat under one of its wings, a favourite spot of mine when I wished for a bit of solitude and time to think of my wife and baby back home in England. Naturally I was very touchy on these occasions and I resented anyone coming to me and talking about squadron matters. The dispersal hut was the place for that as far as I was concerned.

DO YOU BELIEVE IN PRAYER?

I saw one of my young sergeants come up to me; he looked very worried.

'Sir, may I have a word with you?' he exclaimed.

I looked up at him and replied, 'You could have done that back at dispersal. I am having a rest at the moment.'

He was about to walk away but I stopped him by saying, 'You may as well tell me what you want, now that you have disturbed my train of thought.'

'I am sorry, sir,' he said, 'but it is so personal that I did not want anyone else to hear. It's something I want to say to you and no one else.'

Perhaps it was because I was a bit annoyed with his intrusion or perhaps it was the surrounding atmosphere which made me say to him rather sharply, 'Well you are in the right place for confessions here.'

He looked rather surprised and added, 'That is what it is, I suppose.'

The answer annoyed me and I said to him, 'If it's that kind of confession, don't you think that the padre would be a much better person for you to see.' I stood up and continued, 'I don't want to give you the wrong advice.' I took his arm and started to walk slowly away from the aircraft and out of hearing of the ground crew who were close by.

I sat down on a low wall and said to him, 'Sit down and tell me all about it.'

His first question rather surprised me, 'Sir, are you a religious man?' he enquired of me. 'Do you ever pray?'

I leaned back and rested on one elbow, then I got up, I thought that this was not the type of question which could be answered lying on the ground. 'Come, let's go for a stroll,' I said. 'I think it will be easier to talk that way.'

As we were walking I said, 'What do you mean by religion? Am I a believer? Do I pray? Anyway what has this got to do with your problem?'

He was almost in tears and I was beginning to feel that he had a real problem and unless I got to the bottom of it, I was going to lose a pilot, one way or another.

He said, 'Do you believe in prayer?'

For a moment I was at a loss what to answer and then I found myself saying, 'Oh yes, definitely, I was brought up as a child to go to Sunday school.' I continued, 'When I was very young I can remember, over my bed were two texts, one was "More things are wrought by prayer than this world dreams of; the other was simply, "Thy will be done". I think these two quotations have been with me all my life and have become more important to me since I started flying.' I paused for a moment and looked at him. He seemed puzzled and so I continued, 'I don't go to church much. In fact the last time was when my baby was christened.' I stopped walking and said to him, 'Now that's enough about me. It's your troubles I am supposed to be listening to.'

He replied, 'Thank you, sir, I now feel that I can tell you what is worrying me. Since I have been here I have always regarded you as very tough. I know it's your job and I am afraid you might think that I am a coward and I am not that. It's just that I have had a premonition that on my next trip, I am going to be killed.'

I started to walk on once more and after a few seconds I turned to him and took hold of his arm and said, 'Have you told anyone else this?'

'Yes, sir,' he replied. 'I have told some of the other sergeants over breakfast.'

'And what did they say?' I enquired.

'One of them said that sometimes you do get premonitions like that but the best thing to do is to ignore it,' he replied.

'Jolly sensible of them. That is a first world war saying meant for film producers to dramatise; it does not do to take it seriously. For example I have never heard it said, even with all my experience, and it's about the last thing I would think of myself and even if I had a dream like it, I would assume that the cheese had been a bit strong and that I had had a nightmare. I will now ask you a question,' I said. 'Are you religious?'

He replied, 'No! I can't say that I am, but there is something about this place that wants to make me believe in something before I go.'

I said, 'Go! Go where? Where do you think you are going to?'

He replied, 'On my next trip.'

I now began to get a bit angry and enquired of him, 'Sergeant are you asking me to take you off the next trip to make sure you are safe?'

'No, no, sir,' he replied. 'I don't want that. I want to get it over and done with, I don't want to live with this fear.'

I knew that I had to do something to stop this lad's way of thinking and the fact that he had told some of the other sergeants about his dream made it worse. Once this kind of scare gets into a squadron things could get very bad and this was not the time anyway. Jerry was making sure that we were depressed enough, what with his continual attacks and bombings.

'Sergeant,' I said, 'there is not a man on this island who is not scared in one way or another and yet they have survived. It's incredible what these poor people have had to put up with, what with being half starved, bombed for the past two years and yet they have the confidence that we are going to win this war for them. Go into the town and villages and see for yourself and you will see the reason for their absolute faith. Take a look at one of their beautiful churches and then ask me if I believe in God.'

By this time we had sat down again and I was wondering what my next move would be. Instinctively I said a little prayer of my own.

'Sergeant, do you ever pray before you take off in your aircraft?'

'No, sir,' he replied. 'I don't really believe in it, after all how can God help you once you are in the cockpit on your own?'

'Sergeant, I am going to tell you something confidential. It is very serious and you can believe me or not. I'll tell you one thing. I don't think I have ever taken off in an aircraft without saying a little prayer first and a little thank you when I land.'

He looked at me in amazement. 'I can't understand that, you don't look the type to do that.'

'Very well, serge, you don't have to kneel on the floor when you pray. All I ever do perhaps when I am starting the engine or taxying out or even on take-off, is say a little prayer, "Dear God take care of me," and when I land

I say, "Dear God, thank you." You don't have to say it out loud, say it to yourself, God will understand.'

He looked at me still puzzled. 'Is that all?' he asked.

'Yes,' I replied, 'God does not ask too much of you. He knows you are busy and won't expect anything other than recognition of His existence.'

'Do you mean to tell me that someone as hard-boiled as you does that?' he asked.

'I am not hard-boiled,' I replied. 'It might be because of my past experiences I am probably more afraid than you are, but I am not ashamed to tell anybody. It's the way I was brought up, it might even be the reason that I am alive today.'

'Sir, do you think that if I were to do the same thing, that I would be taken care of? Would it be good enough? It would seem to me that I was now ready to pray because I would get something out of it.'

'It's never too late to start,' I replied. 'Some people on this island save up all their lifetime in order to have their confession heard on their deathbed and to receive the Holy Sacrament. They know that it is never too late to ask forgiveness for their sins; not as though you have done much sinning yet,' I added.

'Would you mind if I said the same thing as you do?' he then enquired.

I laughed. 'Of course not, there is no copyright on those words so long as you mean what you say, when you say them. Make sure the next time you take off, you do it because this afternoon you will be on readiness with me, which brings me to the next point.'

'You are aware that my number two has probably one of the hardest positions to fly. Not only has he to look after my back but he is in the thick of it once we intercept the enemy aircraft, especially where there are bombers because their gunners always go for the leading section if they can.'

He looked as though he was now getting interested and said, 'Sir, I know that Sergeant Park is your number two and that he is up for the DFM so he must have had a lot of combat experience by now.'

This was time for my piece de resistance. 'Well you are going to fly in that position on our next trip and it will prove either that your prayer has been answered or that your dream has come true, but bear this in mind, I would never put you in this position if I thought that you were going to what you call, bite it.'

I continued towards our dispersal and told him that everything we had been talking about was as far as I was concerned, confidential and would not be mentioned to any of the other squadron personnel, either what I had told him or what he had told me. He promised he would respect this confidence.

As I was about to leave him I said quietly to him, 'Now don't forget the words, "Dear God, look after me" and when you land "Dear God, thank you".'

'Thank you, sir,' he replied. 'I feel much better now, if someone like you can do it, I am sure I can. Thank you very much, sir.' He then went to join the other chaps.

As he walked away, I called out to him, 'Remember, when you are up there in your Spitfire, hundreds of Maltese people are also praying for your safety.'

I laughed as I heard one of the other sergeants say to him, 'Teacher's pet now, Lenny?' His reply was in no way religious.

I went into the office and then called Sergeant Park who was down as my number two on the flight board; he was a good pilot with six enemy aircraft to his credit. I asked him what he thought of Sergeant L, who like him was a New Zealand lad.

He replied, 'I heard him saying at breakfast about him biting it today and it upset some of the other lads, but I soon told him in my best New Zealand slang what I thought and he shut up. Can't let the old country get a bad name, can I, Bill?'

'Nigel,' I said, 'we both know that whatever happens on our next trip when we have an interception, that lad has got to come back in one piece even if the whole bloody squadron has to look after his arse all the time he is in the air. We can't have this kind of talk under any circumstances, especially with so many new boys around.'

I went up to the board and continued, 'I am putting him as my number two and I want you to lead the second section and look after him, whatever he does, stick on his tail because I will make it a straight in and out on the attack and then everyone's on his own except my number two who will have you behind him until he lands.'

Parky looked at me and said, 'A bit drastic, isn't it? I will do my best as I realise what you are trying to do. After all I know he has had very little operational experience on Spits and I feel sorry for the poor sod.'

I then changed the board accordingly. There were a few puzzled looks when the pilots saw what I had done, but no questions were asked as to why I had done it.

The leader of 'B' Flight had just come into the room and looked at what I had done and then asked me why I had done it. I told him it was to give the new lads some confidence, so I was putting one of them up with me. I also suggested that he kept an eye on him if possible. A successful sortie would buck up morale, I said.

He agreed with me and no more was said or thought of the situation.

Two hours later we were airborne. We were to intercept some bombers with fighter escort that were approaching Valletta Harbour. We had time to get the right height and I had soon positioned the squadron to make a frontal attack slightly to starboard so that I could open up on the Ju 88's and then pull up to port side to where the fighter cover was spread.

I looked at my number two and waved to him and he replied by putting a thumb up to me. I was pleased with the way he had been holding formation and was fully confident that he would pass his test as it were, once we were under fire from the enemy bombers.

We attacked from almost head-on and I told him to take the right hand Ju 88 and keep with me as I was going for the leading aircraft. The attack was very short; a couple of seconds' firing and I saw the two leading aircraft hit by cannon. I pulled up in a steep climb to the right. I looked in my mirror and saw that my number two was right behind me and Parky was right behind him.

Things then got really hectic as one of the other squadrons was going into the fighters above us and then it became a free for all. It took all my time and skill avoiding crashing into other aircraft. The sky was now full of aircraft as another Spitfire squadron had joined in and it was impossible to tell who was who in the melee that followed. I called out over the RT for my chaps to withdraw as I knew they must be out of ammunition by now. They made for base individually.

I stayed outside the enemy formation who were now close to Valletta Harbour and the ack-ack was coming up fast and furious and the enemy was turning back. I landed back at Luqa and on landing I looked over to the pen where number two's aircraft would be parked and it was there. Next to it was Parky's, so I knew that in more than one respect this sortie had been successful.

I climbed out of the cockpit and looked at the damage done to my wing and saw that it was repairable. I then made my way to dispersal where the others were discussing their victories with the Intelligence Officer.

I noticed Sergeant L waving his arms about and telling how he had shot down one of the Ju 88's. It was the first time he had fired at an enemy plane so he was very excited. I went over to him and took his arm and told him to come outside with me. When we were alone I said to him, 'Well, serge, you have made it.'

'Yes, sir,' he replied. 'I did exactly as you told me.'

'Did you say the other bit when you landed?' I enquired.

'Yes, sir,' he replied.

I then said, 'It works then, doesn't it?'

'Yes, sir. Yes, sir,' he replied.

'Well, don't you ever forget it.' With that I told him to go and make out his claim for one Ju 88 which went into the sea with one I had shot down.

I made out my combat report and went out to my aircraft and behind me I saw Flight Sergeant Park. I stopped and waited for him and the first thing he said to me was:

'Bill, I know why you had to take care of Sergeant L but please don't ask me to play God again.'

As I had not mentioned a word to anyone about what had taken place that morning about prayers etc, I was puzzled as to what he meant by that remark. So I said, 'What the hell do you mean? Playing God. You were asked to look after him and you did it quite successfully.'

'Guardian Angel then,' he said.

I laughed, 'That's better. It takes a lot of promotion to get the top job. One thing though,' I continued, 'the fact that nothing happened to him is worth a dozen Jerry aircraft; we won't have any more dreamers thinking they are going to bite it.'

It had been a very successful sortie and we had no losses for four enemy aircraft shot down and several damaged.

I went back to the others and Sergeant L was being congratulated by his pals. He no longer looked like a little boy he was now a young man and with his new-found courage and would be a valuable asset to the squadron.

I don't know why it was but I was feeling a bit uncomfortable about having the lad on my conscience. I had told him that he was safe because

I had inferred his prayers had done the trick and yet inwardly I knew it was Parky who had protected him all the time even to the extent of not shooting down an enemy plane. I knew that he was conserving his ammo in case number two was attacked. I was more pleased than ever that he had been recommended for the DFM. He was an ace in more ways than one.

It had been a tiring day and, when we went back to our hotel, it was my intention to have an early night but it was not to be.

We had finished dinner and I was sitting in the lounge and was waiting to talk to the 'B' Flight commander. He came in with a couple of beers, handed me one and sat down beside me. I instinctively knew that something was wrong.

For a few moments he did not say anything and I did not attempt to start the conversation because I had a feeling I was not going to like it.

At last he opened his mouth, 'Bill, your Sergeant L had quite a chat with me this afternoon. He told me what you had said to him after he had told you of his fears that he was not going to come back from his next sortie. He said that you had told him to say a little prayer each time he flew. Why? If you have so much confidence in prayers and were able to give him so much confidence in them, why did you get me and Parky to look after him all the time. You probably don't know but Parky got shot up and at one time I thought we were both going to finish up in the drink.'

He took a drink of his beer and my anger was building up, not at what he had said but because the sergeant had broken his promise to say nothing to any of the others.

He must have seen my anger but he was now in for the kill. He continued;

'If you had so much confidence in what you told him, why did you not let him take his chance like the rest of us? At least you would have proven that your theory was right or not.'

I was shocked by his statement and the truth of it hit me hard. He was right, why hadn't I had sufficient faith to let his own prayers take care of him?

I said, 'Dave, I know that you are right, but as far as I am concerned, he had to come back from that sortie and so I took no chances. I will have to seek my own peace of mind, after what you have said, but thanks all the same for telling me. I am not sorry for what I did, but remember this,

Dave, it could have happened to anyone of us. In my place you would have done the same to protect one of your men.'

I went to get up to go to my room but Dave held me back. 'Oh, no, you are not going up until you have bought me a drink.' This broke the ice and all Dave said was, 'Sorry, Bill, I think it was the combination of Parky and prayer perhaps.'

We talked with the other chaps and I had soon forgotten about the day's flying. Some of the chaps were going home soon and that was the main topic for the rest of the evening.

I did not get a lot of sleep that night as I kept thinking about what Dave had said and I knew that on the face of it he was right. Perhaps in a few days I will have got over it.

In the following days I often thought of what Parky had said – 'Don't ask me to play God again' – and what Dave had said and it was made worse by the actions of the New Zealand pilot concerned. I did not speak to him about his having told Dave about what I had told him that morning. I wanted to forget the whole episode.

But it was not to be. As much as I wanted to forget it, it was impossible; the sergeant had obviously been taking me seriously and every time he passed me taxying in his aircraft he would grin at me and put his thumb up. I knew what he meant by it; he had said his little prayer and was letting me know each time I saw him. His thumb almost cried out to me, 'I've said it.' It got to a stage where I began to avoid his aircraft and his blasted thumb; he was biting my conscience every day I saw him.

MY LUCK WAS RUNNING OUT

The days passed by and food was getting shorter and it was becoming an awkward situation as far as readiness was concerned. If you were on dawn readiness, at breakfast time you could with a bit of luck get a fried egg (hard done so as not to spill it on the others), one slice of bread and if you were really lucky a small tomato. If you wanted a couple of hard-tack biscuits you could have them but there were not many takers.

We got so many volunteers for dawn readiness each morning that we had twice as many pilots on duty as aircraft and although it meant doing a sweep over Sicily the egg was worth it.

Our new CO had now arrived and wanted to take over the squadron and have two flight commanders like they did in England. Malta was not England and neither of us flight commanders liked the arrangement, but we had to put up with it, new broom and all that sort of thing. The CO made out the flight board and pilots got shifted round some.

It was 25th October and I was showing Parky the flight board and had just put up our official scoresheet for the month of October so far. It was: 36 destroyed, 8 probables and 32 damaged. I said to Parky, 'I think things are going to quieten down a bit now. I think Jerry has had enough.'

I had just completed the sentence when the alarm went for us to take off again and we were soon airborne and intercepted some Me 109's bombers with fighter escort. A dogfight ensued and the squadron was soon broken up and it was every man for himself. It was impossible to see what was happening because there was always an enemy aircraft on your tail or somewhere near you and at the same time you were firing at the enemy one of them was firing at you. After what seemed a lifetime we ran out of ammunition and made our way individually back to base and let the other squadrons take over.

It was not long before I had landed and found out what had happened. We had lost two pilots, one having baled out in the sea. We had four aircraft shot up, two badly. My own had been hit but was repairable. We were left with six aircraft to finish off our readiness period.

I went over to the others to hear what had happened and who was missing. I knew that the CO's aircraft was not in its pen and I had seen one pilot bale out but did not see the aircraft number properly.

The flight sergeant came to me and told me that Flight Sergeant Park had not returned yet and I immediately thought of the second Spitfire I had seen go down into the sea.

I was told by one of the pilots that he had seen Flight Sergeant Park's aircraft hit the sea and he thought he had seen a parachute coming from it. Someone else had seen a Spitfire crash into the sea, but that went down with the pilot still in it. I asked the pilot who thought he had seen Parky go down, if he could pin-point the position and he said that he could do because he took a bearing on it for the Air-Sea Rescue.

I hastily rang the Air-Sea Rescue and they told me they had received the information but it would take some time to get there and it would be getting dark soon. As we were still on operations, I rang operations to ask permission to go out and search for Parky or to protect him if he was in his dinghy. We could also protect the rescue launch. This would leave four aircraft on readiness. I was told that I could take off with one other and search until dusk, but no later as they would not light up the runway when we got back.

I was told that our new CO had not returned so he must have been the one going down in his aircraft. I chose the sergeant who had seen Parky's position and we took off to that area which we searched for almost an hour and as it was getting dark, we had to return to base and leave it to the Air-Sea Rescue.

It was a miserable night, waiting to hear the news about Parky and I was glad when the next day came, although we were soon scrambled against some Me 109 fighter bombers and fighters. We intercepted them about twenty miles out to sea; there were about 25 of them and I was going to settle a score for Parky. I picked out one on the wing and with my first burst of cannon, blew it out of the sky and within a couple of seconds I was turning into a second one. I started to fire at it and was so intent on hitting it, that I did not see the one behind me. I managed to lose it as it opened fire and I fired at the one ahead of me. I had run out of ammunition after a second or so and with another Me 109 on my tail I took evasive action and dived down to sea level and headed for home. We had got four down for no losses. Parky must be smiling, I thought.

We soon got another CO. This time he was a very experienced Battle of Britain pilot with Middle East experience and a DFC and Bar. He was a Canadian and a very friendly chap. I knew we were going to get on well together.

By the end of October we assumed that the blitz was over and we went on the offensive for a change. We carried out sweeps over Sicily with our fighter bombers. What a lovely change from being on the receiving end.

The next couple of weeks were much quieter and some of the pilots had been told they were being relieved as there were many more pilots and aircraft arriving and the food was better because the convoys were now coming through. I thought it would not be long before I got my posting back to England. I had two stone to put back on, but it would not be in Malta.

I FINISH UP IN HOSPITAL

One evening the CO decided that we should go into Valletta for a few drinks and relaxation. We had more than a few but it was a change and a well deserved one at that. There were the CO, we two flight commanders and another officer. We were walking up the hill towards our hotel and only had about a hundred yards to go. Both sides of the street were covered with bombed out buildings and there were a lot of heaps of bricks on the pavements. As we walked along the pavement I hit my hand on a steel or iron bar which was projecting out of a building but which I did not see in the moonlight. I pulled on it as I thought it dangerous and as I did so, the wall it was in came down on me and a very large stone block fell onto my foot. The officer with me helped me to get it off my leg but I found I could not walk on it and the CO and the other flight commander carried me to the mess.

It was too late to call the Doc and as there were no cuts except grazes on my leg and foot I decided that it would wait until morning. During the night the pain got worse and my leg and foot were swelling and bruising and the pain was almost unbearable. It was early morning when the Doc came and he immediately took me to Takali Military Hospital for treatment. I had broken some bones in the foot and injured my right leg and the Doctor told me that I would be walking on crutches for a long time. I was told that I had to stay in the hospital and I would eventually be invalided back to England, but it would take some time.

All my visions of being home with my wife and baby for Christmas disappeared, I envisaged being in Malta for at least another two or three months.

I had my leg and foot in plaster and it weighed a ton or so it felt. I could only get around the ward with a pair of crutches.

In the same ward was a Ju 88 pilot and by coincidence it was the one I had shot down in a head-on attack. He was leading the raid. We had a chat about that day in a mixture of French, English and German, but one thing stood out in plain English. He told me that the most terrifying thing that had happened to him so far was the sight of twelve Spitfires all firing cannon and machine-guns and coming head-on at his formation. He said that all the front gunners of the Ju 88's had frozen stiff with fear and could not fire their guns at us. It was a terrible sight and the look on his face as he said it spoke for itself.

I found it hard to be unfriendly with him although he was probably bombing the life out of us a few weeks before, but seeing him wounded and unable to walk soon made me a regular visitor to his bedside for a talk. The other officers in the ward were an Australian Beaufighter pilot, two army officers and an Italian Naval captain next to me.

On 5th December 1942 the colonel in charge of the hospital came to my bedside and handed me a telegram and a bottle of whisky. I could not at first believe what I was seeing but I took it, perhaps it was Army issue. I opened up the telegram and saw that it was from RAF Headquarters; it read:

Acting Flight Lieutenant William Thomas Edward Rolls DFM, RAFVR, No 126 Squadron

Award of the Distinguished Flying Cross. 4th December 1942

Since being awarded the Distinguished Flying Medal this officer has destroyed a further four hostile aircraft bringing his total to ten. One day in October 1942, although enemy fighter planes; were attacking overhead, he led his section in an attack on eight

German heavy bombers escorted by fifteen fighters. During the ensuing combat he personally destroyed a Ju 88. Acting Flight Lieutenant Rolls has shown outstanding leadership and determination as a flight commander and has led his flight with great courage and skill.

The colonel congratulated me and told me that the whisky was to celebrate the award.

My first reaction to the telegram was naturally one of pleasure; but the most important part of the telegram, was the part about leadership; this meant more to me than how many I had shot down. I then thought to myself; if this award was for shooting down ten aircraft and as I had in fact shot down another seven since that day, perhaps I would be getting a Bar to the DFC at a later date but that was not important. I was secretly thrilled by the award of the DFC and was dying to let the lads in the squadron know; after all they had helped me get it. It was as much theirs as mine.

That afternoon a couple of my brother officers came to visit me and congratulate me. One of them handed me an envelope in which was the ribbon of the DFC so that I could have it sewn on my tunic. I quickly opened the bottle of whisky and we each had a drink. I was going to leave it until after dinner that evening before inviting the others in the ward to help me celebrate; but one of the nurses came to my bed with a tray of glasses so we all had a drink or two, anyway we soon emptied the bottle.

I showed the nurse the ribbon and she took my tunic from behind the chair and asked me for the ribbon so that she could sew it on for me.

When my visitors left, they left a parcel for me and, lo and behold, it was another bottle of whisky. We would have that after dinner I thought.

In the ward with me was an Italian Navy captain who was badly injured, but in spite of that he insisted on shaking hands with me and somehow this gesture took away the pleasure I had over the award. It made me realise that this man and the German pilot were supposed to be my enemies, and yet I had the same feelings about them as I had for my Australian friend and the two Army officers. They were actually congratulating me, their enemy. There was something wrong somewhere. My only consolation was that I was never likely to meet either of them again in combat.

The nurse came back with my tunic and pointed to the ribbon under my wings. It was almost too much for me to stop bursting into tears. I was so happy and proud and was waiting for the day I could show it to my dear wife and family.

I started thinking of all that had happened since I first joined the RAF, of all those mates I had so many happy times with, but were now dead. I thought of the small distance across the sea in North Africa where Johnny was buried.[1] So near and yet so far. Why had he been so eager to get back on operations and why had the idiots put him on Hurricanes? I felt more and more depressed and it was only when I felt the nurse tug at my coat and ask me if I was all right, that I realised where I was and what had happened in the past few hours.

During the evening an Army officer came to me and my Australian friend and told both of us that he was trying to arrange a passage to Gibraltar for us in a submarine which ran the blockade between Malta and Gibraltar with special stores.

We told him in very short terms that no way would we go in a submarine and would rather go in a rowing boat than a sardine can. I was especially adamant about my refusal because I had been in one very early on and suffered from claustrophobia and felt that I was choking to death; I knew then that I could never go in one again. The officer was a bit annoyed

---

[1] Flight Sergeant J White, DFM, No 73 Squadron, died on 13th June 1941. He flew his Hurricane V7383 back to Sidi Barrani area and was attempting to land at Landing Ground 05 when his aircraft spun into the ground. He died of his injuries without recovering consciousness and his aircraft was totally destroyed. The reason for the crash could not be determined with certainty, but it is reasonable to assume that his aircraft was damaged by AA fire over the target, or he may possibly have been wounded, causing him to lose control of his aircraft.

because it was his job to get us back to Gib as quickly as possible and he was not a bit concerned as to how he got us there.

I was getting more depressed than ever as I could see me being in Malta for Christmas. Having refused that offer I could not expect them to worry too much about us. I knew that there was sometimes an aircraft which did that run but there was a waiting list for it as operational pilots and Army officers had first priority for any seats and as it was only a Lockheed Hudson it could take few passengers anyway.

That evening developed into a spot of drinking but the night developed into a nightmare as the pain killers for my leg were fighting the whisky and by the time morning came I had a bit of a temperature. For some reason or other I took my log book out of my cupboard and turned to my last entry, 20th November 1942.1 knew that I was not going to do any more flying from Malta and so I drew a line under that entry and added up my totals. Having no CO to sign the entry I had to sign the entry as flight commander. Another page was completed.

I had now done over four hundred hours on Spitfires alone and had shot down seventeen enemy aircraft. I was amazed when I counted seventy-eight pages full in my log book. How many lives had I had if I accepted my uncle's view that in the first world war one page was one life? So much for his reckoning. My main thought was: what is the next page going to contain? Would there even be another full page? Whose life would it be next time?

I felt myself getting hot and started to sweat profusely as I saw the nurse coming over to me.

'What are you doing with your log book? Reminiscing, thinking of all those lovely young girls you have left behind?'

'How wrong you are, nurse. As a matter of fact I was thinking of all those young men that I knew and who are no longer with us.'

She then took the book away from me and put it in the cupboard. 'That's the last thing you want to talk about or even think about. You have got to get your temperature down if you wish to catch that plane in two nights' time.'

'What plane, nurse?' I asked. 'I have heard nothing about that! Who said so?'

She put her fingers to her lips, smiled and then tucked in the blankets and went away.

I don't know about her telling me to get my temperature down but I was elated to think that I was so near to going home; but was it true?

That afternoon I was officially told that an aircraft was coming from Gibraltar the next night and would take both the Australian pilot and myself to Gibraltar where we would stay for a week to fatten up before going back to England. There we would both go to Uxbridge Hospital (RAF) and then perhaps on leave when the legs and plaster had been seen to.

I would be home for Christmas just as I had told my wife the day I left for Debden.

I had to get my temperature down, so said the nurse. What temperature? I have no temperature. I feel as fit as a worn out fiddle but I would get on that plane whatever my temperature.

It was on the night that my friend Don and I decided to get rid of the last of the scotch and we said a premature farewell to the others in the ward.

At about ten o'clock I tried to get to sleep but because of the excitement of the thoughts of going home I could not sleep and started thinking about the past again, especially Hornchurch and old Parky and his farewell party in the *White Hart*. In a short time, he and two others at that party had been killed in action. Where was it all going to end? How many months or hopefully years had I got coming according to the law of averages, before I was with them?

I felt weak in the stomach and knew that I wanted to go to the lavatory badly. I sat up in bed and turned to get my crutches but saw that they had not been put back by the orderly in time for lights out. I called out for the orderly but I was afraid I would wake up the others in the ward. I looked at the bedside chair, thinking I could lean on it and push it along the ward to the toilet at the end; but I knew that I could not manage it. I thought perhaps that I could hop on one leg but the plaster cast was too heavy. By this time I was in a panic. I knew I could not contain myself much longer. It had to be the chair and as I went to pick it up I saw hanging on the back of it a thick malacca walking stick. I assumed that it belonged to the Italian Naval Officer in the next bed. I would borrow it, which I did and made my way to the toilet with difficulty.

The lighting was subdued in case of air-raids but I could see my bed and made my way back. I reached my bed and was about to put the stick back on the chair. I could see the figure of an old lady who was sitting on the chair, holding out her hand to take the walking stick. I had the shock of my life and I froze as I looked at her. On her head was a small black bonnet perched towards the back of her head. I could see her grey hair tied with a black lace band. I looked down to her feet and saw the black lace-up boots poking out from her long skirt and as I looked up to see her face. It was the cherub face I had seen before in a shop at Romford, the old lady who had wanted to buy the Spitfire clock and which cost dear old Parky a fiver. I thought of her words, 'If it goes as long as I do, it will be worth the ten shillings.' A hand reached for the stick, I screamed and then everything went blank.

The next thing I remembered was the orderly giving me something to drink. He asked me what was wrong with me and what I was doing out of bed when I screamed.

I tried to explain about the old lady in the shop at Romford just before I came to Malta; about how I saw her on the chair and gave her the walking stick back.

'You could not have gone to the toilet without your crutches and they are not here, so what's this about a walking stick?' By now the Italian and some of the others were awake and the Italian officer in the next bed said, 'He had a walking stick when he went to the toilet and when he came back he just stood by his bed and yelled out and then fell on the floor.'

'What walking stick?' enquired the orderly. 'There is no walking stick here.'

He then said something which sobered me up completely, 'Sir! Do you know what time of night it is? It's eleven o'bloody clock.'

I again felt cold all over. At last I had found out the secret of the clock and Park's, 'The old lady's clock's stopped.' This had no doubt saved some of us from being killed that day.

'Sir, you had better get back to sleep and forget tonight or you might not be allowed back in a couple of days' time.'

I got back into bed and pulled the bedclothes over my head and then it all came back to me. Betty my batwoman at Hornchurch and her 'today is the eleventh and will be a lucky day for you'. I wonder if I will ever be able to tell her how right she was. Eleven is your lucky number, well if that is so and we are supposed to take off for Gibraltar on the night of the tenth, we will land at Gib on the eleventh; if it turns out to be right, I will believe it; after all I flew to Malta on 11 August that was a lucky day for me. 'Bandits eleven o'clock, sir, it's eleven o'bloody clock' ...Gradual oblivion took over and I could almost hear the old lady saying, 'God bless you, boys. If the clock goes for as long as I do, it will be worth ten shillings.'

The next thing I remember was the nurse tugging at the bedclothes, and I saw she was laughing.

'I hear you had a nightmare last night. It's the cheap booze I expect,' she said.

'No, nurse, it was the spirits.' I replied as I turned over and tried to go to sleep again. It was no use I had to get up as the colonel was coming to see us that morning.

Later that morning I was pronounced fit to travel and I now knew that we would soon be on our way.

CHAPTER SEVEN

I Am Going Home

The next morning we were told that our Lockheed Hudson had arrived in Malta and would be modified with two beds for Don and myself. This was marvellous news; at last we were believing that we would be home in time for Christmas.

No one had mentioned about the previous night and what had happened to me. I think it was accepted that I had been having a nightmare and had imagined it; I was only too eager to let it go at that.

We were given a rough medical and were told that we would be leaving the hospital at nine o'clock and would be taken direct to the aircraft for a take-off about 10 pm. They always flew to Gibraltar at this time so as to avoid interception and would arrive about dawn.

The rest of the day was spent thanking the nurses and Army personnel who had done so much for us during our stay in the hospital. I had a chat with the Italian Naval officer and the German Ju 88 pilot. I think we all understood that regardless of nationality, when one is suffering, companionship cuts all barriers.

At nine o'clock we were in the ambulance on our way and an hour later we were ready for take-off.

It was a peculiar feeling when we took off as I had done so many times before from that same runway and on the lift off it felt as though my bonds had been cut and I was free at last. I did not even attempt to look out of the window to see the island receding in the darkness of the sky.

The trip to Gibraltar was uneventful but cold, but who cared? Every minute I was getting nearer home and at least it was a much better trip than the one I had from the carrier when I first flew to Malta. It took twice as long though and it was getting light as we landed at Gibraltar.

I was impressed by my first sight of the aerodrome as it was beginning to build up because of the contemplated invasion of North Africa; however we were soon put in an ambulance. I thought we would be going to the hospital or officers' mess; but instead we were taken to the Bristol Hotel.

We certainly got the VIP treatment here and in no time our bags were taken to our respective rooms where a maid brought in a tray of hot coffee and toast. The manager told us we would have time for a bath and breakfast would be served in the dining room in one hour's time. This was fine as it was what we both wanted and we were as hungry as could be, so we were not going to waste much time if we could help it. We had a marvellous week at the hotel, plenty of food and entertainment in the night clubs. I was putting on some weight at last.

On Thursday morning we were told that we would be going home on a twin engine Catalina flying boat and that we were to be at the harbour movements by eight o'clock that evening.

When we got there we saw the aircraft taxying out of the harbour so we went back to our hotel after having been told by the movements officer, that two VIP's had taken our place so we would not have got off even if we had been early. This was a disappointment but we still had some time until Christmas so we were not unduly worried.

The next day we were told that this time we were going on a French piloted Catalina and would land at Portsmouth and would be sent to hospital there or nearabouts. The only trouble was that the weather forecast was terrible, storms in the Bay of Biscay which was the course we were taking. This time we were at movements well before time and learned that we would be the only passengers and that we would have bunk beds for the journey and that it should be a more pleasant trip than our last one because we were not flying so high. It all sounded too good to be true.

Eventually we were introduced to our pilot and crew and thanked them for taking us. The pilot told us that the weather was getting worse but he reckoned we might just miss the main front by flying further out to sea. It did not worry us one bit as we had had enough flying in bad weather and were used to it.

As I got into the window of the fuselage, as I stepped down onto the floor it was further than it looked and I landed a bit heavy on my bad leg and a pain shot right up my back. I got onto my bunk and knew that I would have to take some Kodene for the pain was now in my right leg. I did so after asking Don to give me a glass of water,

We were soon airborne and I had never been in a take off in a seaplane and it was a bit scary as I thought we were not going to get off at all. Eventually I felt the lift off and felt much happier that we were now on the last stage of our journey, that's what I thought at the time.

For the first two hours it was not so bad, a bit rough and noisy but we were at least going towards England; that was the main thing. I don't know how long it was before we actually hit the storm but I heard the navigator say that we were in the Bay of Biscay with a strong headwind. The next hours were the worst I had ever experienced in the air; we were tossed about like a shuttlecock and I don't know how the pilot could control the aircraft, the noise was like a lot of machine-guns hitting the side of the fuselage, it was hail stones. This went on for what seemed ages and I knew that we had been airborne for at least ten hours. I could see nothing out of the window and the pilot must have been flying on instruments as forward visability was non existent.

The other crew members were marvellous and kept us supplied with hot drinks. One of them told us not to worry as the pilot was first class and would get us to England even if he had to taxi the aircraft all the way on the sea.

I don't know how long afterwards it was when the navigator came down to see us. He told us that we could not make Portsmouth as we were so far off track due to the storm and headwinds and they were trying to make a point in South Wales where the weather was a bit better. He also told us to get on the bunks and strap in as we might be making a forced landing at any time. This statement did not worry me as I knew that we would make it safely and I was not worried about where we landed as long as it was in Great Britain. In the three weeks I had been off flying I had not had the chance to say my own private little prayer on take off, but I had remembered to do so when I got in the Lockheed and when I entered the Catalina and on the journey so far had put in a lot of overtime in praying. I also remembered what I had been told by Betty and Aunt Fran, 'You will be surrounded by water, but you will survive it.' It looked as though this was going to be the event they were talking of.

The visibility was still bad and suddenly I felt the bang as we hit the water and the bouncing of the aircraft. It was very frightening and on one of the bounces I crashed up against the side of the fuselage and my leg hit one of the projections on the side and the pain was terrific and I immediately felt sick and for a moment thought we were going to sink.

From that moment on I hardly knew what was happening and took some tablets to help the pain. I vaguely remember someone saying that we would have to be towed in to port as we could not make it on our own. What seemed hours afterwards and bouts of sea sickness out of the side window, I saw a dim shape of what looked to be like a destroyer and a small boat coming towards us. From then on my mind was a blank, all I remember was being helped out of the fuselage and getting soaked as the waves came up the side of the fuselage. I remember being wrapped in a blanket in a cabin of some sort.

The next thing I could remember was that I was lying in bed in a hospital of some sort and at the bottom of the bed were two figures in white coats and one of them had a small power saw in her hand and was doing something to my leg. My first reaction was that they were cutting my leg off; but as the nurse saw that I was awake she laughed and said that they were taking off the plaster and would put a new one on. My leg had swollen and the plaster had got wet evidently.

I soon learned that I was in a Royal Naval Hospital at Swansea and that the aircraft had now been towed into port. It was hoped that Don and I could be put on a night sleeper to Euston and from there would go to RAF Uxbridge hospital.

This was great news as it meant that I would be able to have a visit from my wife and family. On arrival at Euston we were to phone Uxbridge and tell them we had arrived and if we could not make it by train, they would send an ambulance for us.

My plaster cast was soon removed and a new dressing applied and another plaster cast was being applied, this time much smaller than the previous one and on the heel of the cast was an iron half hoop so that I could walk on my heel more easily. Only two toes were left outside the plaster and it felt much easier than the other one had done.

I saw that my parachute bag was near me. It was dry but my clothes were missing. The nurse told me that they were being dried out and pressed and would be ready later. I was sorry when it came to the time to go to the railway station as I had not been able to thank the pilot for his skill in getting us all back safely, I told his navigator to thank him for me.

It was an easy journey to Euston in a first class sleeper and we arrived at about six o'clock in the morning on Sunday, 20th December 1942. Don had a sister who lived in Kensington and he said that he was going to visit her first. He would phone Uxbridge to tell them that we would be there in the evening under our own steam. I had decided that as I was only twelve miles from Euston I was going home first and would go to the hospital that evening. When we arrived at the platform, we saw an ambulance and decided to go out the back way of the station in case it was for us. We both called a taxi and went our own ways for the time being.

During the ride to my home, the taxi driver asked me about where I had been. I told him about the flight home and he could hardly believe what had happened to me. He asked me what the small silver cross on my tunic was for. 'Is it a copy of the George Cross because I know Malta is called the George Cross Island?'

I told him it was not an official decoration but one we pilots of Malta were proud to wear.

'My wife would do her nut for that,' he said.

Within the hour we were at my home and he took my bag to the front door as I was getting out of the cab.

'How much do I owe you?'

He waved his hands. 'It's the least I can do for you, sir.'

I unpinned the cross from my pocket and gave it to him, 'Give this to your wife for a Christmas present.'

He took out his hankerchiefand placed it in it.

'You don't know what this means to me. Thank you very much!'

'Thank you' I replied, 'for the free trip.'

I was almost broke and would have had to ask my wife for some money to pay him. As it was I was able to knock on my front door in private.

When my wife answered the door it was nearly half past seven and she had the shock of her life when she saw me standing there on crutches. She had not received either of the two telegrams I sent from Malta or any of my letters for the past four weeks. She did not know I was in hospital or that I was on my way home. She soon got over the shock and as I picked my baby son up I knew that I was about to start one of those new lives my uncle was always talking about. Even the pains in my foot seemed to have gone; my only worry was what the hospital was going to say when I phoned up to tell them that I was at home, instead of going straight to them. At 10 o'clock I decided that I had better telephone someone and let them know where I was.

It took me some time to get a senior member of the staff or RAF as it was a Sunday and most of them were at church. Eventually I spoke to a matron and explained who I was and where I was. She asked me if I was in need of treatment and I explained that the Naval Hospital had changed the plaster and given me tablets; I also told her that they said the plaster would not have to be changed for at least a week.

'In that case then,' she replied, 'You may as well stay at home over the Christmas and come and see us the day after Boxing Day. I will inform the admin branch.'

She then asked me for the reference on the Navy release form I had been given, and for my own rank and number. She told me that if I was having trouble with my leg I should get someone to take me straight to Uxbridge Hospital. I thanked her and could hardly believe my luck.

When I told my wife that I was going to be home for Christmas, she remarked, 'Well, you did tell me the day you left for Debden that you would be back for baby's first Christmas.'

Thanks to all those people who had made it possible, the hospital staff in Malta, the movements people, the two air crews who flew me back and to the Royal Navy who looked after me after we had force-landed and to the odd prayer or two, I was able to carry out that promise, I made to my wife five months earlier.

It was a wonderful few days before Christmas, preparing a Christmas tree for our baby; what a contrast from the two previous Christmas days at Acklington and Hornchurch. Christmas Day 1940 when Johnny White and I were on night readiness up at Acklington, just the two of us and the ground crews; now poor old Johnny was at rest in some desert spot in Libya. I felt a little guilty when I remembered what John had said to me the last time I saw him, which was at Buckingham Palace Investiture, receiving our DFM's.

'It's not the same without you, Stickey and John. I am going to ask for a posting back on operations,' he had said.

He died four months later.

One could say that it was the luck of the draw that I was still alive, but I did not know what the future held in store for me and so I was determined to make the best of the time I had with my wife and baby, the future was not in my hands, the present was all that mattered. I did not know where I would be in four months' time so I conveniently forgot the past; it was the easiest way to survive.

After a very enjoyable Christmas, I decided that I would go to Hornchurch to fetch my car which was in the garage of the officers' mess. I made arrangements with my elder cousin in the garage at East Ham, to take me, in case the battery was flat, or that there was no petrol in it. It was a pleasant surprise to see it was so nice and clean, even more so, when the engine started on the first turn of the ignition key. There was also plenty of petrol in it. I had let a couple of my old squadron pals use it while I was in Malta and they had left it in running order when they left Hornchurch.

I had already figured out how I was going to drive it; I would use my right foot with the plaster to press on the accelerator, I would not be able to use the footbrake so I would use the hand brake and gears to control my stops when necessary. At first it was like a kangaroo when taking off from start but I soon found out that it was easier for me to push my right foot instead of pressing it on the accelerator and in this way at a steady thirty miles an hour I managed to get to my house. My cousin had been behind me in case I could not manage and he would have towed me if it had been necessary, this was the original intention.

Having the car made it a lot easier for us over the holiday and it was with regret that the day after Boxing Day I had to go to Uxbridge; but at least I had transport from now on.

Nothing much happened at the hospital except that our plasters had been changed. We were told that we would be there about three weeks and would then go on leave, until we were posted back on duty. One amusing incident occurred on New Year's Eve.

We heard that there was going to be a party in the main hall for the nurses and RAF officers to bring in the New Year. Don and I decided that we would like to go to it, if not to dance, then to have a drink or two with the nurses. At about nine o'clock we made our way down to the hall on crutches and got as far as the entrance hall where an irate sister told us in no uncertain terms to get going back to our room. At that moment I was very annoyed to think that after the last five months we had gone through, we were not wanted by the very people who were supposed to be looking after us. (I later saw the reason for it; it would have upset some of the nurses to see us not being able to dance and their pity would have overcome their own enjoyment).

We had no option but to leave the hall and make our way back to our room. On the way we were about to pass my car when I asked Don if he would like to go down to a very nice pub at the end of the town, and have a few beers to see the New Year in ourselves. He readily agreed and we were soon on our way to the west end of Uxbridge to this lovely pub which lay back off the main road. It was easy to drive that little distance and park in the car park.

When we went in the bar it was crowded but when the people saw the two of us on crutches, they quickly made way for us and put us at a table where there seemed to be a party going on. We were given two seats and at the same time, a drink was put in front of us to drink someone's birthday, which we did readily. Very soon we were talking to all of them and we told them about Malta and that we had just returned from there. You can imagine the reception we got after that. When the time came for us to go, it was a hard decision to make because they all wanted us to stay and see the New Year in; we knew that we had to get back before midnight and before the party in the hospital broke up, so it was with great reluctance that we left the bar.

I think that the people who came out to the car park to see us off, were greatly surprised that we had not got a driver to take us back. I told them that it was only a couple of miles of straight road so there was nothing to worry about.

We said our farewells and good wishes and thanks for the very pleasant evening and we were soon on our way back. It was easy going and not a lot of traffic as we were going along the high road, but as we reached the road which leads out from the station a bus came out and turned towards us. I could not pull up in time and we hit it on the side. Fortunately we were not going very fast.

We both got out of the car at the same time as the bus driver did and when he saw both of us on crutches he roared out laughing, 'What the hell do you think you are doing driving on crutches?' he said laughingly. I soon explained what had gone on that evening and he asked us if we were all right and then pulled the wing of the car back as it had been bent against the wheel.

'Can you manage to get along the road by yourself?' he said.

I replied, 'Yes it's only a little way.'

'All right, lads, I suggest you get back to the hospital quickly and quietly; we'll forget about the little bit of damage you have done to my bus.'

I thanked him for being so considerate and got back in the car and went on to the gates of the hospital. We had to go by the main hall where the dance was still in progress and we thought we would have a look in, perhaps after the Sister had had a few drinks she might be agreeable to let us stop to see the New Year in. We went into the entrance and came face to face with an air commodore who quickly told us to get out, which we did.

The next morning we were both told that we were being taken to Halton Hospital until we were posted and we soon found ourselves and our belongings in an ambulance on the way to Halton. No explanation had been given as to the reason for the move.

We arrived at Halton just before lunch and were taken to the CO of the hospital. The driver had told us that he was going to have lunch first and would unload our gear when we knew where we would be going.

I did not like the look of the place and what was more I did not like the idea of being so far from home without my car, neither did Don but we could not do anything about it as we did not know what it was all about.

The CO asked us if we knew why we had been sent to him as it seemed little treatment was necessary for either of us, it was a question of time to heal the bones.

I was about to say that I also did not know the reason when I had a bright idea.

'Sir, I can only assume that it was because of us trying to gatecrash the nurses' dance and crashing my car into a bus last night.'

He did not say a word but just picked up the phone and told the person on the other end to make sure that the ambulance for Uxbridge did not leave without us. He then told us to go to the mess for lunch and we would return to Uxbridge. He would be in contact with Uxbridge in the meantime.

We were back in time for tea and in our same beds but as yet no one had said a word to us; the nurses carried on as though we had not been out even.

A few days later we were sent on leave for two weeks. My cousin soon straightened out my car and the leave was enjoyed by all of us.

On returning after leave, the plaster was removed and a strong bandage applied which was much better. I was now given a walking stick which was a thick Malacca cane and this reminded me of the old lady and what had happened in the hospital in Malta. I had this feeling all the time I used the stick and would not be sorry when I no longer needed it.

I received a notice of posting that I was going to be attached to PR8, a publicity branch of the Air Ministry and I would be going to Northern Ireland with a 'Wings for Victory' Exhibition and would be expected to show the flag and give lectures and talks. I would not be doing any flying for the next six months.

I was not unhappy about that as I had had enough for the time being and I welcomed the posting. Northern Ireland was a much better place than the Middle East or Far East.

I was to have another week's leave before going to London for my briefing at PR8.

I was ready to leave Uxbridge and was about to go to my car when one of those million to one quirks of fate occurred.

I was walking down a narrow road towards the car park when I saw coming towards me a figure that I immediately recognised. It was my old instructor, now Squadron Leader A M Worger-Slade, the man who had given me the chance to fly and was indirectly responsible for my own success as a fighter pilot.

I stopped in front of him and saluted. He smiled, 'Hello, laddie. He pointed to my DFC ribbon on my tunic, 'I've read all about you and your exploits, congratulations.' He then shook my hand, 'I knew you could do it, laddie.'

I was at a loss for words, his term laddie was one which had given me all that encouragement in those early days at Gatwick when he let me do an unofficial solo flight. I was so proud that I was able to once again show him that I had lived up to his expectations. It was one of the most memorable occasions of my life.

Postscript

The officer responsible for my posting to PR8 must have had a sense of humour when he told me that it was for a rest period away from flying. It was without doubt, the hardest work load for that period, I had ever had in my life. The Exhibition 'Wings for Victory' consisted of twenty-six large stands covered with photographs and delicate lighting, plus heavy ground objects, eg bombs and parts of cockpits. There was a corporal, an LAC, an airman and myself. We had to do all the erection and wiring up each time we moved and then dismantle it after the exhibition. It would then be taken by lorry to the next venue which was normally three days away. As an extra duty I was expected to give talks in the evening to various groups and attend luncheons to try to sell War Bonds.

In some of the halls we visited it was a real puzzle as to how we were ever going to get the exhibits in and this meant a lot of extra moving them about and they were heavy.

The one consolation was the people we met in various towns in Northern Ireland and in some London areas. We made some very good friends, which made all the hard work bearable.

In September 1943 I was posted to Air Armaments School, Manby,

Lines, for a six month course after which I became a Specialist Armament Officer in March 1944. After short spells at 12 Group HQ and Biggin Hill, I was posted to Hornchurch and in November 19441 was attached to the Bombing Analysis Unit, under Professor Zuckerman and helped get the unit together with the adjutant and other officers.

We went to France on 30th June 1944 and eventually made base at Versailles. There were many units spread all over France and I visited them to see about photographic requirements and any armament requirements. We later joined up with the United States Air Evaluation Board and eventually I was demobbed early in 1946 and was mentioned in Despatches.

I went into Government service in the Scientific Advisers Division of the Ministry of Works, thanks to Professor Zuckerman who recommended me for the post of films officer.

During the writing of this book, I had many sad moments and many happy ones but the one big consolation I have is that I have been able to put on record some of the actions of my old squadron, 126 Malta. I had, on occasions, to visit the Public Record Offices at Kew and I was most shocked to find that the squadron record books for the period August 1942 to November 1942 had only been copies as the originals, according to the Ministry of Defence, had been lost. Most of the entries were in the same hand, obviously on the same day and the pattern of entry was . ... Scramble, no action. I was infuriated that all those young lads I had known who had lost their lives, had no gravestone or obituary, were as far as the records go, non-existent. There was a complete absence of combat reports.

I have sent copies of my own log book entries to the Ministry of Defence and this book may show that the pilots and ground crews in Malta were every bit as brave as those in the Battle Britain and fought under harsher conditions as far as food, etc. were concerned.

The people of Malta have not forgotten all those servicemen who helped them in their hour of need; they have built a Museum for the Navy, Merchant Navy, Army and Royal Air Force, as a constant reminder to those who gave their lives for their future.

APPENDIX I

No 72 Squadron Pilots in the Battle of Britain

Rank 1940

Plt Off.	H R	Case	Killed★
Sqn Ldr	A R	Collins	
Sgt	H J	Bell-Walker	
Fg Off.	P S	Davis-Cooke	Killed★
Plt. Off.	T D H	Davy	Killed
Plt. Off.	R	Deacon-Elliott	
Plt. Off.	B	Douthwaite	
Plt. Off.	B W	Brown	
Flt. Lt	I H	Cosby	
Plt Off.	R D	Elliott	
Fg Off.	T A F	Elsden	
Sgt	J S	Gilders	Killed
Sgt	N	Glew	Killed
Flt Lt	E	Graham	

Sgt	M	Gray	Killed★
Plt. Off.	D F	Holland	Killed★
Sgt.	M A W	Lee	Killed
Sqn Ldr	R	Lees	
Sgt	A C	Leigh	
Plt Off.	A I	Lindsay	Killed
Plt Off.	J P	Lloyd	
Plt Off.	E E	Males	Killed★
Sgt	N	Momson	Killed
Plt Off.	N R	Norfolk	
Plt Off.	J J	O'Meara	
Fg Off.	O St John	Pigg	Killed★
Sgt	R F	Plant	Killed
Sgt	M H	Pocock	
Plt Off.	P D	Pool	
Plt Off.	N C H	Robson	Killed
Sgt	W T E	Rolls	
Plt Off.	D	Secretan	
Flt Lt	D F B	Sheen	
Flt Lt	F M	Smith	
Sgt	R C J	Staples	
F. Sgt.	J	Steere	
Plt Off.	N	Sutton	Killed★
Sgt	Parra	Terry	
Fg Off.	R A	Thomson	
Flt Lt	J W	Villa	
Plt Off.	R J	Walker	
Sgt.	J	White	Killed
Plt Off.	E J	Wilcox	Killed★
Plt Off.	A L	Winskill	
Plt Off.	D C	Winter	Killed★

★Killed during the Battle of Britain

The following poem is from a selection of poems on the RAF which were sent to me years ago by Mr A. Impey. It is his tribute to 'The Few', and is reproduced with his kind permission.

'The Few' were great men,

Looked on with awe,

Who to battle on high did

In the clouds soar,

With the Spitfire and Hurricane

They were supreme,

And in those little planes

A perfect team.

The Hurricane and Spitfire -both a good plane –

Helped the 'Huns' downfall, time and again.

The sky was their kingdom

(Each plane a throne)

It was swept clean of the

Enemy's drone.

Where are they now,

Those gallant men

Whose names will be mentioned

Time and again?

Wherever they are I may say

This, you see,

God bless you, mates, for

Keeping us free.

APPENDIX II

THE AUTHOR'S 'SCORE SHEET'

Spitfire, 72 Squadron, Biggin Hill. Croydon. Kenley.

Date	Place	Destroyed	Probable	Damaged	Remarks
Sept 2nd 1940	England	Me 110	–	–	Wing blew off
Sept 2nd 1940	England	Do 17	–	–	Blew up in flames
Sept 4th 1940	England	Ju 86	–	–	Crew bailed out
Sept 4th 1940	England	Ju 86	–	–	Crash landed Sept
8th 1940	England	Do 17	–	–	Crash landed Sept
8th 1940	England	–	–	Do 17 Port Engine hit did not sec a/c after	
Sept 14th 1940	England	–	Me 109E did not see it crash but it was smoking		
Sept 14th 1940	England	Me 109E	–	–	Crashed in sea (Dover)
Sept 20th 1940	England	Me 109E	–	–	In flames over Canterbury

Spitfire, 126 Squadron, Hornchurch.

Mar 17th 1940	France	Fw 190	–	–	Exploded at 3,000 feet
Mar 17th 1940	France	–	Fw 190	Hit engine, saw smoke but did not follow	
June 2nd 1940	France	Fw 190	–	–	Both fired at it, flamer shared with

Spitfire, 126 Squadron, Luqua, Malta.

Aug 13th 1942	Off Linosa	Ju 88	–	–	At first claimed half with CO. But *Ohio* crew later confirmed we shot two down
Sept 19th 1942	Sicily	Do 24	–	–	Caught fire on sea
Oct 11th l942	Malta	Reg 2001	–	–	Caught fire crashed in sea
Oct 11th 1942	Malta	–	–	Reg 2001	hit engine did not see crash
Oct 12th 1942	Malta	Ju 88	–	–	Crashed in Valletta Harbour
Oct 12th 1942	Malta	Macchi 202	–	–	Blew up in air
Oct 12th 1942	Malta	Macchi 202	–	–	Crashed in sea
Oct 13th 1942	Malta	Ju 88	–	–	Attacked head on hit leader who crashed into sea
Oct 16th 1942	Malta	Ju 88	–	–	Head on attack, crashed in sea
Oct 20th 1942	Malta	Me 109f	–	–	Crashed on onshore Malta

Total confirmed:

Destroyed:	17 plus half
Probable:	4
Damaged:	1

Note: *a claim was very seldom made for a damaged aircraft, only when it had relation to the other claims.*

EXCERPTS ON THE AUTHOR'S COMBATS FROM THE 122 (BOMBAY) RECORD BOOK

Aircraft Type & No.	Crew	Duty	Time Up	Time Down	Remarks	References
1st May 1942						
Spitfire MTD	P/O Poulton	Off				
MTB	S/L Fajtl	Sweep				
MTG	Sgt Hubbard					
MTH	P/O Crisp					
MTZ	Sgt James					
MTT	F/L de Hemptinne		0915	0940	Close Escort to Hurribombers. R.V. made but operation cancelled owing to bad weather when formation reached Chatham.	
MTO	P/O Bland					
MTM	P/O Muller					
MTS	Sgt Barratt					
MTV	P/O Rolls					
MTN	Sgt Ribout					
MTB	S/L Fajtl					
MTF	Sgt Dunsmore					
MTZ	P/O Crisp					

Aircraft Type & No.	Crew	Duty	Time Up	Time Down	Remarks	References
Spitfire	MTH P/O Durkin					
	MTD P/O Poulton					
	MTG P/O Fowler					
	MTT F/L de Hemptinne	Off				
	MTO P/O Bland	Sweep	1530	1705	Rodeo operation with Hornchurch	
Wing.	MTM P/O Muller				French landfall made at South of Gris	
	MTS Sgt Barratt				Nez. French coast swept from this point	
	MTV P/O Rolls				to 5 miles south of Boulougne. P/O Rolls	
	MTN P/O Maynard				had starboard exhaust manifold damaged	
					when 2 Fw 190's dived out of the sun no	
	MTF Sgt Hubbard				combat ensued the enemy aircraft making	
	MTC P/O Crisp				off as rapidly as they came.	
	MTH P/O Durkin					
	MTD P/O Poulton					
	MTG P/O Fowler				Circus operation with Boston Bombers.	
	MTZ Sgt Nadon	Off			R.V. made over Bradwell. French landfall	
	MTT F/L de Hemptinne	Sweep	1835	2020	made at Gravclines at 23,000', proceeding	
	MTO P/O Bland				south to St. Omer. Coming out cast of	
	MTM P/O Muller				Calais English landfall made at Deal.	
	MTE Sgt Ribout				Yellow 3 was seen spinning down with	
	MTN P/O Maynard				the tail shot off his aircraft. Yellow 4 had	
	MTB S/Ldr Fajtl				a running fight with five enemy aircraft	
					over the channel, which finally broke off	
					7 miles off Dover. Enemy cas. NIL. Our	
					Cas. One Spitfire VB P/O Poulton.	

SUMMARY OF EVENTS, HORNCHURCH, 1942

5th May

Sergeant G NADON (Red 4)

'Just after we turned over Lille I saw 12 Fw 190s about 500 feet above us. An e/a got on to my tail which came in from starboard, and Just as I saw him my a/c was hit in the tailplane and hood – cannon in tail, m/g in hood and each aileron (Cat "A"), I did a steep right-hand turn towards him, during which I saw a FW directly to my right going vertically down. The e/a broke away and I dived down from 21,000 to 15,000 feet, getting protection from another wing of Spitfires, eventually landing safely at Hornchurch.'

P/O J BLAND (Blue 3)

'I was Blue 3 and just after the turn over LILLE 12 bandits (Fw 190s) were reported 500 ft above & lying well back, flying in three sections of 4. Red and Blue Sections were attacked simultaneously & I saw Red 3 & 4 break across with an e/a on Red 4's tail. I attacked this e/a from line astern in a steep turn, about 30° deflection, giving a 5 sees burst of m/g & cannon. The e/a broke away and appeared to be completely out of control, but I did not stop to observe further results, as the Squadron was completely broken up by this time and I was alone. P/O ROLLS (Red 3), however, saw this e/a going down obviously out of control with its tail apparently missing. In view of his confirmation I claim this c/a as "probably destroyed" – it was not actually seen to crash – but request consideration of having it stepped up to "destroyed". I Joined up with Yellow 4 (P/0 DURKIN) and we escorted P/OJICHA of 313 Sqdn, whose aircraft was damaged, back to England, crossing the coast at Manston.'

P/O W T F ROLLS, DFM. (Red 3)

'When I heard the warning of bandits attacking, I saw a Fw 190 on my tail, who opened fire. I did a steep turn to the right to allow Red 4, who was well out on my left to fire at it. He evidently missed and I saw the e/a dive away. I started to follow, but saw Blue 3 doing a quarter attack on the same e/a. I continued my dive, seeing both the c/a & Blue 3 break away. As I was still in my dive and closing in range I still followed, and saw the e/a which apparently had had its tail shot off, execute a "flick roll" at about 400 m.p.h.! It continued on its downward course, upside down and practically tail first. Seeing this e/a was definitely finished, I saved my ammunition as I imagined it would be needed pretty soon.'

P/O R VAN de POEL (Belgian) (Blue 4)

'When Red & Blue sections were attacked by the Fw 190s, I avoided one on my tail and tried to catch him as he broke away, but just as I came out of a steep turn I received a cannon-shell in my port wing from another c/a. I informed Blue 1 I should have to bale out as I was diving & couldn't control the aircraft. I tried once again to get the aircraft under control, this time successfully, eventually flying back over Belgium and crossing out over DUNKIRK at 0 feet. I climbed a little when over the Channel and got a homing,

5th May (cont)	eventually landing safely at HORNCHURCH.'
	CAMOUFLAGE F/Lt HALLOWES reports seeing Fw 190s with light grey camouflage and yellow tapering streaks on the nose-cowling. There was a black cross mid-way down the fuselage, and black crosses on the wings almost hidden by the camouflage. P/Os BLAND & ROLLS & Sgt-Pilot NADON report seeing the upper surfaces of Fw 190s camouflaged "a dirty, greasy yellow colour, with somewhat mottled effect".
14th May	Weather improving slightly but not good enough for operational flying. Quite a lot flying of all sorts was indulged in by the Squadron, including air-firing, cine gun trips, formation flying, formation weaving etc. Some excitement was provided during the afternoon by P/0 Fowler's sports car, which went up in flames, most obligingly just outside the Fire Section. Both P/0 FOWLER and his passenger baled out rapidly! The Fire Section got really enthusiastic & the fire was extinguished in a most workmanlike manner, but the car is definitely u/s at present.
15th May	A persistent ground mist made flying difficult early on & although the weather improved somewhat later, no operational flying took place. Practice flying consisted of formation exercises, dnc gun and test flights. In the evening many of the Squadron went to "Laburnum Grove", a Priestley play performed by a very good ENSA Company. A thoroughly good show.
16th May	Weather improving slightly, but apart from convoy patrolling there was no operational activity in the squadron. Flying for the day consisted mainly of practice formation flights, sector rcccos and cine gun trips. Nothing of any importance to record.
17th May	The most successful day the Squadron has had up till now, though not without loss to themselves. Led by W/Cdr

17th May
(cont)

Powell, DFC, who destroyed a Fw 190, they further accounted for 2 Fw 190's destroyed, 3 Fw 190's probably destroyed, 4 Fw 190's damaged, a locomotive, a lorry, 2 machine-gun posts and a number of Bodies. F/Lt. Barthropp, DFC and P/O Muller did not return. The squadron took off at 10-45 hrs. and RV over Beachy Head at 500 ft, 11-05hrs., the operation being Ramrod 33 – a diversionary sweep. French landfall was made at Mardelot, 20,000 ft. Intense flak was seen from Boulogne and also smoke pouring from the marshalling yards there. the formation moved towards St. Omer and Audruick slightly below and heqading North. The W/Cdr gave the order to attack and a scries of dog fights ensued.

S/Ldr PREVOT (Red 3).
The C.O. got on to the tail of a FW 190 at 200-150 yards range and gave it several short bursts. White smoke started pouring out and the E/A went into a spin, finally crashing into the Audruick area. This e/a is claimed as destroyed. The C.O. continued alone heading North at zero feet and saw a convoy of 5 lorries with trailers (definitely not guns) on the road from Gravelincs to Calais. He attacked the fourth lorry of the convoy and saw cannon shells exploding over it, finally leaving it in flames. Just before crossing the coast east of Calais he saw a m/g post with 5 Boches who started running. He opened fire and the Bodies fell. He then set course for home landing safely at Hornchurch by 12-15 hrs.

P/O ROLLS, DFM. (Red 2).
I was the W/Cdr.'s No. 2 (Red 2) and went down with him when he attacked the Fw 190's. I got in a 2 sees. burst at one Fw 190 which came past me from port to starboard and saw white smoke issuing from it. I followed it in a dive down to 11,000 feet approx., the range dosing from about 200 to 50 yds., giving it about a 2 secs. burst of m/g and cannon. Very shortly after-wards the c/a exploded in mid air and an undercarriage leg and wheel came past over my port wing. I daim this e/a as destroyed. I pulled out of my

dive at 3,00ttfcct and started climbing, reaching 10,000 feet approx. S.E. of Guines but shortly after saw another Fw 190 very close on my tail. I went into a very steep turn and after about a turn and a half got on to his tail, managing to get it a 2 sees. burst (m/g only) from about 15 degrees port. I saw white smoke coming from what appeared to be the port wing root but could not observe further as I was overshooting. This combat, however, was seen by F/Lt. Thomas of 64 Squadron who states that this e/a was completely out of control going down over and over "very sloppily" obviously finished and not worth while going after to make sure. In view of his confirmation I daim this e/a as a "probable." After overshooting I half-rolled down to 0 feet and set course for home joining up with Blue 1 and 2 (122 Squadron). I saw Blue 1 (F/lt. Griffith, DFC) make his attack on the gun post and a number of Bodies strewn over the ground. Crossed back over the Channel landing safely at Hornchurch by 12-15 hrs.

F/Lt GRIGGITH, DFC (Blue 1).

Coming out of the general mix-up I got down to about 10,000 feet when I saw and attacked a FW 190 from astern and slightly above. I gave it a burst of 3-4 sees (cannon only) and then saw that the port leg of the under-carriagc had dropped. The e/a started to give off thick greyish-black smoke and went into a steep dive travelling very fast and spiralling slowly. I went down to 2,000 feet when I overshot so pulled out but the e/a was still in his steep dive at this height. My No. 2 (P/0 Bland) confirms seeing the under-carriage leg and the smoke from this c/a whidi I daim as a "probable." After pulling out of my dive I made for the coast at a height of 2,000 ft. when I saw a gun post cast of Calais with 20 to 30 Germans firing rifles and m/g's at me. I gave them a squirt and observed many strikes from cannon and m/g's on the post and also saw the soldiers fall. This was also seen by Red 2 who had joined up with me. My aircraft received much damage during the various incidents and is Cat "B" although it brought me back safely to Hornchurch.

17th May *(cont)*	P/O PREST (Blue 4).

I was in Blue 4 and on receiving the order to attack the Fw 190's I followed Blue 3 (P/O Muller) into the general melee that ensued but then lost sight of him. I made a port beam attack on a Fw 190 from about 800 yards range getting in a 6 sees. burst (cannon only). The c/a went into a steep dive with thick black smoke pouring from it. I claim it as a "Damaged." I was then attacked from behind by 6 Fw 190's and my aircraft was hit by cannon shells in the starboard wing and fuselage (Cat "B"). I spiralled down into cloud at 3,000 feet where I shook off the e/a, went out over the coast east of Calais and crossed the Channel at 0 feet arriving safely at Hornchurch by 12-15 hrs.

F/Lt. HALLOWES, DFM and bar. (Yellow 1).
The c/a started climbing towards us as soon as we were seen and I carried out a quarter head-on attack from above on 2 Fw 190's, giving approx. a 1 sec. burst from a distance of 600/500 yds. I saw strikes and 2 yellow flashes just in front of the tailplane of one of them and this I claim as damaged. I then climbed and carried out a quarter astern attack on another Fw 190 at 500 yds. range, giving 2 bursts of approx. I sees. each. Strikes were seen on the port wing.

1st June	Weather fair. Pilots did test flights in the new Spitfire IX.

Air Firing practice at Southend by two Sections of "B" Flight from 1000-1100. Convoy Patrols were also flown and air sea rescue work by three Sections from 1543-1710. At 1850 the Squadron was airborne as a unit of wing on Circus 180. At 1907 they went out over Dungeness and at 10,000 crossed in over Gris Nez at 1925. They went round behind Calais as bombers peeled off to bomb and went out over Gravelines. They then flew down Channel 5/10 miles off the coast and crossing in again at Gris Nez swept via Guines and Devfres finally going out over Ambleteuse at 1955, and landed at Base at 2013. Flak was seen in the Guines area by no enemy aircraft. Pilots taking part were, Red – S/Ldr L O Prevot, P/O K C Giddings, F/Lt W D Williams, Sgt D F Hubbard: Blue – F/Lt L P Griffith, P/O

1st June *(cont)*	W A Prest, P/O W T Rolls, Sgt G R Nadon: Yellow – P/O J L Crisp, P/O J E Fowler, P/O R W L Mulliner, Sgt W E Dunsmore. The Squadron was then released.
2nd June	An extremely busy day, starting bright and early. At 0605 the Squadron took off as unit of wing on Circus 181. Meeting Kenley Wing and Humbombers at Beachy Head they went out over Dungeness and crossing, flew down the French coast 5 miles offshore making landfall at Le Crotoy at 0'. Shortly after crossing eight Fw 190's were seen 1,000' above and ahead of the Squadron. The enemy aircraft dived and dog fights ensued as a result of which we claim one Fw 190 destroyed (P/O W T Rolls and Sgt G R Hendon shared), one Fw 190 probable (S/Ldr L O Prevot), one Fw 190 damaged (P/O W T Rolls), and one Fw 190 damaged (S/Ldr L O Prevot). We suffered no casualties whatsoever, and all our aircraft landed safely at Base at 0800. Pilots taking part were Red – S/Ldr L O Prevot, P/O J E V Wilkin, F/Lt W D Williams, P/O W A Prest; Blue – F/Lt L P Griffith, Sgt G R Nadon, P/O W T Rolls, Sgt J P Barratt; Yellow – P/O J L Crisp, P/O J E Fowler, P/O R W L Mulliner, Sgt W E Dunsmore. A well earned breakfast and then up again at 1004 as unit of wing on Rodeo No. 69. R V Hastings at 1020, they went out over Dungeness and made Frandi landfall at 17,000' at Gris Nez. They proceeded in the direction of St Omer but before reaching there swung right towards Montreal near which Fw 190's were seen at the same height as the Squadron in the Hesdin area, and a further thirty Fw 190's were seen flying north towards Boulougne. The Squadron continued on its course and crossing out over Berch turned again when ten miles out and made back towards Le Touquet. Twenty three Fw 190's were then spotted ahead and below and the Squadron went down to the attack. The enemy aircraft scattered, but S/Ldr L C Prevot engaged in a head on attack as a result of which he claims one Fw 190 damaged. We suffered no casualty and eleven of our aircraft landed safely at Base at 1154, and the twelfth at Mansion at 1140. Lunch, a short rest then off again

2nd June
(cont)

on Circus 182 at 1640. Out over North Noreland and climbing to 25,000' turned right off Boulougne and flew mid-channel between Gris Nez and Dover orbiting continuously. Nothing exciting happened except that when 5 miles W of Gris Nez two pilots of yellow section – P/0. Crisp and Fowler joined by 2 Me 109's who started firing at them from 500 yards astern. Our pilots dived to sea level, Joined up with a Polish Squadron, and returned to Base. We suffered no casualty and all A/C. landed at base at 1850. Pilots taking part were – Red – S/Ldr Prevot, Sgt Peet, F/Lt Williams, P/O Wilkin. Blue – F/Lt Griffith, Sgt. Barratt, P/O Rolls, Sgt. Nadon. Yellow – P/O Crisp, Fowler, Durkin, and Sgt Dunsmore. That concluded the days activity – operationally at least. After dinner, being released, the pilots sought recreation off the camp.

Aircraft Type & No.	Crew	Duty	Time Up	Time Down	Remarks	References

2nd July, 1942

Aircraft Type & No.	Crew	Duty	Time Up	Time Down	Remarks
Spitfire MTC	P/O J L Crisp.				Shortly after crossing 8 Fw 190's were
MTA	P/O J E Fowler				seen above and ahead of the Squadron.
MTF	P/O R W Mullmer				Dogfights ensued as a result of which we
MTH	Sgt W E Dunsmore				claim one Fw 190 destroyed (P/O Rolls
					and Sgt Nadon shared) one Fw probable
MTP	S/L L O Prevot			1155	(S/L Prevot) one Fw damaged (P/O Rolls)
MTY	P/O Giddings			1130	one Fw damaged (S/Ldr Prevot).
MTT	F/L L P Griffith			1150	
MTL	P/O W A Prest			1140	Rodeo No.69.Went out over Dungeness
MTX	P/O W T Rolls	Offensive		1145	and made Flench landfall at Gris Nez.
MTM	Sgt G R Nadon	Sweep	1000	1145	Fw 190's were seen in the Hesdin area.
MTE	F/Lt W D Williams			1135	The Squadron crossed out over Berch,
MTD	Sgt D F Hubbard			1135	but turned again when ten miles out and
MTC	P/O Crisp			1145	made back towards Le Touquet. Twenty
MTA	P/O Fowler			1145	three Fw 190's were seen ahead and below
MTF	P/O R W Mulliner.			1140	the Squadron and we went in to attack.
MTH	Sgt W E Dunsmore			1140	S/Ldr. Prevot claims one Fw 190 damaged.
					All our aircraft returned safely.
MTE	F/Lt W D Williams				
MTU	P/O J Wilkin				
MTC	P/O J L Crisp				
MTA	P/O J E Fowler				
MTZ	P/O J G Durkin				
MTF	Sgt W E Dunsmore.	Offensive	1640	1850	Circus 182. Went out over N. Foreland
MTP	S/L L O Prevot	Sweep.			and climbed to 25,000 feel and flew mid
MTO	Sgt W W Peel				channel between Gris Nez and Dover
MTY	F/L L P Griffith				orbiting continuously. Only two c/a were
MTS	Sgt J L Barratt				seen, but nothing exciting happened.
MTX	P/O W T Rolls				

3rd July, 1942

Aircraft Type & No.	Crew	Duty	Time Up	Time Down	Remarks
MTT	F/L L P Griffith	Patrol	0840	1000	Convoy Patrol.
MTO	Sgt W W Peet				
MTB	P/O J G Durkin	Patrol	9025	1055	Convoy Patrol.
MTF	SGT W E Dunsmore				
MTC	P/O J L Crisp	Patrol	1015	1130	Convoy Patrol.
MTA	P/O J E Fowler				
MTV	P/O W T Rolls	Patrol	1100	1215	Convoy Patrol.
MTX	Sgt J L Barratt				
MTB	P/O J G Durkin	Patrol	1145	1300	Convoy Patrol.
MTH	Sgt W E Dunmiore				
MTM	Sgt G R Nadon	Patrol	1235	1405	Convoy Patrol.

Index